WHEN IRON
GATES YIELD

A. MacDonald.

GEOFFREY T. BULL

GOD HOLDS THE KEY
CORAL IN THE SAND
THE SKY IS RED

WHEN IRON GATES YIELD

GEOFFREY T. BULL

HODDER AND STOUGHTON

FIRST PUBLISHED 1955
ELEVENTH IMPRESSION 1959
FIRST PAPERBACK EDITION 1960
FOURTH IMPRESSION 1965

PRINTED IN GREAT BRITAIN FOR HODDER
AND STOUGHTON LIMITED, ST. PAUL'S HOUSE,
WARWICK LANE, LONDON, E.C.4 BY C. TINLING
AND CO. LIMITED, LIVERPOOL, LONDON AND
PRESCOT

CONTENTS

Part I

WAR ON THE PLATEAU

Part II

WAR ON THE SOUL

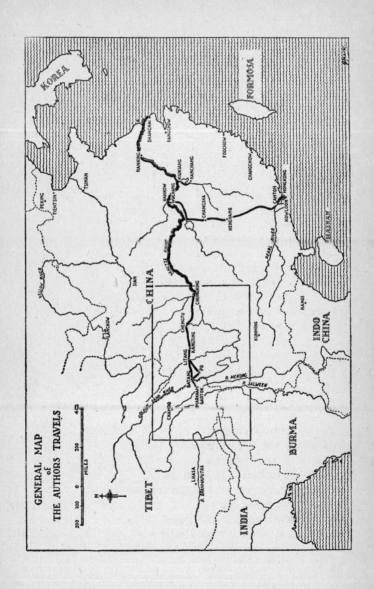

GENERAL MAP
of
THE AUTHORS TRAVELS

DRAMATIS PERSONAE

George . .	George N. Patterson, my fellow worker.
Con Baehr . .	An American missionary.
Mr. and Mrs. Kraft	China Inland Mission missionaries.
Robert Ford .	British radio operator with the Tibetan Army.
Pangda Tsang .	The family or household of Pangda.
Pangda Rapga .	One of the Pangda brothers, an ardent nationalist and an ex civil governor of the Tibetan province of Markham.
Pangda Dopgyay .	Brother to Rapga, also a Tibetan nationalist. He was ex military governor of Markham and exercised great influence in Chinese controlled Tibet prior to the Communist revolution.
Cidenla . .	Pangda Dopgyay's wife.
Jigme . . .	Pangda Dopgyay's eldest son.
Tsering Dorje .	Pangda Dopgyay's head servant.
Gezang Drashi .	A "commander of a hundred" in Dopgyay's private army and personal guardian of Jigme. Also a trader and steward of Dopgyay's lands and goods.
Bundi . . .	Commander-in-Chief of Pangda Dopgyay's private army.
Juga . . .	One of Pangda Dopgyay's servants.
Azung . . .	A steward of Pangda Tsang's property in Tibet.
Badjay . . .	A horseman.
Aku . . .	Pangda Rapga's personal servant.
Dege Sey . .	This means the Prince of Dege, he is commonly referred to by his military title of General. He was the military governor of Markham at the time of the Communist led attack on Tibet by the Chinese People's Liberation Army.
Geshi Assam .	A lama.
Chao Hsun . .	A lama.

John Ting Tien } . .	Chinese evangelists.
Pa Shamba . .	A peasant, the author's landlord in the village of Po.
Ga Ga . . .	The author's servant.
Chiang . .	The Kuomintang magistrate of Batang.
Mrs. Ren . .	His daughter.
Joseph Wang Naomi Pastor Li } .	Batang Christians.
Timothy Hsiao Chu	
Liu Chia Ju . .	A scholarly Batang Tibetan.
Liu . . .	Political officer of the Kuomintang in Batang.
Liu Wen Hui .	Kuomintang Governor of the Province of Sikang, who surrendered to the Communists.
Chang . . .	The Vice-Governor of Sikang serving under Liu Wen Hui.
Pu Tso Wanje .	Leader of the Communist underground movement in Batang.
Kungo Dzong .	Civil Governor and Magistrate of Markham.
Gun Ga . .	My Tibetan teacher.
Lt. Chang . .	English-speaking Chinese junior officer of the People's Liberation Army.
Chien Wang } .	Staff Officers of the P.L.A. undertaking escort duties.
Yang Liu Hu } . .	P.L.A. Officers employed on interrogation and indoctrination.
Fan . . .	Officer in charge of interrogation at the No. 1 prison for counter revolutionaries outside Chungking. He held the rank of 'Ko Chang'.
Chang Li Diao } . .	Prisoners.
Wang Ling Chi .	A prisoner, ex KMT Governor of Kiangsi and Szechwan provinces and ex Commander of KMT land forces.

MAPS

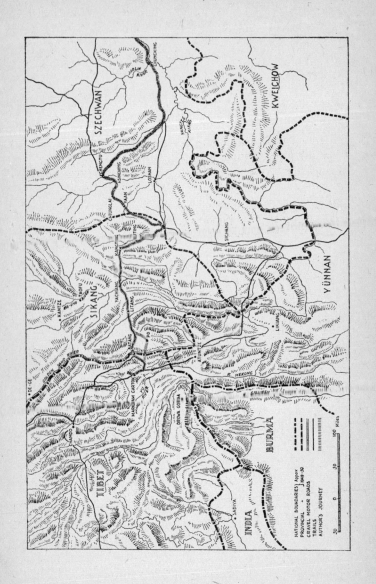

AUTHOR'S PREFACE

FOR several years all over the world, Christians have been praying for me. News has come from all five continents of the unceasing intercession made of the Church for my release. In ever increasing volume, the believing prayers of countless thousands have ascended to the Throne of God.

That to-day, in soundness of mind and body and preserved in faith, I am found once again in freedom, is due solely to God's grace, achieving the impossible, in answer to the cry of His people.

This book has been written during the period of convalescence and with much sense of weakness, but I trust it will come to each one who reads it, in the power and strength of God. The single purpose of its issue is to declare His grace, His faithfulness and His power, wholly sufficient for every extremity of service and trial.

May it stimulate a spirit of worship towards God our Father, an intense devotion to Christ Jesus our Lord, and a fervent praying in the Spirit for our brothers and sisters who stand as lights in the growing darkness, engulfing the "People's Democracies".

As to the content—it is divided into two parts. The first covers the tense period of January to October 1950, when the Tibetan interior was the focal point of a great spiritual struggle and a hotbed of intrigue. It records something of God's ways with me in my life and work alone amongst the Tibetans at that time, my entry into Tibet proper and the ultimate invasion of Tibet by the "Chinese People's Liberation Army". The second part gives a fairly detailed account of my arrest and the subsequent three years and two months of captivity spent in the prisons and detention centres of the People's Government of China, where I was subjected to their notorious system of "brain-washing." This whole story, in almost every detail, is known to them and now to all who have prayed and to any with a heart to read, I send it forth.

"I will extol thee, O Lord; for Thou hast lifted me up, and has not made my foes to rejoice over me . . . Thou hast turned for me my mourning into dancing; Thou hast put off my sackcloth, and girded me with gladness; To the end that my tongue may sing praise to Thee, and not keep silent."

Part 1

WAR ON THE PLATEAU

CHAPTER I

LONE APPOINTMENT

"I must walk to-day and to-morrow, and the day following. The third day I shall be perfected." Luke 13.

THE great arms of the valley, draped with fir, stretched out and upwards to embrace the greying sky and, far above, the jagged rocky fingers of the heights were already clasping at the mist and clouds. Away to the south I could see a distant trail, slashed up through the forests, till it broke across a grassy ridge to the west and beyond. How my heart burned to tread that road. I stood, watching the figure of my fellow-labourer move slowly on towards the lonely pass. The sound of horses' hooves grew fainter and fainter and the departing riders were soon lost to view in the lower ravine. Somehow my eyes remained fixed in that great direction. Beyond the mighty passes to the west flowed the almost legendary river of Golden Sand and, beyond the 'big river', the foreboding and little known country of Tibet. I turned at last, strangely alone in all that uttermost country. My nearest European neighbour would now be some twenty-one days eastward, through high nomad and bandit country, to the Sikang and Szechwan border; my only companions, the Tibetan people, to whom I had been sent. Yet we believed that one must go and one must stay, if we were to attack this satanic stronghold and, by the power of God, see Christ enthroned in ruined souls, as yet still cringing in the shadows of the Potala.

"Will you ride the grey?" The jocular teasing voice of Pangda Dopgyay, ruler of the valley, broke in upon my musing and roughly faced me with the stern reality, that I was expected to ride the superb but fiery animal, which George had left behind. It was all but a literal choice between suicide and humiliation. The only other horse available was Bundi's charger. Bundi, a great, burly, good-humoured fellow, was the captain of the local militia and very proud of his steed. "You can ride mine if you like," he offered with a twinkle. It was a case of exchanging a lion for a tiger, when all I could handle was a kitten. I wilted visibly. There was nothing for it but to accept at least temporary defeat, my only consolation being that I still had my life in hand to stage a come-back. I clambered on to the war-horse, a young fellow took the halter and I was led back slowly to the village. The ploughed fields were hard with frost and the winter air bit keenly at the face. The boy and I jogged slowly forward, engrossed in our own silence. . . .

It was now January 1950. Nearly three years had passed since George and I had landed at Shanghai. The great human tangle of Shanghai's millions had appalled us. There only seemed one thing I could remember now of that teeming metropolis. It had never ceased to haunt me. Little babies, wrapped up in bundles of filthy rags and left deserted on the pavement. Then there was that last evening. Could I ever forget it? We boarded the river steamer. A dim light struggled bravely to illumine the cramped little cabin. Four bunks, four missionaries and a disproportionate amount of baggage in a room about the size of a coalshed. Outside, the wharf lights glared into the darkness and the weird yodelling cries of the coolies rent the night air, as they struggled with their bamboo poles to load a cargo of gigantic bales. The stench and the confusion were indescribable and the squirming mass of humanity, cooped up between decks, was pitiful to behold. In the quietness of our cabin we had bowed in prayer. All China lay before us and, to the far west, Tibet, land of our calling. Would we hold our course? Would we be true to Christ and press the battle to the gates? Suddenly, in his beautiful voice, Con Baehr had begun to sing. Its music was to ring all through the way of tears as yet unknown:

"King of my life I crown Thee now,
Thine may the glory be,
Lest I forget Thy thorn-crowned brow
Lead me to Calvary.

Lest I forget Gethsemane,
Lest I forget Thine agony,
Lest I forget Thy love to me,
Lead me to Calvary."

George Patterson and I, after a short time of learning the language in Central China, had eventually arrived at Kangting, then the provincial capital of Sikang. We spent eighteen months there, learning Tibetan and making valuable contacts among the many Tibetans living in the district. There, too, we had met the Pangda brothers, who were powerful Tibetan nobles and enthusiastic nationalists. At their invitation we had travelled with them some three to four hundred miles westwards across the Tibetan plateau to Po, their mountain stronghold situated but a short distance from the River of Golden Sand.

The 'big river', as it is called by the Tibetans, is really part of the upper reaches of the Yangtze. At that time, in 1949 and 1950, it formed the political and military frontier between Kuomintang-controlled Tibet and those parts of Tibet controlled by the Lhasa Government. Lhasa had its own army and administration and maintained as much independence from China as possible. As Communism gained ground in China proper, this independence grew more marked and the Sikang Tibetans also longed to free themselves from the Chinese yoke, which had become almost nominal. From this disturbed border country, George and I hoped to strike into the heart of Tibet proper.

What an age ago our departure from Shanghai seemed and now George was on his way to India, with permission from the Lhasa Government to cross right through S.E. Tibet. These three years we had known God's triumphant leading. We had seen Him overcome all barriers, supplying all our needs and gloriously fulfilling His promises to us day by day. In the consciousness of His appointment, He had brought us right across China at this crucial moment in history and, in His own sovereign purposes, thrust us into this key village hundreds of miles deep in Tibetan-inhabited country. Even with the authorities, He had given us favour. Permission to cross Lhasa territory was a crowning answer to prayer. Now, under His mighty hand, even the iron gates of Tibet itself were opening to His servants. As we parted, our souls were caught up in one great desire to move on in the full stream of His unfolding will, till Lhasa yield, till Satan bow, till the song of the redeemed echo and re-echo throughout all the peaks and grasslands of the great sub-continent of Central Asia, till the whole world should know in this demonstration of His triumph something more of the greatness of our God. . . .

The horse jogged on. Only a stone's throw now and we would be in the village. The squat, fort-like dwellings clustered together on the verge of the millstream, looked somewhat unkempt against the great forested bowl of the mountains. From the eaves of the flat roofs, here and there a tattered prayer flag fluttered pathetically at the unseen foe. Tumbledown stone walls and chopped lengths of tinder surrounded the dung-filled courtyards, where dogs bared their fangs and bayed fiercely at our intrusion. We passed down the main street, no more than a haphazard right of way formed by the gaps between the houses, to the wooden bridge. At the water's edge lay a big black stone, where the muscular housewives of the hamlets pummelled and thrashed their ragged garments into a semblance of cleanliness. Grubby-faced, lovable sheep-skinned urchins looked up from their play amongst the heaps of refuse. How they loved throwing stones, aiming with deadly accuracy at perhaps a yak's horn or some bird hopping among the rocks. We ascended into a wider roadway and before us stood the great white mansion of Pangda Dopgyay and his family. Here, as lord of the manor, and as a baron in his own right, he ruled from his castle over all the surrounding country, exercising feudal control over the majority of the inhabitants; the nomad pasture-grounds, the arable valleys and rights of communication. The three storeys of whitewashed clay walls, with neat rows of high trapezium-shaped windows, beginning about twenty feet from the ground, dominated the courtyard into which we now entered. Numerous hunting dogs slunk hither and thither before the threat of a whip, whilst the tame stag, a magnificent animal with huge antlers, peered regally and condescendingly upon us from the approaches of his stable. I walked through to the farther side and, climbing up on to a sun-baked clay roof, covering the entrance to the semi-underground hovel of our landlord, I found myself once more in front of our little log cabin. Ga Ga, the boy, after some fumbling, managed to loosen the foreign padlock and I walked into our temporary home. From the smouldering logs in the open hearth, a grey sooty smoke was coiling its way resentfully towards the hole in the roof appointed for its exit. Just how much smoke actually passed through that square foot aperture in the mud and brushwood was always open to question. The white leaves of the books lying on the primitive bookshelves, nailed precariously to the horizontal pine trunks, had long since turned a dirty yellow and all the logs above the fire had become encrusted with layers of soot and tar. With smarting eyes I peered through the gloom and made a bee-line for the only window, a mere cutting in the logs, also about a foot square. I hastily removed the block of wood which served the dual purpose of a shutter and a board for cutting yak's meat. The atmosphere eased a little and the smoke slipped away furiously, just as some group of ragamuffins might scamper away when caught unawares. I looked round on our jumbled furniture. Before the door were stacked several yak-skinned boxes serving as the larder, and to the left another one used as a medicine chest. From a nail hung odd saddlery. Blackened pots and a frying pan lay littering the floor about the fire. All was as we had left it, yet something was different. I glanced down at the two low couches made of rough planks and spread with rugs. I knew what it was. But an hour ago I had been in company. Now I had returned alone. From the east, the revolutionary hordes of Red China were sweeping all before them. To the west the rusty hinges of Tibet's long-bolted door were creaking under the pressure of the Almighty's hand. All around, there breathed an air of Satanic power, superstition and intrigue. He had appointed me to stand in solitude upon the threshold of crisis, yet the only loneliness I had need to fear was that of a corn of wheat afraid to die. He that sent me was with me and in His power I yearned to walk to the third day, the day of a finished work.

*   *   *   *   *   *

One morning a few days later, I turned to Ga Ga and said: "Saddle the grey, I am going to conquer it." It was a glorious Central Asian sky, one immense light-filled dome, supported on a rim of grassland ridges and stupendous fells. The blue was so blue that one felt it almost tinged with blackness at the zenith. The dazzling sunshine poured itself lavishly upon the indifferent earth, iron with the frost, and we moved lightheartedly over the rough fields, inhaling the crisp mountain air. A mile outside the village all was still, save for the ordered yet exhilarating sound of an axe biting a tree in the forest. To-day was the first performance. For any Tibetan children tending goats or cattle on the lower slopes, my pathetic handling of this magnificent animal would afford an unexpected circus to help them while away the hours. Day after day the boy and I led it out into some secluded corner of the valley, where I would mount and then be thrown about in terror along its plunging mane. My chief resort when carried into a headlong gallop was, with all my strength, to turn its head to the hillside and let it thunder straight at a slope of not less than 45 degrees, if such could be found. Surely the old saying: "More things are wrought by prayer than this world dreams of" was never more true than in my taming of the grey. I knew only too well how much my acceptance by the Tibetans depended on it. No man is more despised by this rugged mountain race than he who shows cowardice. Although I had been born and bred in the hum of London's traffic, yet the impossible was achieved. Whatever others might say, for me at least it had been a spiritual conquest!

We returned, the horse was tethered and, skirting the ponds of stagnant manure, I went down into the landlord's cave-like dwelling of mud and stone, which formed the foundation of our cabin. These few weeks the whole valley was agog with preparations for the New Year festivities. Barley beer was in the brewing and grain in great quantities was being scorched into popcorn. Trade in cheap highly-coloured Chinese silks was the order of the day and a stream of the poorer folk kept coming to ask me whether I had a shirt to lend for the great occasion!

Inside the smoke-ridden dungeon of a place, I was now received with smiles and buttered tea by Pa Shamba. His wizened old face crinkled with pleasure, as he motioned me to sit down on some old sheepskins spread on the earthen floor. In a moment we were joined by his wife, a typical old Tibetan woman with a face as wrinkled as one of last summer's apples. Her hair was steely grey and cut short like a convict's, in recognition of some Buddhist vow. His daughter, the veritable slave of the family, begrimed, ugly yet exuberant, also found a place near us. We sipped the greasy but refreshing liquid from the dirty wooden bowls. The first topic was the New Year's beer, then the village odds and ends, after which came questions about Pangda Dopgyay. Finally, the apprehensive enquiry: "Is there any news about the Chinese?" I looked up at the crude plough slung across a few wooden props in the stone wall, then at the roughly carved wooden ploughshares lodged above it. "Don't they break when you are ploughing?" I asked casually. "Oh yes," he said, "we use about a dozen on our field, and you know that's not very big. We shall be making some more for the spring." What unbelievable toil, I thought. Suddenly the old fellow turned to me and murmured half confidentially: "I want to ask you a question, I somehow don't like asking those lama fellows. Do you think you can answer me?" Without waiting for my reply he went on, speaking with increasing seriousness. At last it came. "How big is a man's soul?" he said quietly. I looked into the fire and then into his worn and quizzical face. "A soul," I replied, "is measured like the wind, not by its length and breadth, or even its height, but by its power." Only as a soul is linked with the Eternal Spirit of the living and true God can it grow to any size. How often I had thought of that arresting phrase, "Hell is no vastness, it is full of little rotting souls." I suppose if we viewed the lake of fire materially, it would be no bigger than a pinhead and yet able to contain all the millions who have shrivelled themselves in alienation from their Creator and Redeemer. Eventually we broke up. The ploughing and the sowing were not easy. I wondered just how much the old chap understood. I wondered, too, just how big my own soul might really be.

The first days alone made great demands. Within thirty-six hours of George's departure a woodcutter had come in, his kneecap split from top to bottom with a blow from an axe. Another fellow with a syphilitic sore, a great punched out wound about two or three inches wide and a quarter of an inch deep, wanted attention. Then there was a mammary abscess to be dressed, following George's successful lancing just before his departure. With very little knowledge of medicine, apart from what I had learned in the war and since I had come to the Tibetan interior I was greatly cast upon the Lord. Although taken for granted in the west, such things as a few stitches, pills and poultices, rightly applied to these stricken people, proved victories indeed and won a respect and confidence of untold value. Often of an evening now, a crowd of the neighbours would gather in the confined space of the log cabin and, by the flickering light of a butterlamp and the glow of the embers, sit spellbound, listening to that wonder of wonders, a gramophone. Some crouching and kneeling on the floor, some sitting crosslegged puffing their long pipes, others sitting on boxes or on my poor bed, they would drink it in, passing candid comments, as Ga Ga proudly changed the records or inserted a new needle. Our programme was a mixture of American hymn singing and Lhasa duets, these latter records being kindly loaned to us by Pangda Dopgyay. Sometimes as the foreign words and tunes came on, I could intersperse odd sentences telling of their meaning. It was the beginning of opportunity. One felt these were times of growing closeness to the people. To see them there, with their wild tousled hair, clad in their heavy greasy sheepskin gowns or coarse homespun "tweed"—to see the hard weather-beaten, yet strong and defiant faces of these Tibetan nomads and peasants—to see the bright eyes and the eagerness of such dirty rosy-cheeked children thrilling to the sound of the music—to see their openheartedness towards the stranger in their midst, drew one's heart out towards them and the Lord of such a harvest field. And sometimes when the rich bass voice of a gospel singer rang out in such a setting, my heart would leap to the great refrain:—

> I'd rather have Jesus than silver or gold,
> I'd rather have Jesus than riches untold,
> I'd rather have Jesus than houses or lands,
> I'd rather be led by His nail-pierced hands.

> Than to be the king of a vast domain
> And be held in sin's dread sway.
> I'd rather have Jesus than anything
> This world affords to-day.

CHAPTER II

PO CELEBRATES THE FIRST MOON

"And it came to pass, after the year was expired,
at the time when kings go forth to battle . . . . they
destroyed the children of Ammon." 2 Samuel 11.

A FEW days and the great festive season would begin. There had
been fewer in the cabin to-night and Ga Ga and I were retiring
early. Outside the temperature was probably only a few degrees
above zero but we dared not pile the fire too high. A week or
two back we had wakened to find the floor on fire! The butter
lamp was just spluttering out and the shadows leaping ever more
grotesquely towards their final triumph in the little room. The
door was firmly closed. Suddenly we became alert. A heavy tread
sounded across the courtyard. Who could it be, at this time of
night? Visions of people dying, an accident or, most paralysing
of all, a complicated childbirth, raced through my mind. I was
just about ready for anything, in this sad country where the
missionary from the west is presumed to be the answer to so
many ills, in fact a new kind of lama, equipped with more expert
devices. There was a thud, as something struck the door, followed
by an unintelligible Tibetan call. Ga Ga opened the door with
some caution and then wide with welcome. A blast of arctic air
chilled the entire cabin with one lethal breath. In the rectangle
of darkness stood the figure of Aku, Pangda Rapga's Nepalese
servant. He was much smaller in build than the Tibetans and
his sharp features stood out clearly, illumined by the rough torch
of pine splinters he was holding before his face. "Come quickly,"
he said, "his lordship wishes to see you." In a few moments we
were groping our way in the small pool of yellow light afforded
by the flare towards the white house, now transformed into a
great sinister shadow, barely discernible in the night. Green eyes
of Tibetan hunting dogs peered hauntingly at us, out of the

gloom, but recoiled immediately from a vicious thrust of flame
by Aku. We passed through the massive wooden doors. Furs of
leopard, tiger, wolf and fox hung from an iron peg, and numerous
sacks and bales lay back beyond the big wooden steps. Up we
clambered to the second floor. Here Ga Ga left us to join the
ribald company of the ruler's retainers and servants, smoking and
joking around the open log fire and boiling cauldron of the great
feudal kitchen. At last we reached the top storey. I pushed back
the curtain of the main room and peeped in. There were three
thick wooden pillars down the centre. The south side was made
up almost completely of large lattice windows looking out into a
sheltered roof-courtyard. Below the windows and reaching round
to the far end of the room was a long low couch, a kind of dais
covered thickly with beautifully coloured rugs. On the little red
table, opposite the place where Pangda Dopgyay usually sat,
whether arbitrating disputes, playing with his children or sipping
tea, burned a small lamp composed of a lighted length of pith
protruding from a bowl of vegetable oil. The room being deserted,
we passed through on to a landing and into the room of Pangda
Rapga, Dopgyay's brother. The two brothers were in jubilant
mood. Of diverse temperament, they were nevertheless united in
their aspirations for the Tibetan people. Dopgyay, humorous,
buoyant, candid and mischievous, besides having an almost
frightening ability to penetrate and understand character, was,
for all his great mansion and fabulous wealth, a man in close
touch with the people. He was a gifted military leader and was
never more in his element than when out riding in the mountains
on his magnificent mule, with a crowd of his trusty warriors
around him. Rapga, ponderous but whimsical, was a philosopher
gifted with astute judgment. In decision, I felt, he would be up-
held by principle, whereas Dopgyay was more open to expediency.
He was also something of a recluse, giving himself constantly to
study. In fifteen years he had gained a fine understanding of
intellectual English, while in his grasp of Buddhist teaching and
the Tibetan classical language, he still outstripped the local lamas.
Although so isolated from the west, he had nevertheless made it
his business to procure and ponder an exhaustive treatise by
Marx, on "Dialectical Materialism"! By one means and another

he had managed to carry on research into different political systems and to form his own judgment. He was surprisingly abreast of international affairs, even on the roof of the world. Few perhaps realised how the hearts of these two men, born of the Lhasa nobility, yearned for their race. Whilst still in their twenties they had launched an abortive rebellion against the tyranny of the Lhasa Government. It had meant many years of exile but, even in the most unfavourable circumstances, they had done their utmost to wrench from the corrupt Kuomintang regime a fair deal and a measure of independence for the oppressed Tibetans. Now in their middle forties, the acknowledged and acclaimed leaders of nearly two-thirds of the entire race, with their other brother holding high office in Lhasa, they hoped against hope that the backward and shortsighted overlords in the forbidden capital would unite with them in resistance against the greatest menace they had ever faced, the Communist-inspired armies of new China. To-night, however, the burdens of the times seemed lighter. New Year was just around the corner and a messenger had come in from Chamdo beyond the big river.

"Pour Abu Guzang some buttered tea," Rapga ordered, using my Tibetan name. Whilst Aku complied, he handed me a letter. "For you," he said. I looked at the blurred pencil scrawl and recognised with great satisfaction that it was from George. I devoured it greedily as a thirsty soul receiving good news from a far country. He was safe at Markham Gartok, the chief garrison town of S.E. Tibet. The Ninth General of the Tibetan Army, Prince of Dege, who was the Lhasa Government's officer ruling all the way from the Golden Sand River to the Indian border, had warmly received him and was entertaining him royally. The General, known as the Dege Sey,* was very interested in the possibility that we might be able to introduce new ideas in education or medicine and was looking forward to seeing me in the coming months. Would I send a supply of medicines with simple instructions for their use, to the General, also an English New Testament, as he had had an English education. Then there was one other item; a cookery book of western dishes! It was all very thrilling. The best of all, though, was when Rapga took from his

* The 'Dege Sey' means the 'Prince of Dege'.

pile of mail a small pink envelope sealed by the Prince of Dege with the Lhasa Government seal and addressed to "Bull Sahib". I tore it open carefully. To my joy, inside was a letter authorising me to cross the frontier at the Golden Sand river and proceed the four or five days westward inside Tibetan governed territory to Markham Gartok, and to take my journey across S.E. Tibet to India if I so wished. This permission granted to us as Christian missionaries, to enter and traverse a portion of Tibetan territory, most of which had never before been travelled by westerners, was unique indeed and a victory of our Lord Jesus Christ, "Who openeth and no man shutteth, Who shutteth and no man openeth." Prayer had again prevailed.

It was late New Year's Eve (mid-February by the solar calendar). Contrary to expectation, Pangda Dopgyay had decided to despatch a messenger into Tibet on New Year's Day. No doubt the growing crisis demanded it. Close communication with the Lhasa authorities and the reliable nationalist elements in Tibet proper was vital for the brothers' plans at this juncture. "Put some more butter in the lamp," I said to Ga Ga, "it looks as if we shall be up all night, if we are to get our packages off to Gartok with to-morrow's messenger." Gradually I managed to sort out some of the more ordinary medicines, and sitting down on a box, I perched the portable typewriter in such a position as to prevent it from crashing to ruin and began to type out the medicines more ordinary uses. The easiest way would have been to quote the old missionary formula, "an aspirin for all pains above the waist and epsom salts for all below", but eventually after much painstaking effort I managed to make a somewhat more comprehensive, although still very simplified, statement. The night dragged on but at last all was ready. I looked at my watch. I announced to the boy that it was 4.30 a.m. and that I was going to bed. On understanding that 4.30 a.m. meant it would soon be light, the boy jubilantly declared he would not be sleeping now and disappeared to hail the New Year's Morn with his cronies.

The first great event of the day was the annual race up several hundred feet of most precipitous mountainside, to an old fort standing on a spur of ground dominating the valley. Various groups of households had each appointed a representative runner. Several hundred villagers gathered before the great white house. Some of them had donned beautiful silk and lambskin gowns, while practically everybody had made their annual change of shirt, so they at least looked clean from the waist up. The numerous newly sewn leather boots, with the usual pointed curly toe and high leg, bound tightly with colourful cloth straps just below the knee, showed just how busy everybody had been this past week or two. At last Pangda Dopgyay, chief of the House of Pangda, came out to the assembled crowds and the fifteen runners lined up on the roadway. He announced with feudal beneficence that there would be prizes for every competitor. Generous quantities of brick tea, bundles of leaves for making snuff and lengths of cloth were then brought out from the vaults of the white house and graded into fifteen separate piles, the first of course being the largest, but everyone, as he had proclaimed, being sure of something. A special prize of a sheepskin was allocated for the man who would come last, as he would have a whole year to live down his disgrace. Every one showed the highest delight at these arrangements and speculation ran high. Juga, one of Pangda's servants famed for his running, was highly favoured. Another young fellow who could lift the giant stone by the village flagpole higher than anyone else also had numerous followers. Ga Ga looked somewhat nervous. I remembered what he had said, back in the cabin: "If I come last, I don't know what my wife will do, she's bound to cry!" For a Tibetan the gain or loss of prestige on these trials of endurance is incalculable. Everyone now wandered slowly over to the foot of the mountain and the runners busied themselves with shedding their sheepskins and other encumbrances. The chief steward, a fat jovial red-faced fellow, with a reputation for just, albeit ruthless, execution of the valley law, stood by with his revolver. One mad crack at the sky and they were off. Seldom could there be witnessed more agile human beings ascending a mountain. The words of the Song of Solomon come forcibly to mind. "Be thou like unto a roe or to a young hart upon the mountains of spices." The altitude was about 12,500 feet (and the temperature well below freezing point), but its effect upon the runners seemed to be negligible. Minutes passed. All eyes were now fixed on the old fort where the foremost runners were almost in. Suddenly a bucket was raised in the air and the first man was thoroughly douched with cold water. "What's that for?" I asked, gaping with astonishment. "Oh, that's to stop them from fainting," was the casual reply. "Who's the winner?" everyone was saying, but nobody seemed to know for sure, the distance being too great. At last all were in and the competitors came back, led by the chief steward on horseback, to the awaiting crowds and the reception of prizes. As they drew near, the oldest households of Po welcomed the victor with great elation. He was one of their men, a comparative "unknown". The second was the young fellow expected to win. Juga looked glum. He had only managed the seventh place, whilst Ga Ga in the tenth place seemed quite pleased with himself. When the excitement died down, we retired to the great house for buttered tea, dried fruits and biscuits. We had chatted together only a few minutes when one of the servants came rushing in to say that Juga had collapsed. "I expect he's sorry about losing his reputation!" chipped Pangda Dopgyay knowingly. Anyway he took a dose of medicine and was quite all right by the afternoon. No doubt his master knew him better than I!

About midday I went out to look at the weddings. The most striking thing about the wedding ceremonies in Po valley is that the parents of neither party are allowed to attend. The bride-groom with his most intimate friends sits on one side of a big square, lined by guests and spectators. On the opposite side of the square sit the bride and her friends. All is carried on in the open air. Before all the guests are spread low tables on which are placed bowls, filled again and again with beer or tea. There is also a spread of dried fruits, home-made biscuits and certain more unusual native dishes. Before the bride are a number of wands about which are draped prayer flags and ceremonial scarves. A number of joss sticks are lighted and perfume the air. In the centre of the square stands the master of ceremonies, reciting at great length and accompanied by unrestrained guffaws and comments from the good natured and appreciative audience. From time to time a friend steps into the square with a gift and hands it to the Master of Ceremonies, who gives an impromptu eulogy of the donor, his gift and the use it will have for the newlyweds. I was an invited guest at one wedding over the New Year. Badjay, the horseman who took George to Gartok, was in charge. The sixteen-year-old son of one of Pangda Dopgyay's most renowned hunters and soldiers, a man who could still shoot down three mountain goats in about four hours on the fells, was being married to the sixteen-year-old daughter of one of the local families. After receiving advice, I presented half a bundle of brick tea, which was duly admired as a generous gift. Other gifts were snuff, coloured cloth, silver rupees, and even a length of silk from the Pangda family. When most gifts had obviously been handed in and the centre of the square showed an appreciable pile of all sorts of useful articles, about twenty of the village maidens, transformed from the dust and ashes of their constant toil to be Cinderellas for a day, trooped in, dressed in exquisitely multi-coloured aprons and long-sleeved red, green and yellow silk blouses. On their feet they had beautifully worked leather top boots which, contrary to expectation, enhanced their movements rather than hindered them. So the dancing began and continued for hours. All this time the bride's head was completely covered in a special cloth. Only for one brief moment did I catch sight of her face and then I noticed that tears were coursing down her cheeks. "Why is she crying?" I whispered to another guest. "Oh, she's leaving home. They always cry on their wedding day," was the somewhat callous reply.

Now followed days of high revelry. The second day of the New Year was the day for the horse racing. A course of a mile long was pegged out with coloured flags, and the great number of magnificent horses brought in from miles around were classified into three groups, according to their build and stamina. Pangda Dopgyay again provided handsome prizes. Our grey, ridden by Juga, was entered in the first class and I was designated with my wrist-watch to time the first three at the winning post. By the time the race reached its climax, however, I, like everyone else, was so excited that I could not decide just how many times my second hand had actually gone round the dial. Racing over ploughed, frozen earth, with every horse specially fed on tea leaves to make it fierce for the occasion, both riders and steeds were liable to be mangled to bits in a mêlée of hooves and clods, if once they stumbled. I suppose it is a tribute to their surpassing horsemanship that there was not one accident. The racing was followed by a big shooting match. Bundi, as captain of Pangda's forces, was more than delighted at winning this contest. He posed like some renowned chieftain, with gun in hand and his two targets at his feet, for a photograph. The spontaneity of Tibetans at play and their sheer enjoyment of the fun itself, is one Tibetan characteristic which especially appeals to the Britisher.

The third day was perhaps the most remarkable and also the most revealing. In the brilliant morning sunshine, some eighty or more riders gathered together, arrayed in their finest and most colourful costumes and with their horses decked in their brightest saddle rugs. The whole company mustered in the wide open yard before the old family shrine. The Pangda's household lama, philosopher and priest of the red sect of Lamaism, was also present, dressed in his deep scarlet robes fully prepared for the integral part he was to play in the proceedings. What an amazing sight! It seemed like one of the tournaments of England's Middle Ages come to life again. Long lances of young fir had been cut, and newly printed prayer flags in red, yellow and green tied to each sharpened stake. These were carried, as by knights of old, in the midst of the flashing cavalcade, up the mountain to a clearing in the forest. Here the prayer flag banners were raised amidst a pile of stone and unfurled defiantly against the cloudless blue. By this time the lama and certain of his assistants were installed on the lower side of the cairn and the chanting of the Buddhist scriptures began. The whole company of Tibetans started to encircle the prayer flags and huge piles of evergreens were heaped on to an immense bonfire set alight just before this pagan altar. Louder and louder became the chanting, and with wild shouts and quickened pace the Tibetans danced around the ascending column of dense white smoke now engulfing the idolatrous pile. The circling became increasingly hilarious, just an orgy of incantation and shouting. Some took big handfuls of grain, throwing them upward into the smoke, and others brought in more and more evergreens. Fresh bursts of flame and smoke were followed by an increased bedlam of voices. Then suddenly the wild circle paused for a brief moment. It was the climax. Each man pulled his revolver from his holster and fired several shots into the air. There was a sudden stillness and one by one the men withdrew to a wide stretch of grass among the trees, where for the next hour a great alfresco feast of bread, yak's meat, wine and beer, was enjoyed with perhaps even more enthusiasm than had been shown towards their religious observances. As one looked at the clouded heavens, the high place of idolatrous worship and the grove of green trees, one could but feel it is indeed of the Lord's mercy that man is not consumed. After everyone had been compelled to sing a solo, as a closing feature of this annual expedition, we took to our horses. The animals had been fed again for the occasion. By the time we reached the lower slopes some were almost uncontrollable. It was my big test with the grey. I could but trust my Lord, who would not fail me or allow me to be disgraced before such a company. Down we came in one mad headlong charge. Some were the worse for drink. The path narrowed and all tried to gain the lead and hold the track. In this sickening and breathtaking helter-skelter, several men were thrown. Although severely jostled, the superior strength of my horse now told. He held firm throughout and when we reached the approaches of the village I was miraculously still in the saddle. Up we came, a whole bunch of us, at a breakneck gallop to the white house. To my horror the whole stream of horses now went into a whirlwind encirclement of the house. Apparently it was the traditional grand finale. The fearsome appearance of the sight was accentuated by the blowing of trumpets and belabouring of drums by a band of lamas in the courtyard, sitting amidst the swirling white smoke of fiercely burning brushwood. The sense of the unreal was complete. Pangda Dopgyay stood in the courtyard gesticulating frantically and shouting at us all at the top of his voice: "Dismount! Dismount!" At the second or third time round he dashed forward, gripped the rein of my horse and at some peril to himself pulled me clear. Others, too, gradually pulled out of the maelstrom and jumped from their steeds.

The whole big courtyard was now spread for a feast. Seats were provided by long orderly rows of tea bundles bound in yak hide. Several hundred people surrounded the yard, some two hundred of whom were guests. Whilst the feast proceeded the whole family of Pangda, the two brothers, their wives and their children, sat on a parapet above the guests, under a specially raised awning emphasising the fact that they were rulers bestowing largesse upon their subjects. I was also given a seat with them on this occasion as a token of their respect. Once the feast was finished, the whole square was given over to community folk dancing, which was most picturesque. At evening time I was invited to the roof courtyard of the big house. The lattice windows were all opened and for many hours I sat watching the whirl of the dancers, and listening to their harsh broken songs, which so strangely enthral. The young fellows were in white shirts and breeches, playing Chinese two-stringed fiddles as they danced, and the young girls dressed as at the weddings the previous day, except that silver and gold ornaments now hung in profusion from their waists, jangling at every turn.

So the New Year passed, celebrated by a thoroughly Tibetan community, according to their own customs and religion. For me it had been a baptism of life alone with this great people in something of its wildness and abandon. After this I never recall anyone despising me, and the sense of distance seemed removed. Perhaps, with God's help, I had taken a step nearer to their heart. Perhaps, the more I was received, the nearer came the time when they would also receive the Christ, Who sent me, but to go all the way to another people means crucifixion in unthought-of measure. It is not so much a question of missionary methods. The most vital factor is a way of living. It is the straitening to that life of the Master which is described so adequately in the taunt, "This man receiveth sinners and eateth with them". It means a life, which is of such purity and love, that to touch the leper no longer means defilement, but the beginning of his cleansing.

CHAPTER III

CLASH OF FORCES

*"The weapons of our warfare are not carnal,
but mighty through God."* 2 Corinthians 10.

IN strong contrast to the atmosphere of gaiety prevailing at Po, was the foreboding spirit of distrust and apprehension that gripped the Provincial capital of Sikang some three to four hundred miles over mountain trails to the east. This town of Kangting or Tatsienlu, situated at about 8,500 feet, with a population half Tibetan, half Chinese, had submitted sullenly to the military rule of the Chinese Red Army's advance units for almost two months. The Governor of the Province, Liu Wen Hui, for long at logger-heads with Chiang Kai Shek, had taken advantage of the swift advance of the revolutionary forces and, by a clever intrigue with pro-Communist elements in the Szechwan and Yünnan Provinces, had led an en-bloc surrender of these three big areas in December of 1949. Almost immediately, forces of occupation had been sent in by the newly formed People's Government. There was heavy fighting on the road into Kangting with Kuomintang guerrillas, organised by the feudalistic secret societies so strong in that part of W. China. The resistance, however, had soon been swept aside and the occupation achieved. New Year's Day had been one of the gloomiest in the history of the town, which for so long had been accustomed to the bustle and prosperity of the terminus of the great trade route running from China right across Central Asia, via Tibet, to India. As the red troops marched in, a number of the new red flags, with five yellow stars, were hurriedly hung out of the windows and the old red flags, with a white sun on a blue field, hastily withdrawn. Apart from these doubtful emblems of loyalty to the new regime there was little colour in the streets, which at this festive season would generally have been festooned in the good old Chinese way.

B

Just as everyone was congratulating themselves behind their closed doors that New Year had passed off quietly enough, a rumour began to spread like wildfire through the caravanserais and narrow alleyways. "The reds are clearing out! The reds are clearing out!" In a short while a new cry was raised. "Chiang's armies are on the way in." It sounded impossible. People began to move about the streets. The previously sober submissive city awoke to rejoicing and defiance. The more numerous flags of the old regime now fluttered everywhere. New Year celebrations began in earnest and in from the north swept the Kuomintang troops. Chang, the old vice-Governor involved in Liu Wen Hui's opportunist surrender, had been left in charge but now of course had to flee for his life to the grasslands. The Nationalist troops did not hesitate to loot his entire property left behind in the town. In Kangting at this time was one of God's most faithful servants, a Chinese evangelist named John Ting. His mind ranged far beyond the mere ebb and flow of political fortune, to the "heavenlies" where the battle for the souls of Central Asia was waging. The present confusion, for him, was but an opportunity. Constrained by the love of Christ and led by the Holy Spirit of God, he and his fellow-worker, Tien Wen Ting, hired a couple of mules and, with a few Tibetan drovers for company, set out to the west. Their destination lay nearly four hundred miles away, through country between ten to eighteen thousand feet above sea level and, let it be remembered, it was still winter time. Nevertheless the need of a little group of believers struggling on alone in the small Tibetan town of Batang urged them on. The establishing of a living testimony to the Name of the Lord Jesus Christ, in that strategic point of the spiritual front in Central Asia, was vital at this time. A few days and the superior Red forces re-took Kangting. The evangelists, however, had moved on in the will of the Lord for a conflict on higher levels than this world knows.

. . . .

In Po the effervescence of the New Year died away leaving a dull flat-tasting aftermath, of wounds, illness and deflated spirits. The Pangda brothers were faced with more and more compromising situations. The underground Communist forces in Batang, three days' journey away to the north-west, had now more or less asserted political control of the community there, although possessing no actual military power, being as they were hundreds of miles from the most advanced Red Army troops. Pu Tso Wanje, their clever and courageous leader, a Tibetan by birth, had appended the brothers' names to the telegram he had audaciously sent to the Communist authorities acclaiming the Governor's surrender. This had nettled them and now Pangda Rapga was further perturbed, as a letter had arrived from Batang from the Communist group, asking him to put an important propaganda pamphlet into Tibetan. He replied curtly that he did not know Chinese, so could do nothing of the kind, but it boded ill for the future. Pangda Dopgyay, too, had received a messenger from Chang the vice-Governor, stranded out in the grasslands, appealing for help on the ground of old acquaintance. It was becoming more and more difficult for them to know what course to take. It was at this time that I first met Azung. He was Pangda Tsang's agent from Ja Gag, across the Golden Sand River, and had come on a visit to Po. He was dressed as a lama in the most gorgeous robes but was known by all to be an absolute impostor. Some said he was crazy, but I think artful would have been the word. In his quaint person and incessant chatter, he provided something of a comic relief, in an otherwise grey situation. As for the people, come what might, the preparation of the spring sowing was the biggest question, but odd rumours passed on by travellers filled their minds with wonderings for the peace of the future.

The servant of the Lord, however, dare not be a mere spectator of events. "He that observeth the wind shall not sow; and he that regardeth the clouds shall not reap." As soon as the New Year celebrations were over, I put forward a scheme I had in mind to old Pa Shamba. I noticed he had a good deal of rough material in the way of timber lying round. "If you will supply the wood, I'll pay for the labour, and we could get another room added to your log cabin," I ventured. Of course we had vaguely chatted about it before but now it would be a good thing if he could get going, before the commencement of the general programme of building planned by Pangda Dopgyay for the coming spring. I explained my design for windows, a cupboard and a bookshelf. The old carpenter, whom Pa Shamba brought along, rather shook his head at my ambitious suggestions, but nevertheless proved a brilliant craftsman. He completed everything in twenty-three days.

During all this time I was very busy. I wanted to move on to more definite preaching of the Gospel, so I continued as hard as possible at language study, taking the Tibetan New Testament chapter by chapter. I commenced also the study of one of the Buddhist classics and maintained almost constant conversation with the people. The only time that I did not leave myself open to their every intrusion was in the early morning, which I felt must be preserved for meditation and prayer, lest my whole spiritual life should be undermined. Apart from this, I could never feel I should close the door or in any way make the people to whom God had sent me gain the impression that I was unapproachable. There were constant calls for medical help. Some were very critical. One young woman married to three brothers, under the very prevalent institution of polyandry, was almost clubbed to death with a butter-lamp by one of her husbands. With pus-filled eyes and suppurating head wounds, she seemed as if she would go blind but, with penicillin and sulphur drugs, her infection was kept at bay and her raging temperature eventually brought under control. The Lord was indeed gracious to her and eventually, after one severe relapse, she completely recovered. When I enquired into the valley law, I found that, although on one occasion a person was shot for theft by the chief steward acting in the capacity of Pangda Dopgyay's administrator of justice, yet no steps would be taken by anyone to protect a woman so ill-treated. "After all, it's his wife," was all the reply I received. The other two brothers, also her recognised husbands, were away, one up on the grasslands herding yak, the other on a long trading trip. Thus she could not even appeal to them.

One day Badjay, the horseman, came in to see me. In sad tones he told me his sister was dying. He implored me to go and see her. Eventually I decided to go and the boy went out to saddle the horses. I gathered together some books and medicine and we set off. The ride was strenuous and fast and we took about an hour to reach the village where his sister lived. At last we dismounted, the horses sweating and the grey bleeding at the mouth. My legs were trembling a little at the arduous ride but we made our way almost immediately into one of the dark rooms of the tumbledown dwelling. Although the sun stood high in the heavens, yet it was like midnight inside. The only window was a chimney, a hole in the roof to let the smoke out, rather than to let the light in. So the fact that there was any light at all was something of an accident. I sat down for a moment by the miserable fire, to collect my senses and allow my eyes to become adjusted to the darkness and acrid smoke. Gradually I became aware of someone lying in a heap of bedding away in an even darker corner of the room. I asked that the crowd of people which had found their way in with Radjay and Ca Ga be asked to leave, also that a piece of pine be lit that we might see. The poor girl was on the very brink of death. It was almost certainly a case of poisoning. Her terribly blistered tongue and raw mouth must have been very painful. She had vomited three bowls of blood and her skin was marked with a rash as if she had been splashed with purple ink. It was difficult to know what to do, or what to say. She was conscious, although her eyes were very glassy and her breathing difficult. I gave her a sedative and ordered some milk to be boiled for her, for she had eaten nothing for three days. As she sipped the milk I asked if she had any enemies. "None," she said, except for one person, who had died across the river in Tibet. She seemed to fear his spirit, so I asked her "Are you afraid of demons?" "No . . ." she mumbled. "If you are afraid, do not call the lamas, for they are just as easily demon-possessed as anyone else," I pleaded. Her glassy eyes looked vacantly into the semi-darkness around us. "Do you know who I am?" I asked her. She looked at me in great weakness. "One sent here by the only true God," I said. "Because of the power of His Son in me I can withstand the power of demons and I am going to pray for you." She was still for a moment, then whimpered softly: "Will I die?" This was her last question. I spoke to her a little longer and then left her lying limply upon her couch in the darkness. I hoped fervently, she might live for another visit. Her husband, a somewhat doubtful character, whom Badjay suspected of being responsible in some way for his sister's condition, stood by as if he could not care less. I gave him strict instructions to supply her with milk, hoping that, as is sometimes the case with this robust mountain race, she might yet recover. So we left this veritable ante-room of Hades and went out into the sunshine. But a few hours and the young woman stepped out into the darkness. I say the darkness, and yet maybe she stepped from the agonising shadows of that shack in the mountains, into the untrammelled brightness of the Father's presence. Not according to what we know of the Gospel is He pleased to receive us, but "whosoever calleth on the Name of the Lord shall be saved." So in the twilight as one came from the true God to her bedside, maybe she called upon His Name.

About this time another tragedy occurred. It was a day of violent wind, reaching hurricane force at times, one of those fearful gales which are typical of the Tibetan plateau. It so happened that the local lamas had chosen this particular day to carry out a certain ceremony for the appeasing of local deities, and the procuring of the general well-being of the district. It was a thoroughly crude affair, having none of the brilliant costumes or finery that the big lamaseries sometimes achieve. A number of the local inhabitants, who could read, or at least said they could, had been mobilised into a chanting squad. Others having a good wind and plenty of muscle were supplied with drums, cymbals and trumpets, collected for the occasion from a local temple! Pangda's household lama officiated. At a given signal the "orchestra" and "lay readers" began to perform. It was both earsplitting and heart-rending. Large numbers of the village folk crowded round and even Pangda Rapga stirred himself to come down to see the act that his friend the lama had put on. After an all too long overture, the devilish ceremony approached its climax and the lama moved forward in his long red robes. Without a flicker on his sallow pock-marked face he performed his priestly act. One by one tsamba effigies, some supported on sticks and some stained red, were handed to him and he threw them on to a mat placed before a huge pile of prepared timber and evergreens. This being completed, the great bonfire was lit and the force of the wind roared through the blazing branches, driving the smoke hither and thither up the valley, in unremitting fury. From this dismal scene of superstition and idolatry I wandered sadly up to the square before the family shrine near the big house. There, other effigies had been placed and incense sticks inserted in boards in readiness for a final stage which I had not anticipated. In a few minutes the whole village, led by the "musicians", "chanters" and the officiating lama, moved slowly up to where I was standing. To a renewed musical accompaniment, a quantity of rice was poured into a waiting hole and the earth solemnly replaced. The sticks of incense burnt slowly downwards and the motley crowd of villagers lingered still, befuddled by the lama and his mystic ritual. Suddenly an awful cry went up. It was as if the judgment of God had fallen. "There is a house on fire! There is a house on fire!" someone yelled. The lama and his accomplices, together with all their paraphernalia, were left to do what they would. The people fled and the wind increased its fury. In a matter of seconds a hayrick on one of the flat-roofed houses was well ablaze. Only minutes and one whole block of some half dozen houses was aflame from end to end. The poor demented women began to cry heartbrokenly at the sight of their homes being destroyed. Others took their little tea churns to the mill-stream for water. Most flew to their own rooftops, where in panic-stricken haste they tore down the hay from their own ricks, lest a spark be swept across from the inferno. A few embers here and there and the whole village north of the stream would be razed to the ground. The most pathetic sight was my little friend, the dumb boy. As he saw the relentless flames licking at the foot of the adjacent fort, he could not contain himself. His home was in the ground floor. Rapidly the fire swept on and in a minute or two the place was gutted. He jumped up and down, the tears streaming down his face, uttering the most pathetic and unearthly noises. The conflagration spread so fast that two women were trapped in the quadrangle in the centre of the houses. There was only one main entrance and this was now blocked with flame. It was fearful for them. One escaped over the roof, but the other, with that incredible courage given in the face of death, plunged out through the flames. The burns covered most of the skin of the upper part of her body. Her face and hands were frightening but the face burns healed almost without a scar, although two joints of one of her fingers had later to be amputated, having been burnt to a cinder. For about ten days I literally fought for her life and in the end God graciously brought her through. All she could say every time she saw me was: "But for you I should be dead." It was a lesson to me, of the attitude I should always have towards my Saviour, Who has delivered me from the eternal flames. The lama's ceremony, having been followed by such devastating results, caused some of the villagers openly to sneer at what he had done. The cause of the fire was all too obvious. He had lit the bonfire just below the place of the outbreak and everyone knew that the hayrick had been set alight by a spark blown across from the bonfire by the fierce wind. This turn of events made me bolder to preach the Gospel.

Shortly after the fire I paid a visit to a young fellow suffering from dysentery and also a dropsical condition. I had been giving him such medicines as I had, and he had greatly improved, so much so that one of his relatives came across to say that they were thinking of taking him back down the valley to his own home. This being the case, I made my way over to see him. I entered a courtyard of a very typical Tibetan house. The ground floor was a large stable and one ascended to the second floor by a tree trunk, in which notches were cut to serve as steps. On the top floor was the usual common room, with an open hearth fire and a pile of logs and branches for use as firewood. On one wall numerous big brass ladles, generally employed in tea-making or in handling the milk and curds hung from hooks. On a farther wall were slung a gun or two and in the centre were wooden pillars supporting the roof, on which were scratched a series of white marks, no doubt of some superstitious significance. The sick youth was housed in a dark dirty room separate from the main living quarters and of much smaller dimensions. I was led in to where he was and I asked that the sliding window, which no longer really slid, be pushed back. At last a little more light poured in, which seemed to accentuate rather than relieve the cheerless scene. The fellow was certainly much better but, if so, it was hard to explain the ceremony now being conducted. In my few days' absence, they had called in one of the poorer local lamas. In fact he was one of my neighbours. I felt rather angry but said nothing. I first saw how the patient really was and then sat down on the floor to talk. A number of folk had gathered and I was sure that this was an opportunity for me to preach the Gospel. I looked at my lama neighbour, sitting there with a paltry offering of grain on a cheap tin plate. How ready he seemed to mutter a few Buddhist charms for the sake of a bowl of tsamba. Keeping an eye on the people's reactions, I began to explain very pointedly the issues involved in the calling in of the lama. I told them who I was—one sent from the only true God, and of the great distinction between the lama's doctrine and the "Jesus doctrine", as they so often call it. The consequence of calling me, and relying on the treatment given, yet at the same time employing a lama, could be serious indeed. God would not allow His work of healing to be attributed to demons. I then went on to expose, or at least take advantage of, recent events, pointing out the absolute inefficacy of the lama's efforts. There was not one person who was willing to deny that the recent lama ceremony in the village had resulted in disaster. I watched the lama now before me. He sat motionless and betrayed no anger. With such attention I went on to tell the marvellous story of Jesus and His love. I concluded with an allegory they would well understand, travelling so frequently in the grasslands and often encountering dangerous bogs. As, floundering in the morass of sin we were completely unable to save each other, how could our neighbour the lama, do anything here? We must look to the One, Who never sinned, even the Lord Jesus Christ, God's Son, Who loved us and gave Himself for us. Apart from Him, there is no Saviour. They listened right through and when I had finished broke up peaceably. As a token of goodwill I left a dose of medicine for the sick boy. Some days later Gạ Ga came running in to say that the man with dysentery had been taken back to his village and that when he arrived they had decided to celebrate. The young fellow in high spirits drank some wine saying: "I am better at last." No sooner had he done so than he collapsed, and in a few moments passed into eternity. The day I preached at his bedside was the last time we were ever together.

The doors of opportunity in the valley were increasing in number. By now it was the end of March, 1950. I had been nearly two and a half months alone amongst the Tibetans. The new room was finished and with great enthusiasm I set about furnishing it. Medicines and books were placed in the specially-made cupboard. This room would be smoke-free, although somewhat cold. For the summer it would be ideal. Through the open windows I had a lovely view right down the valley. For seating I had to see Pangda Dopgyay. He kindly loaned me a good number of yak hide boxes of brick tea to serve as seats and couches. These, covered with rugs, and arranged in a square together with a camp bed, occupied one half of the room, leaving the other half free for a dispensary. On the walls I hung up texts in Tibetan, one of which was: "This is a faithful saying and worthy of all acceptation that Jesus Christ came into the world to save sinners, of whom I am chief." I also pasted up four big picture posters: one of the Good Samaritan, one of the Prodigal Son, one of the Sower and the other showing a cross, some nails, a crown of thorns and a whip, together with a little silhouette-diagram of three crosses on a hill. On this was a quotation in Chinese: "The Lord hath laid on Him the iniquity of us all." The last addition was a borrowed table of the low Tibetan type. This was my total furnishing for the time being, but it was like a palace to me. Folk came in constantly and admired the new quarters, peered at the texts and "showed off" what they could of their ability to read. The children were most intrigued with the pictures and wanted to know what they were all about. It was all a great joy and a real step forward. The landlord was now able to come up and live in the log cabin, which I still shared with his family for cooking. I was beginning to feel really one of the local inhabitants and felt very conscious of their increased acceptance and confidence. Often in the early morning I would go to the farther side of the valley and there pray in the first rays of the rising sun as it lipped over the eastern ridges and shot out its long golden fingers to where I stood. On returning to breakfast I could see the scarlet-robed lama standing on the roof of his shrine, holding a great conch shell to his lips, and I would hear the doleful blast, sounding out down the valley to every hobgoblin and foul fiend. Two forces had begun their first encounter in the valley of Po. Sometimes the loneliness would creep over me but then I would recall the greatness of His calling and the knowledge of His supremacy.

Two days after the completion of my little Gospel room, to my amazement I heard somebody call my name in English. "Geoff, Geoff," came a cry from the ploughed field just below my window. I rushed out and there, to my almost uncontrollable joy, was John Ting. Ever since we met in Chungking in 1947, we had moved on together step by step. First to Chengtu, then to Kangting, and now hundreds of miles in the interior to be united again in such circumstances was too wonderful for words.

CHAPTER IV

BATANG CONFLICT

"The street shall be built again and the
wall, even in troublous times." Daniel 9.

"WELL, what do you think of my going to Batang at this time?"
I questioned Pangda Dopgyay. He looked thoughtful. "Of course
it's a risk," he said, "but you can take it from me the young
Communist group in Batang can't do a thing until the Red Army
gets through from Kanting. At present all Tibetans from the
Chinghai border to Yünnan are standing with us. Without military
power they are helpless. Would you dare to go though, at such
a time as this?" "Yes," I said. "And I am expecting to go with
John Ting to-morrow." "Abu Guzang is a brave man," he re-
torted in a tone of voice that could mean anything from flattery
to mockery. Then speaking seriously once again, he said, "There
is only one thing, if you get the slightest inkling that the red troops
are on their way in, cut straight back here as fast as you can.
I wouldn't like to guarantee anything once they arrive. As for
us," he said, "we are up against it, we came in here with high
aspirations but Lhasa and their Army are just hopeless. The
Communists have offered me a big job, believe it or not! I sometimes think they are like the One you preach," he went on
blasphemously. "I just sit here and do nothing and they make
sure some important position falls into my lap." I failed to see the
analogy, but did not take him up. One could see behind his
humour and cynicism a man baffled by his circumstances,
although events were yet to prove him a master of expediency.

It was Sunday, and I left Pangda Dopgyay to his own thoughts.
Over in the new room of the log cabin, John Ting, his co-worker
Tien and various other folk, mostly Batang people, travelling
along the same route together, had gathered for a service. This
would be our first "Gospel Meeting", as such, in Po valley.
Before we started, we discussed what language we should use.

As the Batang people are mostly bi-lingual and at least two Chinese were present, we decided to use Chinese. Brother Tien sang some choruses in which we joined as best we could and then John suggested I should preach a little. I had not spoken much Chinese for some time but, keeping much to the Scripture, I was able to bring out a few points from the story of the Cross. Seeing Mrs. Ren, daughter of Mr. Chiang the Batang magistrate and mother of three children, with us, I especially emphasised the thought "there stood by the cross of Jesus, His mother", hoping that she herself would take a clear stand beneath the cross of Jesus, for she had in earlier days heard something of the Gospel. John followed and spoke with considerable power from the poster on the wall, dealing with the crucifixion. The three days we had together were indeed never to be forgotten. I entertained my guests to what they called "foreign food". This was eggs, boiled, poached, scrambled or fried, with rather hard and heavy scones of wheat flour, being my nearest approximation to bread. Then there was butter, dried and fried yak's meat and wild honey. For a beverage, I still had a tin of cocoa which, with the liberal supplies of local milk, was very useful. I spared them the tsamba and buttered tea, which I sometimes took myself, but to which they were not fully accustomed. At that altitude the greatest lack was fresh vegetables and fruit. Rice also was something of a luxury. As far as we were concerned it was good, wholesome fare. As we were leaving on the morrow a certain amount of preparation had to be made. My boots had to be "buttered" and such clothes and other odds and ends as we might need, stuffed into saddlebags. I often used to think of Job, who washed his steps in butter. Amongst the Tibetans it is a very plentiful product, though often rancid before it is used. It is about the only fat in the interior and is utilised for lighting, cooking, tea-making, ointment and the preserving of leather, etc. John was delighted with Po and we made an excursion round the valley in the afternoon. One of the streams we had to cross was still thick with ice, so the journey over the high pass of about sixteen thousand feet on the morrow would almost certainly be at below zero temperatures.

I managed to get John Ting and Tien off fairly early the following morning, as their animals were well loaded and I knew

it would be unfair to expect them to travel at any speed. I
followed about two hours afterwards on the grey. We took the
path northward up the valley, which soon narrowed to a ravine.
A sparkling mountain torrent poured through the canyon. On the
steep slopes, a forest of pine trees clung to the massive moss-
covered stones, forcing their giant heads up to the light. Gnarled
roots and fallen trees, rotting in the dank atmosphere, constantly
barred our path, which rose and fell like some never-ending
switchback. We crossed and recrossed the stream until, after
several hours' riding, we broke out of the woods, to find ourselves
in a stretch of grassland with the mountains beginning to lie well
back. The magnificent panorama of menacing crags and huge
rocky buttresses, which could now be seen in full perspective,
awed one's spirit. There is a sense in which beauty is over-
whelming and its constant beholding quite exhausting. An hour
or two through odd copses and once more over the river, this
time by an old timber cantilever bridge, brought us to real nomad
country. One could see the black low tents dotting the undulating
grassy folds and, on the expanse of pasture, herds of sheep and
yak roaming afar. On my very fast horse I managed to catch up
the main Batang party just before they arrived at the nomad
encampment. It was well on in the afternoon and we decided to
spend the night with the nomads. We were given a fierce but
warm welcome as the dogs leapt at us from their stakes and the
woolly-haired nomad folk, in their rough sheepskin gowns, came
running out to lead our horses into a suitable tethering place.
We unsaddled all the animals and turned them loose to graze.
After a few rolls on the brown grass they cantered off to enjoy
their well-earned relaxation. We walked into one of the tents
where the camp people had arranged for us to pass the night.
It was quite a commodious one, being about twenty feet square.
The nomad tent is generally made of yak and goat's hair twined
into a peculiar coarse fabric, which is waterproof and yet still
permits a small amount of light to penetrate. It is roughly cup-
shaped, being supported by ropes, which pluck it upward at
various points, then pass over a series of poles set around the tent,
finally being pegged down some five or six yards back. From the
entrance flap to the back of the tent is a slit in the canvas about a

foot wide, which lets in the light and gives an outlet to the smoke from a built-up fireplace occupying the centre of the tent. This opening is covered by another flap when rain or snow are excessive. Inside the tent, on the right of the entrance, yak calves are sometimes staked at night in order to protect them from the intense cold and the prowling wild beasts. The edges are lined with boxes and bags of tsamba, although sometimes firewood is used for the same purpose, namely to keep out the draught. On the left of the entrance, the "household" utensils, such as churns, chopping board, mixing bowl, etc., are piled. Towards the back of the tent is often seen a little shrine and some small dirty idol of Buddha or one of his alleged incarnations. A ladle or two will hang from ropes slung across the tent roof, and saddles, bridles and ropes will be seen stacked in some corner. On the floor are spread old sheepskins. In such dwellings out on the windswept grasslands the nomads successfully combat the elements, eke out their existence and rear their families. They are a robust and fearless people, whom one is compelled to admire and whom one readily learns to love.

Once settled in, we spread out our bedding on our saddle-rugs around the fire, took our fill of some tsamba and buttered tea, and then chatted away into the twilight. There was some opportunity of witness before we retired. The nomads were still pottering around for quite a while but at last we were left in the silence. I hardly seemed to have been dozing more than a few minutes when I awoke to see the woman of the tent blowing the fire with some goatskin bellows. I looked out through the slit above my head. It was still pitch dark. It must have been something like three o'clock in the morning. About half past four we all began to move. There was an exacting day ahead. John had arranged with the horsemen to reach Batang by nightfall, which would mean at least thirteen hours' riding, including the crossing of a high pass. By the time we had arisen and got some hot tea inside us, it was the dawn. Peering out through the door of the tent, I could see the planet Venus, scintillating in the pale blue of the morning sky, one dominating point of light above the steely ridges. In the tent John was folding his bedding and humming the familiar hymn tune. "He's the lily of the valley, the bright and morning star." It somehow gave a real ring to the day. Although up so early, we were still behind the other travellers at the start, which was rather dangerous on that pass, where bandits had shot a man and a woman only a few weeks back. After some time, we caught up and proceeded together, climbing hard for several hours. It was not until well above the tree line, about 15,000 feet in these regions, that we glimpsed the summit of the pass. The ice fields were numerous and at times dangerous. I was thrown once and John twice as our horses fell, but mercifully we received no injury. At the top there was surprisingly little snow, so the last stretch gave us no real difficulty. As the Tibetan drovers came over the top they cast a stone on the cairn and uttered blood-curdling shrieks, which they do as an acknowledgment to the "guardian" demons. Now began a descent of many hours. Once down to the tree line we all stopped, lit several fires and made a hot drink. The worst of the journey had been accomplished. Mrs. Ren's maidservant had climbed right over the top, carrying one of the children too small to be taken on horseback—an instance of the unbelievable stamina of the Tibetan people in their own environment. It was now about eleven o'clock. After an hour we started off again, continuing all day until about four in the afternoon. After a wonderful descent through the forests we dropped down to the village of Jumbading. The men and animals, not to speak of ourselves, were already thoroughly tired, but there was still much daylight and we continued yet another two or three hours down a winding narrow path at the bottom of a grea abyss. At last, turning a bend in the road, a well-watered plain stretched out before us and, in the centre of it the old walled city of Batang. Beyond the flat roofs of the town lay a lama city with high battlements and gilded temples. We clattered down past the wall of a monastery, across a small stream and, to our surprise, met Mr. Chiang, the magistrate, out for his evening stroll. I dismounted, he introduced himself, and we exchanged cordialities. After a few words I passed in through the city gate, leading the grey, still brimming with energy, even after such a strenuous day. Except for two buildings, the entire city is built in the Tibetan style of architecture. The streets are narrow and flagged with stone, worn smooth with the feet of centuries. I found the main

street and asked for Pangda Tsang's agency. The horsemen
arrived and we went straight into the courtyard of a two-storey
building. The agent, a somewhat lean-faced but friendly Tibetan,
took me up into a big room, which I shared with the horsemen
for the next three days. John and Tien were accommodated
temporarily by some of the Christians. My host looked after me
well, cooking all my food, and the men with me from Po treated
me very much as one of themselves. It was a treat to sit down on a
long couch and look out of the window at the darkening sky.
Away up on a mountain above the town a forest fire was raging,
giving the ridge a crest of flame. In the street below some school
children marched by, singing the new Communist songs. As the
sound died away, I was faintly conscious of other young voices
singing choruses in the "preaching shop" next door. Suddenly
I was startled by the sound of iron striking the paved way. Looking
down the street, I saw a man stripped to the waist and painted
like a skeleton. In his hand he had a long heavy chain and was
running madly up and down the street shaking it this way and
that. I wondered whatever he was about, but almost immediately
there followed a Buddhist procession carrying idols and sticks of
incense. I was sorry to see Liu Chia Jü, a scholarly Tibetan I had
known in Kangting, walking slowly along holding a joss stick.
What I had just seen and heard greatly challenged me. To-day
in Batang were three forces, eager to claim the people, three
clashing loyalties, three conflicting sets of interests. There was the
Lord Jesus Christ, Son of God, Saviour of the world, and the two
soul destroying alternatives Communism and Buddhism. Spiritually, however, the issues were only Light and darkness. To be in
the arena at such a time was an honour indeed, yet I knew only
God's grace could sustain me and bring me through victoriously
from all the conflict yet to be.

Over the town in several places flew the flag of the new regime,
yet no Communist official had been to see me. In the mornings
I was able to walk quietly up and down on the flat roof of the
hostel. The passage the Lord gave me was: "Jesus therefore,
knowing all things that should come upon Him, went forth and
said unto them, 'Whom seek ye'?" The initiative never left His
hands. Therefore I took my passport and handed it to Pangda's

agent. "Will you notify the local authorities ot my arrival?" I said. This he agreed to do and, after some time, returned, passport in hand, saying that all was in order. After this I was never approached by any of the local Communists as to my presence in the town. The Lord, through the contacts He had given us, had graciously overruled. In a sense, perhaps, I could also say, "My time has not yet come".

The evening I arrived, two of the local Christians came to greet me. They were Joseph Wang and Naomi. Joseph was twenty-three, spoke Chinese and Tibetan fluently, and English quite well. He was the adopted son of American missionaries, who had penetrated these parts years ago. Naomi was a whole time Christian worker aged about forty. Naturally she was not at all good looking, having a disconcerting cast in one eye, but spiritually she rejoiced in the adornment of a fine Christian character. They welcomed me and arrangements were made for me to move over to some quarters they were preparing for me, in a room of one of the Mission houses. I had very much wanted to stay in town to be nearer the people, but the mind of the Christians was that I should live more closely with them rather than live alone in a hostel, which they felt was most unsuitable in every way. If they had known just to what extent I had been bitten by some of the other "residents", they would probably have been even more insistent on my leaving my present quarters.

John and Tien were installed in a room quite near my new place, also situated on the old Mission property, now deserted and much of it derelict. Once in the new room I was able to talk on occasions to Joseph in the little kitchen where we cooked our food. When alone he outlined to me the position of the town. He said that when the American missionaries pulled out, two or three months ago, they had quite a bad time. Fifty or sixty young people, stirred up by the Communists, had come up to the compound and forced one of the missionaries to open all his baggage. They took away an ordinary receiving set and gave him a receipt. When the missionary protested, he was actually struck by one of them. At last they had got away, receiving, as George and I had done, permission from the Lhasa Government to travel to India, but the whole thing took a very nasty turn. The town itself was divided into two factions. One of the wealthiest local people, a man called Liu, was the political officer of the old regime in the town. He, with Liu Chia Jü, the heads of the lamaseries and certain others, represented one party, whilst most of the young people of the district, under the leadership of Pu Tso Wanje, the Tibetan Communist leader, represented the other. The small Communist group had set up a kind of local authority although Chiang, the ex-Kuomintang magistrate, was supposed to remain in office until the new officials came in to take over. All telegrams from the Communist authorities out in China proper passed through the local unit of the Communist Party. This meant that Chiang, the old magistrate, had virtually been deprived of all his power. The most uncertain factor in the place which made the red youth hold back, was that the two hundred ex-Nationalist troops, who under Liu Wen Hui's surrender should now be loyal to the new regime, had refused to lay down their arms to the local Government group. They, with their Kuomintang commander, insisted on remaining fully armed until the real Red Army arrived. This of course was a complication, for no one was foolish enough to imagine that the ex-KMT troops were now ready to fight for Mao Tse Tung, just because their notorious Governor, whose chief fame was in opium traffic, had "gone over" to the people. One day whilst we were together, a Tibetan came in and had a chat. He said he had just been down the south road to Tali in Yünnan to the Communist H.Q. there, carrying letters and documents for the local group. He seemed quite pleased with himself. "Although the double trip has taken several weeks; they gave me two thousand rupees" (about £50), he volunteered cheerfully. Who amongst the Tibetans would not be prepared to work for the Reds, if they paid a figure like that to a runner? I reflected.

The next few days were taken up with feasts. Liu Chia Jü, artist and scholar, invited me to his home. "I am keeping very quiet these days" he said, "doing a little painting in the day, then taking a walk in the country towards evening time. I avoid most people in the present situation." We also had a feast at the home of the widow of one of Tibet's most famous nationalists in recent years. It was on that day that news came in that all resistance on the mainland of China had ceased. Now only Tibet had to be "liberated". The sympathies of those present were not hard to detect. This meant that outside Lhasa-controlled territory, apart perhaps from odd tribal chieftains in isolated areas, the Pangda brothers were the only rulers not to have surrendered to the new regime. By subtle encroachment, however, and by absence of action on the part of Lhasa, their influence and power were being rapidly neutralised, until they would be powerless to do anything other than accept the new situation as inevitable.

The third feast was the most surprising. I received an invitation from the commander of the garrison troops, as did also John and Tien. We could, of course, hardly refuse, although one did not quite know what to expect. At the appointed time in the afternoon, we attended the old Tibetan fort below the town, a massive two-storeyed square building with battlemented walls and flat roof. At the entrance stood two cannons used by the Pangda brothers, in their revolt against the Lhasa Government and clashes with the Chinese in years gone by. What a story they could tell! Above us the red flag and five yellow stars of the People's Government fluttered triumphantly. It was going to be interesting to see who was invited. We went in through a courtyard and upstairs to where several tables were spread in two rooms. When all had arrived we were led in. To my surprise I was placed at the head of the first table as the guest of honour. I looked round. The ex-KMT commander, who still refused to yield his guns to the new local authority, was certainly playing a dangerous game. There in the fort with the flag of the new regime flying from its mast he had gathered together just about everyone of anti-Communist leanings he knew. It was no doubt a kind of demonstration of his loyalty to Chiang Kai Shek and the old set-up, which he probably wanted me especially to notice, since I was the personal friend of the Pangda brothers, who still held the actual military supremacy through the whole area. Amongst those present were Chiang the magistrate, Liu the KMT political officer, Liu Chia Jü, Geshi Assam, a leading lama, and other lesser personalities. To my amazement I found another lama there, Chao Hsun. He was a Chinese, a university graduate devoting himself to Buddhism in

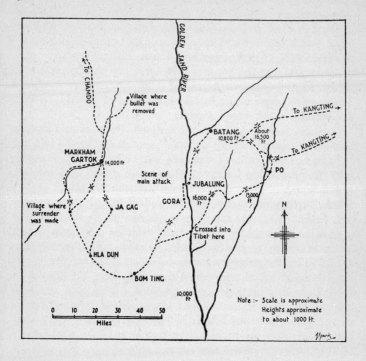

This is a rough sketch map showing the mountain trails traversed by the author in the region of the Golden Sand River. This river is part of the upper reaches of the Yangtze and marked the political boundary between Chinese Tibet and that part of Tibet controlled by the Lhasa Government, when the Chinese Communist armies attacked in October 1950.

the Litang monastery. I had met him in '49 when passing through that town. It was strange to see him again. Chao Hsun was learning Tibetan and he accepted an offer of a Tibetan New Testament.

We had some good spiritual talks with him later on. After the feast, which was in the Chinese style of about sixteen or so dishes of beautifully cooked vegetables, meats, etc., followed by rice, we went out into the grounds of the military commander's residence. Here I found that some of those present were preparing to escape to Lhasa before things really clamped down. This then was Batang in the throes of crisis.

Next day John had a quiet talk with me. "What should be done if there is adultery in the Church?" he asked. This he said not because he did not know the answer, but, being Chinese, it was his way of approaching a rather difficult matter that he wanted to put before me. I nevertheless gave him the Scriptural answer before helping him to say what he wanted to say. Then he went on, "You know, some say there *is* adultery in the Church. The man they name is a 'keen' brother too." "It is not . . .?" I exclaimed. "Yes, it is," he replied with great sadness. The day following Pastor Li invited us all to a meal with others of the Church fellowship, some of whom truly loved the Lord. Dear old brother Li had, like many in these parts, forgotten his age but reckoned himself about seventy seven. He was a sincere man, whom I grew to appreciate as a true soldier of Jesus Christ. He would stump around with his old stick, on the handle of which were carved the three Chinese characters, hope, faith and love. "Whenever I feel downhearted" he said, "I just look at my stick and my heart rejoices again." Another old brother was one of the elders named Chu. His life had been one of hard toil and much poverty but in his own way he loved the Lord, although he was not able to minister much from the Word of God now. That the Christians held together at all, in the circumstances, was quite remarkable. Everything was on the verge of disintegration. There was a great need for the clearing of the rubble, a purging of the defiling elements, and the knitting together in a holy love of all the living stones actually present in Batang. It seemed a hard thing to do to raise a temple, when all that faced one was the shambles of a wrecked testimony, but God could do it and do it quickly, should

He so desire. John and I, sharing a deep exercise of heart, continued on our knees together, for the Lord's arm to be made bare. John's words came back to me: "You realise it is Pastor Li's daughter who is concerned?" he had whispered. It was a complicated situation and more came to light as fellowship with one and another deepened. During these days I also had the joy of meeting brother Timothy Hsiao and his wife, Sino-Tibetans, who, deep down, were really devoted to Christ. He had some medical training and was the medical officer of the town, running a dispensary for all in the Gospel Shop. The Gospel was either preached or made known in the distributing of tracts nearly every day, which was a bright spot in the gloom. Naomi had a lot to do with this courageous effort. With the fellowship of the two or three something could be done. The Lord would cause the wall to be built even in troublous times.

So we continued in prayer. Services were held in the old Mission house in Tibetan and Chinese, every meeting being conducted in both languages. But on the seventh day, Badjay and another Tibetan messenger came in to Batang at break of day, having ridden almost non-stop from Po. They were armed to the teeth, each man having a gun, revolver and dagger. We tore open Pangda Dopgyay's letter. "My wife is dying. Can you or Hsiao come at once?" I thought of Cidenla, his wife, and the four children, ranging from the baby of four to Jigme of fifteen. Timothy and I knelt in prayer in my room. Within an hour we had decided that we should both leave immediately for Po. Subsequent events proved this was truly of the Lord, as new steps forward in testimony resulted in both places. It gave John more adequate time to collect data of the actual position in the Church and to deepen his fellowship with such spiritual elements as were there, whilst I was with Hsiao, deepening my fellowship with him and also having his help in what might prove a remarkable opportunity of witness. The first day, we only made a comparatively short distance, as one of the horses nearly died and had to be abandoned the following morning on the roadside. We spent the night sleeping next to the cows in a small hovel on the trail. The next day, having hired a fresh horse, we rode from 4.30 a.m. to 7 p.m. with no more than an hour's stopping on the way.

Pangda Dopgyay gave us a royal welcome. He had a room prepared for us in the big house, looking out on the roof-courtyard.
Cidenla was a little improved. In his desperation he had broken
into my dispensary and, with some penicillin of his own and some
distilled water he had managed to find, he had given some kind
of injection, an astonishing feat for a Tibetan. He had probably
seen it done a number of times when his children were treated for
measles in Kangting. Whether because of or in spite of the injection, the fact remained that his wife, although still with a
temperature of about 103, was nevertheless alive. There was little
doubt that she had pneumonia. As she could not take M. & B.
tablets, it had to be penicillin. She had apparently gone out on the
roof and stood in a cold wind to watch the great sight of a forest
fire blazing straight up from the valley floor to the tree line. This
had resulted in her present condition. She had a history of diabetes
and now began to spit blood. It looked as if tuberculosis had set in.
Pangda Dopgyay was most distressed and ordered a mass "prayer"
meeting. Every man, woman and child in the district who could
mumble, recite, chant or otherwise mutter some Buddhist saying
was mobilised and, several nights at sundown for about two
hours, they sat in the long porchway of the family shrine in one
great tattered crowd, droning out a united incantation. I felt, with
this, that the moment for direct testimony to the head of the
valley had arrived. With such a burden on my heart, the Lord
graciously provided the opportunity. Pangda Dopgyay knew we
were doing everything in our power to save his wife, as we were
getting up every three hours during the night to give injections.
He knew the ground on which I stood. He had heard the Gospel
before in Kangting, so I faced him alone with the issues involved.
I had not spared the poor. Should I spare the rich? I had never
seen him sit so still or so submissive. This time there was no joking,
no blasphemy, no mockery, but utter seriousness. He was a man
perhaps nearer breaking than he had ever been. Political and
domestic crises had brought him very nearly to the end of his
resources. When I had at last finished, he offered no rebuff and
attempted no back-answer, even as he had made no interruption
whilst I was speaking. A moment or two and he rose, walking
quietly away to some other part of the house. . . .

A rider came galloping in from the south. Bundi brought him to Dopgyay, who enquired of his mission. Two days' journey down the valley some six hundred runaway Kuomintang troops were planning an advance on Po. They had cut right across Sikang from Kangting, jumping out of the Red Army's grip on that city, and were expecting to be in Po in 36 hours. They wanted to be assured of Pangda's co-operation. Almost at the same time another messenger came in. This time from the north. Dopgyay tore open the letter. A peculiar grin spread across his face. Perhaps the most peculiar he would ever grin in all his chequered career. It was from the Batang Communist leader, Pu Tso Wanje. Could Pangda Dopgyay at all costs resist the Kuomintang bandits? In Batang they were fortifying the American Mission Compound and mustering as many guns as they could. The Red Army would not be long now. To say it was an incredible situation was putting it mildly. To side with the KMT troops would be to invite trouble with the Red Army, which might be through very soon. To resist a KMT marauding party would mean a pitched battle, as they would almost certainly be in a desperate state for supplies and the looting of Po would solve many of their problems. The fact, that the two brothers, as a result of Pu Tso Wanje's telegram, had been reported over the radio as surrendering, would add to the ill-feeling of the KMT troops. I thought of the recently so cock-sure Communist young people in Batang, now scared for their lives and their revolutionary gains. If the six hundred KMT troops did break through to Batang, there was little doubt that they would murder every one of them they could lay hands on, and the two hundred armed KMT troops already in Batang would probably be the first to start, once they saw hope of a relief from outside. I wondered, too, just how Dopgyay would handle it. This situation would be a nightmare to most people, but it found him in his element. When the news went round it caused quite a stir. I think the most nervous was Pangda Rapga's wife, who was very perturbed to find there might be war in Po valley on the morrow. I saw Pangda Rapga. He said he was confident they could mobilise five thousand men in a few days, but reckoned they probably had enough personnel locally to handle any trouble that might arise. Outside, Dopgyay and

Bundi were giving orders. Guns were being massed, tested and then allocated. The defence was to be conducted in two bands. Po valley was ideal country for defensive warfare, there being a bottleneck ravine at both ends, impassable ridges on the west and high passes and extensive grasslands to the east. The first band was ordered to guard the very restricted southern entrance to the valley. The second band was to be stationed in the fort above, where the New Year race up the mountain had been run. They were to be on vigil all night. Meanwhile replies were sent to both the KMT troops and the Batang Communists. I did not hear the letters dictated but, from all that was going on and ultimately transpired, it was obvious that Pangda Dopgyay must have stated to the Communists that guards had been set, which would satisfy them to some extent. To the KMT troops he no doubt sent a conciliatory note of explanation, offering an alternative route or even giving orders for certain supplies to be delivered to them surreptitiously. Riders were despatched almost immediately to the south. It was a great relief to everyone that the days passed by without incident. The only ones disappointed were probably the soldiers themselves, who, I think were looking forward to a good scrap, for such is the Tibetan Khamba's temperament.

Within a month Hsiao and I were back in Batang. It was necessary for me now to live with him and his family. The old Mission property had been reduced to a shambles, having been turned into a fort by the Communist young people. The main doorway had been bricked up and holes made in the walls. As a result it was no longer fit for habitation. Batang had apparently had a real scare. I tremble to think what would have happened if the KMT had really got through. We heard later that these KMT remnants had tried to get away to the S.W. into S.E. Tibet or Burma, but met Red Army columns coming up from the Yünnan border which engaged them. After some fighting they were finally dispersed. Some of them I saw being led into Batang under escort a few weeks later on. They were certainly unsettled times. Brother Hsiao gave me two books to read. *A thousand miles of miracle in China* and *Goforth of China*—both relating "Boxer rising" experiences. I wondered whether history would repeat itself.

By now it was the second week in May. It had been difficult for John and Tien with all the interruption to do much. Without concrete proof of sin in the Church it was difficult to act in such cases. Once we were back, meetings were restored. The first three weeks John took the bulk of the preaching. During this time we had a good talk with Joseph, telling him frankly what we had heard. John said that he had been maligned once in this way and realised the agony of mind through which one passes. We wanted to have fellowship with him and to comfort and encourage him if all these reports were really untrue. The main thing was to watch his reaction to such an approach. The outcome was that he more or less convinced us he was innocent. Meeting after meeting John preached on. The pastor's daughter was obviously upset. The last three weeks, at the invitation of the Christians, I preached constantly, mostly in Tibetan, although I gave my testimony once in Chinese. I experienced marvellous enabling and we decided to act once more. We again had an opportunity to speak alone with Joseph. This time, somehow, I felt I must go all the way. It seemed a terrible risk to accuse a brother in the Lord but I felt things had come to a head. We talked on and on into the evening. Then just at midnight he broke down and confessed his guilt. We knelt while he sobbed out his heart to the Lord in prayer. The Holy Spirit was moving. Next morning I told Hsiao that Pastor Li must be told. Hsiao said, "He's an old man, his heart is in a terrible condition. It will probably kill him." I felt grieved. "That which is for the glory of the Lord and the purity of the testimony cannot result in anything disastrous," was all I could reply. John and I both felt we should move right on and God would give His own grace to our aged brother. We met the old man in his garden. He first rebuked us for carrying on so late in his house the previous evening without telling him the reason. We could only apologise profusely and then state what we had to say. So we told him the worst. "She is only seventeen," he said. Although he wept a little, he was very still. He turned to us realising how much we felt for him and how much we loved him, and knowing that we were prepared to stand with him. "According to Chinese custom," he said, "I could kill my daughter for this, but we are the Lord's children; it cannot be this way with

us. Give me two days for prayer and I will make a decision."
The first stage was over. The Lord was triumphing in His servant.
That evening there was a meeting for the church folk. Somehow
there had been a misunderstanding and they had arranged no
speaker. I shall always remember how the old man rose up,
opened his Bible at 1 Cor. 13, read it and then preached with all his
heart on the love of God until he broke down in tears. Practically
no one but ourselves knew what had transpired, so the effect
upon all the other people gathered there was somewhat un-
nerving and there was a feeling that something was about to
happen.

Within two days he had a conference with us. He said that
he had had a severe shock. The previous evening in his home,
from upstairs there was suddenly the shot of a gun. Joseph had
been staying with him the last week or two. He had gone up
expecting the worst. He burst into Joseph's room but he was
still sitting there all right. Since he had confessed he had been in
a dreadful state of apprehension. Whether he had attempted
suicide and lost his nerve at the last minute the old man could
not tell, but he had fired the gun in the room. Joseph merely said
he had been cleaning it. We could only believe the Lord had
averted a tragedy. It meant however that the whole matter must
be dealt with immediately. Pastor Li's plan was, first, that Joseph
should write a signed and sealed statement of repentance and
then that everyone of any spiritual reality in the church, brother
or sister, should be called to a special meeting at which there
should be a public confession and the matter judged. Would
we get the statement from Joseph? When we approached our
young brother he expressed willingness to comply and the
document was duly completed in English and Chinese, John and
I signing as witnesses. This also served as legal proof of the
matter.

The meeting was convened in the home of the pastor, the first
of its kind, no doubt, in the history of Gospel testimony in that
town. About ten people were present apart from ourselves.
Joseph's statement was read. It sounded terrible. The girl, whom
I felt for very much, but who for the testimony's sake must go
through the ordeal, was made by her father, amidst awful sobbings,

to stand and acknowledge her guilt. The old man then collapsed on the floor, weeping convulsively and crying aloud. I sat silent and still. To-day the local Christians were judging sin in their midst. They must do it as they would, and I was determined whatever happened not to interfere. At last, order was restored, and our old brother sitting quietly in his chair again. The meeting was drawn to a close and I was invited to speak to the company. God gave me ability beyond my own and, speaking in Chinese and Tibetan, I addressed first our brother and sister who had acknowledged their sin, pointing out the certainty of God's loving forgiveness on the ground of the precious blood of Christ shed at Calvary. I then rebuked sharply the other believers and so-called "elders" as being partly responsible through lack of shepherding, and fear to act as they should in these matters. Dear Hsiao dropped his head, as he was one who could have helped so much.

Afterwards we broke up, as various practical things had to be settled. We left the believers talking in close fellowship with one another, perhaps in a way they had not done for many years. Joseph was to leave Batang immediately and return to his wife, whilst the care of Pastor Li's daughter and the child to be born, at his insistence, was left in the Pastor's hands.

At Hsiao's home there was a happier event by far. A little baby boy was born to him and his wife. I was called on to give this little one a name. I suggested John or David. They chose John. I shall always remember the bright testimony and joy of Mrs. Hsiao. She was radiant in the Lord and with the thrill of her new born child.

It was obvious that my present work was done. The friendly ex-KMT magistrate called me secretly. "I have special information that Red troops have already left Litang," he said. "I think you should leave immediately for Po." I thanked him. I knew that there was no question but that I should go.

The following day we gathered outside Batang, a little group knit together in a new-found love for one another. The birth pangs were passing, a new thing was being born. The possibility of a New Testament Church was coming into being from the ruins. The Lord would build and the gates of hell should not prevail against it. We prayed, bade farewell, then with a sudden wrench I turned the grey about and headed once again towards the mountains.

CHAPTER V

VALLEY OF DECISION

"The vision is yet for an appointed time, but at the end it shall speak . . ." Habbakuk 2.
"To every purpose there is time and judgment." Ecclesiastes 8.
"Surely there is an end and thine expectation shall not be cut off." Proverbs 23.

WE had reached a small patch of grass amongst the boulders about eight hundred feet from the summit of the pass. Our baggage, a strange assortment of furniture, green vegetables, flour and other bits and pieces, was strewn about whilst the animals grazed at a short distance. We had just had a meal and I strolled off a few hundred yards to stretch my legs after so long a while in the saddle. Suddenly my whole being was electrified. Up against the skyline I could see the silhouettes of men armed with rifles, coming over a spur of rock. A few yards along the road, prayer flags marked the spot where two recent murders by bandits had taken place. We were on one of the more notorious sectors of the road. I stood for a moment, watching anxiously. The men continued to descend in single file until between thirty and forty had come into view. I rejoined my Tibetan companions, who were looking uneasily in the same direction. By the ordered nature of their advance, I felt sure that we were about to encounter forward units of the Red Army. We, of course, could do nothing but wait. All the animals had to be reloaded before we could get under way again. Within ten minutes the first men were almost upon us. Sure enough, I was right, and as the leading officer came up, I went forward to greet him. He and his men were obviously utterly exhausted. He sank down on to a piece of rock. "Very tiring over the pass," I said sympathetically. He looked up, almost too fatigued to speak. "Here's my card, I am a

Christian missionary in these parts. Any time I am down at Batang you'll know who I am," I said cheerily. He looked at me quite blankly. A moment or two and his men came trudging by. He turned towards them, rose very wearily and, lunging somewhat unsteadily down the trail after them, left without so much as asking me a question. I stood gazing at the receding figures, dressed in their yellow cotton padded uniforms and blue plimsolls, each carrying a load of about sixty pounds. Power had not yet been put in their hands and until it was I would be immune in all circumstances, for the vision must yet run its course. How wonderful to be completely in the hands of the Lord. "Get things loaded now, Ga Ga," I told the boy. It would be as well to put as much distance as possible between us and the detachment which had just gone by. In an hour or so our party was over the pass. We spent a night with the nomads again and then, as the river of Po valley was in spate and the narrow ravine would be impassable, we made a detour over another high pass, coming down through the forest into the village another way. The Pangda brothers were glad to see me. Things were on the verge of breaking up. Their big plans for Tibetan independence, with lack of co-operation from Lhasa and no real foreign help, had been successfully neutralised by the Communists, who had now sent in their advance forces to contact them. Every attempt was being made to woo them to the Communist standpoint. They wanted Pangda Dopgyay to go to Peking. They offered him a good position. The detachment we had just met had passed through Po, leaving three officers and three other ranks behind, to continue working on the Pangda brothers. One of these, named Chang, was a secretary of Pangda Dopgyay whilst in Kangting, but he had now been roped in by the new government as a liaison officer. I knew this fellow quite well and when I had an opportunity with him alone, asked him: "Are you really a Communist?" "No," he said, "but at present I just go round doing this kind of work." Later we talked together with Pangda Rapga and one could see that Chang had not come to any deep convictions about the new regime or its policy, but had merely been coerced into his present task. I think that, underneath, he still wanted to be as helpful as he could to his old masters, in the serious dilemma in which they now found themselves. As was our custom at Po, Pangda Dopgyay and I had our midday meal together. This now became a most delicate situation, as two Communist officers of the People's Liberation Army were always present to eat with us. They were in a sense guests and yet intruders. They wanted to draw Pangda Dopgyay but Pangda Dopgyay would not be drawn. As far as they were concerned I was an unknown quantity, although automatically presumed to be an imperialist. When they had gone Pangda Dopgyay would tease me good naturedly over the whole thing, going over some aspect of the conversation which had more particularly been aimed at my discomfort. A sense of humour was a great mercy in such a situation.

One day, in my little Gospel room in the log cabin, one of the Communist officers came to see me. He was very affable on the whole. We talked about the civil war in China. I was quite direct with him, as I felt no reason to be otherwise. I said I thought it a great pity that after the second world war China could not settle her domestic problems peaceably, for then her position and prestige were very high and she could have taken a leading part in Asian affairs. The throwing away of such a golden opportunity and the resorting to such a terrible civil war, I thought, were most regrettable and indeed shameful. This put him somewhat on the defensive and he went to great pains to try and prove that all the blame was on the head of the bandit Chiang Kai Shek. From this I spoke of man's real condemnation. It was in the rejection of light. Taking down a Chinese John's Gospel, I turned to chapter three, showing him the words, "this is the condemnation that Light is come into the world and men loved darkness rather than light because their deeds were evil." This trend in the conversation was not to his liking, so he turned on me and said: "All you preachers are deceivers of the people". "As to who is a deceiver, three to five years hence, your own regime will reveal. If you do not fulfil what you have promised the people, would it not be right to say you are a deceiver?" "O, yes," he said quite glibly, "but we shall do what we promise without the slightest doubt." He cast an accusing eye at a number of suspicious looking cases below the medicine cupboard. "Is that a wireless transmitter?"

he rudely questioned. "No," I replied, "it is a box of surgical instruments and the other box you see is a typewriter." He was unconvinced. I watched him as he talked. He was sitting, as it happened, with his back to the big wooden cross of the poster on the wall. How unconsciously and with what strange coincidence was his attitude portrayed. There had been some candid speaking on both sides, but he nevertheless took with him a copy of each of the Gospels when he finally left me. I watched him go across Pa Shamba's roof, a soul for whom Christ died. Up on the hay rick hung a wireless aerial, connected with the Communist quarters in one of the big houses nearby. We were certainly living under observation. Had I left it too late, or misjudged the time? When should I leave for Tibet? To go alone seemed inadvisable as I wanted to stay there, not just flee to India. George had hoped to return but there had been no news now for months. The ideal seal of the moment to me would be if at least one of the Pangda brothers would move over the River of Golden Sand to Tibetan soil. It was a tense and searching time, yet the triumphs of the Lord's grace in Batang assured me that the time for entrance to Tibet had not been mistaken or overlooked, although it was quite obvious that a decision must be made shortly. So I continued before the Lord. I must at all costs dare to wait, even with indiscretion according to human standards, for the moment of His appointment. If I moved in His will, then all that later transpired would be in the working together for good of His great purpose.

Nearly a month went by, every day lived under the eyes of the Communist intelligence officers. Jigme was always out shooting with them. Lessons were thrown to the winds except when his father locked him in his study room. The Kangting days, when his guardian Gezang Drashi was always with him, were now a thing of the past. A messenger from Tibet hung about for some days in the outskirts of the village, keeping out of sight of the Chinese soldiers. He was waiting for letters from the Pangda brothers to carry back to the Lhasa Government. During this time I kept in close conference with Pangda Rapga. In secret, he told me how he feared lest his brother be deceived by the Communists, or act contrary to principle, in the question of loyalty to the Tibetan people. Bundi came in one day to my log cabin and sat down, just we two alone. "What about Pangda Dopgyay?" he asked. "We are all just breaking our hearts," he said. "There is talk of his going to Kangting to talk with the Communists and we think it would be a terrible disgrace for him to go. He could send a representative if it were absolutely necessary, but for he himself to go, we feel it is dangerous and most unwise. Any one of us would gladly die, if we could only fight." The big burly fellow spoke with great emotion. Ever since the rebellion in the old days he had stood by Pangda Dopgyay and he was baffled at his master's regard for expediency. I pointed out that Dopgyay had been beaten in battle more than once and knew what that meant. Against impossible odds, Pangda Dopgyay realised that to resist the whole People's Army of China without Lhasa's support, with no foreign help and with insufficient time for preparation, was just suicide. An alternative course had to be thought of in the new circumstances. As an explanation to a Kamba Tibetan I knew it was of little worth. So far as he was concerned, he would rather his blood be spilt in the snow, with the Chinese hordes trampling his body into the rocks and bracken, than to be found alive and defamed forever by the stigma of compromise. He left sadly, baffled and disappointed. About this time the Lhasa messenger slipped out of Po village undetected, carrying letters to the Lhasa Government. He also carried what proved to be my last letter to the outside world for nearly three and a half years.

"The vision . . . though it tarry, wait for it, because it will surely come, it will not tarry." The word of the Lord to Habbakuk, together with other scriptures recorded in that letter, eventually received in England, reveal the exercise of heart in those critical days and the longing to fulfil His great calling according to the hour of His appointment. Another runs, "to every purpose there a time and judgment". He Who had sent me to Tibet, would He not take me in at this eleventh hour to fulfil His Word? Towards the end of July, one morning I looked out of the cabin door. The miracle had happened, the detachment of the People's Liberation Army was preparing to leave. The radio aerial was dismantled, the horses were being loaded and by about nine

o'clock they were moving out. They left from a deserted courtyard. They had arrived unwelcomed and departed unsung. As
soon as they disappeared into the forest it seemed as if a dark
cloud had passed away and the sunshine had broken through
again. This indeed was the God-given time for advance. There was
nothing to hold me now. All His years of discipline and guidance
in my heart seemed now to have reached their climax. I had an
official pass from the Lhasa Government in my hand. All things
at Batang and Po had come in a very clear course of circumstance
to their own at least temporary conclusion. The Word of God
had by very remarkable Scriptures steadied me for decision. I
therefore went over to see Pangda Rapga immediately. I entered
his room and he greeted me with the words, "I am leaving for
Tibet within three days. Lhasa has said that I shall be received
and that I need have no fears of treachery from them because of
our bygone differences." As we chatted he continued, "At such a
time as this, personal loss can count nothing. I must go. Only
thus can I be clear in my conscience in my loyalty towards my
people!" His going, for me, was the last seal. This was the moment
of God's Own appointment for me, to enter into Tibet in the full
stream of His purposes. I could move forward in full assurance
of faith.

The two brothers were constantly in conference. Such possibilities of a rift between them as had earlier been indicated were
now healed. On what basis it was as yet hard to see. Away up
on a hillside, alone with the Lord, I considered the whole question
before me. I made my decision to cut clear of Po and move into
Tibet. When I announced my intention to the brothers, Pangda
Dopgyay spoke to me like a father. He said, "If you go and then
the Chinese armies overrun Markham Gartok and you are caught,
it may prove very serious for you. If you stay, though, I am going
to Kangting and may be able to speak for you to the authorities,
regarding your position here. If you go across to the other side of
the big river it indicates a stand. Our old arrangement, whereby
I supply you with goods in Sikang and you give me rupees in
Calcutta, you realise would have to be terminated? In the circumstances it would be both impossible and unwise. If you do go
though, I will give you a contact in Tibet with another trader

known to me." His understanding and helpful way showed the regard that had been built up over the period of our acquaintance and one only hoped that it would count for the Master after we parted. With Rapga I had to make certain arrangements. I suggested that we travel together, but after consideration his political insight suggested an alternative plan. If we should travel together, it might lead to misinterpretation by the Communists, should it come to their ears. "You follow me three days behind," he said "and then meet me in Tibet proper before we get to Gartok." I took his advice, although I had no inkling that if I had not done so, it might have proved disastrous. Again the Lord was over all, that until my present course had been fulfilled no man should lay hands on me.

On July 23rd, 1950, a great company of riders saw Pangda Rapga off on his journey into Tibet. One thing I could not understand was that Pangda Dopgyay's most trusted and personal head servant, Tsering Dorje, was travelling with Rapga. About an hour or so down the valley we parted and I turned back to Po with Pangda Dopgyay. His trip to Kangting was now in full preparation. Such servants as were going were being refitted with clothes. A special tent was being made. He was determined to go there in some style, and as a representative of his people. As for me, the log cabin was emptied of its goods and chattels. We planned on six loads. These were to include Scriptures, books, medicines and instruments, a tent, certain household equipment, tools, silks for trading or bartering, a typewriter, and a certain amount of clothing. About twenty-five loads of other medicines, scriptures, etc., I prepared to leave for the time being in the cellars of the big house. The dividing up and packing of equipment was an unexpectedly strenuous task, but we were ready to leave by the morning of the 26th.

It was my last evening in Po. Just seven months had elapsed since we had come to live in this remote valley, where so few, if any, had ever heard the name of Jesus. Dusk was fast approaching. How often after a day with the people or in arduous study, or returning from some sick person, I had looked down from the windows of my room to see the shadowy fingers of nightfall slanting down from the western ridges and the last glories of the setting sun gilding the eastern heights. It was in such moments that I had been most conscious of loneliness, and yet most conscious that I would not change my pathway for all the world could give. Four simple words from the Song of Songs had fixed my soul in Christ. "Thy love is better . . . Thy love is better!" I closed the windows and lit the butter lamp for the last time. I looked at my watch. It was almost half past nine. To-morrow, in the will of the Lord, I would be away on that trail slashed up through the forests, then over that grassy ridge to the great country beyond. I was just retiring when a voice called, as before, in English, "Geoff, Geoff." I looked out into the moon-lit field below. "John!" I exclaimed in utter astonishment, "wherever have you come from at this time of night?" "Down through the forest," he said calmly and led his horse towards Pa Shamba's compound. "Well, brother, come in. This is thrilling; I'm leaving to-morrow." In rather sad tones he replied, "I am on my way back to Kangting, my wife has somehow or other managed to swallow a needle. I may have to take her down to Chengtu to get an operation."

The next day, after bidding farewell to all at the white house, I returned to the cabin. Dopgyay had given me a beautiful present of a big Tibetan rug of many colours and a foreign suit he had hardly worn. His wife gave me a very fine razor. According to Tibetan custom I also made certain gifts to them, the most appreciated being a pressure cooker, which would enable Cidenla to cook her chicken soup the more quickly in that high altitude. Accounts were also settled and at last I had reached the moment of leaving. To-day it was a quiet, unannounced departure. The big farewells had all been carried out the day Pangda Rapga left. I said good-bye to personal friends; then John Ting and I walked down about half a mile beyond the village. We felt the parting keenly. There we stood, in a remote spot of Central Asia, two of the Lord's children, of different nationality but welded together in the spiritual destiny of the Central Asian peoples. Where our paths lay, neither of us could tell. All I knew was that my face was set towards Lhasa. As for John, he must return into the teeth of the godless system engulfing the millions of his people. We could but commend ourselves into the Hand of the Lord for the glory of His Name. Chungking, Chengtu, Kangting, Po, Batang. Perhaps one day in Chamdo, so we moved on, in His pathway set for our feet.

CHAPTER VI

INTO TIBET

"A man can receive nothing, except it
be given him from heaven." John 3.

I LOOKED back through the trees. Some miles up the valley I
could still glimpse the great white house. I should perhaps never
see Po village again, yet in the mystery of God's will and purposes,
He had seen fit that the shifting fortunes of the house of Pangda
should serve the interests of the abiding Kingdom of His Son.
By early afternoon, we were over the first pass. In a hollow, Ga Ga
and I located the horsemen, who had travelled ahead with the
loads. After a good drink of tea we pushed on, down into the
woods again. Being summertime it was most pleasant, with the
sunshine twinkling through the leaves. So unconcerned were we
with the trail that, before we had time to save the situation, one
of the mules walked below a tree trunk, slanting across the road,
and nearly wrecked one of the boxes. No serious damage was
done and we came out of the woods to a few houses skirting a
stream. This valley was linked with the Batang trail that we had
traversed some two months before. Another hour over a wooded
hillock and we entered a valley remarkable for the fact that in it
were situated two quite large villages, within about half a mile
of one another. Between the two was an old deserted shrine. It
proved an ideal place for camping and there we passed our first
night. Next morning we were away early and soon began to climb.
It took us most of the morning to get above the tree line, but by
about one, we were in nomad country and decided to have a
meal in one of their tents. From the nomad encampment, we
proceeded up a wide deserted valley, the pasture land deteriorating
all the time until there was only rough scrub. After two or three
hours following the course of the valley slowly upwards, all vege-
tation ceased and we found ourselves in a wilderness of rock. The
second pass now loomed before us. It was a gruelling trail

stretching over three barren ridges. Rarely in all my travels in
Central Asia have I seen such a desolate landscape. It might have
been on the moon itself. On the roadside lay the carcase of a
mule amongst the rocks. "That belonged to the Moslem trader
who left Po a little while back," conjectured one of the horsemen.
It was pitiless country. Not a blade of grass, not a trickle of a
spring, no sound, no life unless it were some vulture circling high
in the great vault of heaven. At last, after driving the animals
hard, we were over the three-headed pass and descending into
yet more nomad country on the farther side. Our highest point
must have been in the neighbourhood of 16,500 feet. We had only
dropped about five hundred feet but felt that we should nevertheless pitch our camp for the night. We had no sooner raised our
big Tibetan tent, than it began to rain and the temperature
dropped violently. A cold, that had been coming on some hours
aggravated by the extra fatigue of the rather strenuous day, made
me feel thoroughly wretched. Although I had spent nearly two
and a half years on the Tibetan plateau, this trip was to prove
me still an ignoramus as to its weather. I had presumed that, being
July, whilst we might encounter some rain, yet even on the
heights temperatures would not be too low. Heavy rain now turned
into hail. The dry ground was soon running with water. We dug
hasty trenches round about us as the downpour, driven by the
wind, battered at our frail tent. It was a hectic time. When would
it stop? I do not think I have ever seen such a prolonged hailstorm.
Fortunately the hailstones were not too big but they began to
pile up, until inches thick in places. I began to feel really ill as
darkness fell. There was no dry tinder and we could only snuggle
down into our bedding and gowns. We had done our best but the
trenches were none too successful in keeping the interior of the
tent dry. Such food as we carried with us we ate. I took a good
dose of sulphanilamide. To go down with pneumonia in these
circumstances could prove disastrous. The storm raged on. In a
lull the boy, with one of the horsemen, went down the track in
the darkness to see if they could contact another nomad tent.
They were away hours and the trip proved fruitless. The next
tent was apparently miles down the valley. Ga Ga, who had also
been feeling none too good, began to crock up on his return and

I had to give him some medicine. The night was awful. I woke feeling like death itself. I felt I must get up but almost dropped to the floor in a faint. I struggled hard to maintain consciousness. As I dropped down on my sleeping bag I put my hand under the tent flap and found about two inches of hailstones still unmelted. Applying them to my forehead, my head cleared again and, eventually, I managed to sleep a little. Daylight revealed that we were in the middle of a raging snowstorm. How long it had been going on I do not know, but the tent was weighed right down with the snow. No one felt any necessity to rise. In fact it was useless to do so. No fire could be lit and there was only the howling blizzard outside. About every half hour from dawn onwards, we beat the snow off the tent to save it from collapsing. The circumstances were unenviable. I still felt ill but, with continued doses of sulphanilamide, my temperature was kept under control. I think even the Tibetans were taken aback by such weather occurring in July. About nine-thirty or so the storm abated and almost immediately the sky cleared. By about ten o'clock the sun was shining and the state of the weather absolutely reversed. The snow now simply fled before the sunshine. It melted with such rapidity that the men began to consider the possibility of moving by about midday. What a time! Eventually with much of our kit and loads sopping wet, we managed to assemble our somewhat disorganised caravan and get under way. We descended slightly through the melting snow and skirted across the side of the valley to a slope, which the men wondered if we would be able to cross, as it was of clay soil. It was, as one can imagine after the volume of water descending upon this region in the previous night, in a deplorable condition. The only thing that made it possible, I think, was that there was a certain amount of rock about, so slithering our way hither and thither we eventually scrambled over a rise, then down on to a long thin ridge of land where the trail was much improved. We were now in wonderful country. It was as if we were travelling on the apex of a roof. On either side the country fell away immediately thousands of feet into ravine and gorge. At last, after several miles, we descended a further few hundred feet to a grassy promontory where, like Moses from Pisgah, I was able to look out from about 15,000 feet over the land of His promise. Before me, stretching away as far as the eye could see, lay Tibet, one great jumbled panorama of hill and valley, peak and grassland. Behind me the rough mountain trails, trodden out by countless mule trains and many a weary traveller down the centuries, straggled back hundreds of miles over the passes, to the Szechwan plains. In all this vast country, God had hewn us a way. No spiritual, political or natural barriers had been able to frustrate Him and now before my very eyes was the open door for which I had yearned for years. O the exceeding greatness of our God! Far below, the swollen yellow waters of the Golden Sand River rolled down through a vast abyss. On its farther side I could see a small delta formed by a tributary stream. The deep ravine it had cut in the mountains could be traced right up to a minor plateau of distant grasslands. I stood overwhelmed by the wonder of it all. God willing, on the morrow, I should be there. As we continued to descend, I found the men were preparing to encamp in the open again. Our start had been so late, they felt it too much of an effort to try to make a village before nightfall. In my weak condition, however, I felt it absolutely imperative to get to a house for the night, to have some properly cooked food and a good rest. They were somewhat disgruntled, but one of them, being the husband of the woman so terribly burned, was on my side. When I found it was a question of buying fodder for the horses, an item which would be unnecessary if we camped out, the whole matter was easily settled. So we continued and were able to reach a small village perched up on a ledge of land, overlooking the river, before darkness set in. It was a real haven of rest. The village folk were kind to us, and I was able to treat one of their children for a sore leg and pass on a Scripture portion in Tibetan to them before I left.

The following morning we set out, both the boy and I, feeling still far from well. The descent to the river, several thousands of feet below, was stupendous in every way. In places the road was non-existent, just a gravel slide down the mountain. At another place, a ledge across a sheer face of rock meant that all the loads had to be taken off the animals, as the roughly constructed trail, doubtfully supported by precarious walls of loose stone, was only wide enough for a man or an unloaded animal to cross on his own. The zig-zag gradients were so steep that one would have done almost anything to be allowed to go uphill again. The jolting of constant descent left one's whole body bruised and jarred. Towards midday Ga Ga and I reached the rocky shores of "the big river", as the Tibetans call it, and gazed out to the farther side. The air was now really warm, the altitude being little more than 10,000 feet. We could see a small village amongst the trees growing on the distant delta and a big three-storeyed dwelling, built against the mountainside immediately facing us. We shouted but there was no movement. Eventually some of the horsemen arrived and one or two other travellers and together we renewed our shouting. Our persistent calling echoed feebly through the cliffs and screes and seemed fainter than a bird's cry in the relentless rush of water, surging through the mighty chasm. At long last something moved. It was a grotesque object not unlike some prehistoric reptile. This first Tibetan mystery, however, soon unfolded itself and straining my eyes I detected what proved to be a man carrying a yak-hide coracle. By skilful downstream manipulation he and an "accomplice" managed to paddle this unwieldy Boadicean craft across the turbid waters to where we stood. Five boxes were carefully lowered into the bottom of this little cockleshell, dancing on the bosom of the river. This seemed to steady it. The wild-looking oarsmen said they could take three passengers. It seemed hard to believe but I stepped "aboard". In addition to this, horses had to be "towed". A further coracle arrived and loaded up with men and cargo. Two animals were placed on a long rein, which was held by a man in the coracle, and the remaining horsemen beat them into the water, until we had paddled out into the current. "There's no danger," one of the men said cheerily, but my trust was in the Lord, Who I felt sure would not allow me to come right across China to this very moment, to be swept back down to Shanghai in the raging flood. As soon as the horses were out of their depth they began to swim desperately to hold their own against the current. The oarsmen of each coracle paddled fiercely and everybody crouched low, while the battle was waged. The current swept us downstream a considerable distance before the shore began to seem anywhere near us. I could see that, a few hundred yards below, the river entered a gorge, where no landing would be possible, but the men in the coracle were more in command than I supposed and, as they manoeuvered their boat successfully out of the main flow, the mad rush downstream slackened. Very quickly now we drew into the beach, quite a distance below the village. We touched in and I jumped out on to the stones and sand. Beneath my feet was Tibetan soil. The iron gates had yielded. God had by His grace and the infinite skilfulness of His hands brought me into the land of His appointment. I walked as in a dream, my heart leaping up with thankfulness.

In my Bible given to me by my old Sunday School teacher, are recorded these words:"Sat. July 29th, 1950. Just before noon, I crossed the river called the River of Golden Sand, which forms the upper reaches of the Yangtse and set my foot down on Tibetan soil under the control of the Lhasa Government. For me a very great event—and also I dare to believe a very great event in the history of the Gospel's advance into Central Asia by the Will of God."

I stumbled over the stones and up to the big three-storey building. I was received by the Pangda Tsang's agent, who entertained me in a room on the top floor looking out down the river. This was a muleteer's hostel and an agency for handling caravans crossing the river. There was an endless bustle with tough-looking characters coming in and out. The day I was there was perhaps especially busy, as a salt caravan was going through the customs. To sit and watch the different groups of men and each individual was fascinating. I had been given a low couch by the window on which to rest. It was for all the world like being amongst a band of buccaneers. Armed to the teeth, with dagger and pistol stuck in their girdles, they cursed and swore, shouted and guffawed. The filth, in the warmer temperature, seemed suddenly intensified. Some were stripped to the waist, their skin a dull blackish copper colour, tanned by the sun and ingrained with grime. My host, a quaint type of man, was so run off his feet that he could hardly speak to me, although this did not concern me unduly. All I wanted to do was to sit. After a while the frontier officer, a "commander of ten" by rank, came in to see me. As Pangda Rapga had passed through two days previously, he did not even ask to see my passport. He had already been forewarned of my coming. His main concern was to see if he could get some medicine from me for his syphilitic sores. When my first tiredness had worn off I wandered out again to the river bank. Along the beach I came across a group of boys about fifteen or sixteen years of age and we quickly got into conversation. I was pleased to find how much they understood me. It was not long before I was able to speak to them concerning the true God, which was a great encouragement to me, having been only a few hours in Tibet proper. As we walked along, the two coracles were propped up on poles on the riverside. One of the boatmen pointed to a rip in the yak-skin. "Your grey horse did that," he said. The idea being that the owner of the grey horse might be disposed to pay out compensation. As the claim was not pressed I could only presume he was a rather optimistic opportunist.

As soon as I had arrived, enquiries had been set afoot for the hire of to-morrow's horses. The officer came to assure me that all had been attended to and that, according to their orders received from the General, I would have a soldier escort. At sundown, after some argument with the landlord, I managed to persuade him to allow me to sleep on the roof under a lean-to. He considered this preposterous. Other guests had never done it. They had always slept in the main room on the couch. Nevertheless I insisted. I knew that, if I did not regain strength and get an absolutely undisturbed night, I would be in a state of collapse by the time I reached Cartok.

Next morning prior to departure we had a short medical parade. The eyes of the villagers were in a filthy and diseased state. All I could do was to put in drops to give them a little temporary relief, for which they seemed very grateful. Meanwhile our little caravan had been assembled. We had new horsemen as we were now to move forward in stages, under the Lhasa Government system of Ulag, a compulsory use of the people's cattle and horses by the government, as a levy of tax. Our journey lay through a long wooded valley, up which we climbed for some hours, until we moved out on to another very broad fertile valley some 13,000 feet above sea level. I looked across its meadows dotted with farmsteads. All was so peaceful and I wondered just how

long it would be before the sound of battle would ring through
it. During the day we changed animals twice. The last stage
brought us to the hamlet of Bom Ting, situated on a hillock,
towards the far end of the broad valley. We spent the night in
the big house occupied by the garrison. The local commander
was away but had left instructions regarding our accommodation.
I had hoped to make a further stage that night in order to catch
up Pangda Rapga's party, but the local people said I could stay
at Bom Ting and still do it the next day. We retired early and
were up with the dawn, so were changing horses at the next stage
by about 8 a.m. next morning. Whilst waiting for the new animals
I went into the "stage" house. I could hear the call going from
rooftop to rooftop for the Ulag horses. The family of the house
showed me into a back room. There amidst all the farm imple-
ments, in a kind of outhouse, lived the father, in isolation. He
looked as if he had tuberculosis. He was delighted to see me and
a ray of hope shone in his eye. I could do nothing for him
medically. He was very sad and asked me about death. It was a
fine opportunity and I was able to give him a portion of the
Scriptures in Tibetan which told of the One in Whom was life.
"Will it be long before I die?" he asked. "We are all only here
a little while," I replied and encouraged him to read the Scripture, which he seemed well able to do. Ga Ga suddenly called
me and I had to leave. We broke away up from the valley, over
some denuded shale slopes, to the grasslands again, where along
a big stretch of the trail were piled heaps and heaps of "mani"
stones. These are stones on which are carved the mystic Buddhist
formula "Om mani padme Om". To us it is meaningless, but it
is revered above all other speech by the Tibetans. The traditional
interpretation is "O the jewel in the heart of the lotus", but one
lama told me that there are some exponents of Lama-istic teaching, who can discourse for three months on the supposed content
of this saying alone. "Mani" piles are a common sight throughout
Tibetan-inhabited country and have been raised by pilgrims and
devout Buddhists, buying such a stone from a carver and then
casting it as an act of devotion on to the pile. We descended into
another valley in the pouring rain, until we cantered into a
ruinous heap of dwellings which styled itself Hla Dun. The name

implies it has association with the gods. I entered a muddy alley-
way, which meandered amidst a shambles of broken down walls
and houses. At the centre of the maze, we stepped into the rather
snug quarters of a "centurion" of the Tibetan army. He was a
man in his forties, rather portly and attended by a wife, at least
twenty years younger than himself. As he talked and entertained
us, I little realised that in three months he would be in eternity.
He could not read, but I gave a tract to a young fellow about
the place who could. We only changed horses here, so moved on
quickly towards Ja Gag, which means, ironically enough, "stop
the Chinese". I shall always remember the next stretch of country.
It was over hill and dale and the flowers were superbly beautiful,
the most common being a kind of red primula, stretching in great
patches of flame in the green grass. At about four in the afternoon we descended a snake-shaped valley and moved out on to
a small plain. Another mile brought us to Ja Gag, a full-sized
village and the sphere of influence of the Pangda Tsang's notorious
agent, named Azung. Although playing at lamas was one of his
chief fads, yet as we entered the big inner courtyard of his sizeable
mansion, he was there to meet us dressed as an ordinary Tibetan,
and in quite a sober turn of mind. The Po charade was not to
be enacted that day. One glance at the faces around me and I
knew Pangda Rapga was there. Aku, Tsering Dorje and others
welcomed me in. I was ushered into the big guest chamber.
Several grotesque man-sized images leered down at me from their
gilded shelves as I entered. At the far end Rapga was sitting on
a raised dais. He was obviously very pleased to see me. On his
left, sitting on a couch at right angles to his own, sat a very old
man, whose appearance was most extraordinary. He wore some
green spectacles of a peculiar shape. I cannot imagine from where
he obtained them. His garments were orange and red but unlike
any lama robes I had ever seen. On his chest he had a kind of
breastplate, a big highly polished circle of brass. He apparently
had known Pangda Rapga when he was very young and now,
on his return, had travelled up to Ja Ga to welcome him. He
could neither read nor write and was of the school of lamas who
believe that all truth comes by meditation, there being no need
of study. Pangda Rapga, a little whimsically, introduced me to

this strange character, as one who did not a little preaching in
these parts. A couch had been provided for me and we sat and
talked. As Rapga spoke of his journey, I realised again how
wonderfully God had overruled in all things. When he and his
escort had come to the little village high up over the river at
which we had stayed the night, an armed party of the Batang
underground communists had intercepted them. It was a miracle
that they did not engage in open combat but Pu Tso Wanje came
forward with a gift of silk, after which he made a speech about
the Communist policy towards Tibet and pleaded with Rapga
not to continue on his journey. With this they withdrew and he
proceeded to the river. I could only wonder what the position
would have been if I had been with him. Other news consisted of
border clashes between Tibetan and Chinese troops and a rather
disquieting rumour that the invasion had actually started, but
this was not confirmed. I was glad to hear that he contemplated
resting a few days before proceeding. I was still sick with a cold
and diarrhoea. Whilst there I had a certain amount of opportunity to do a little simple medical work and to testify to some of
the people. The strange old lama was baffled to think I had come
as far as I had. "Whatever makes you do it?" he enquired with
a most puzzled look on his face. The answer was anything but
what he expected. "Because of the danger in which you stand,"
I replied. "Danger? Who's in danger? We are not in any danger."
His answer reveals the typical attitude of the majority of the
Lama priesthood and, for that matter, of most of the Tibetan
people themselves.

In the question of religion they view themselves as being of the
"inner doctrine". All other faiths are "outer doctrine". The very
idea of some foreigner coming from afar to preach to them is in
their minds of necessity an utter absurdity. When we consider
that the One we proclaim, we do so on His authority and at His
command, as the only Saviour and as the only mediator between
God and man, then the difficulties of preaching the Gospel to the
Tibetans will be apparent. They hold Buddha and his incarnations, the whole priesthood under the Dalai Lama and the 108
volumes of their scriptures, as the component parts of their three-
fold god. "By the three gods" is a constant oath on the lips of all

Tibetans and their self-complacency in this dark religion is complete. Azung, always full of pranks, started to tease me one day as he was showing us around his god room. We were looking at the rather common Buddhist idol with a myriad hands. "Isn't that a fine god?" he said, expecting me to assent. "No, it's not!" I said. This started the ball rolling and a time of testimony ensued. Another day I was on the roof giving out medicine with a group of Tibetans round me. It was a question of syphilis, and so often on that point it is easy to broach the question of sin and the real remedy, as being not in the medicine but in the Lord Jesus Christ. As I walked around the roof afterwards I was disconcerted to see a man watching me closely. I turned and our eyes met. Suddenly we recognised each other. "Gezang Drashi, Gezang Drashi. Why now I remember!" This man, one of Pangda Dopgyay's centurions, used to escort Jigme every day to our Chinese house in Kangting for English classes. "Are you at peace? I live just near here—it is good to see you again," he welcomed me. These were happy days for me. No one interfered with my movements and it was thrilling to be about the Master's business in this great country.

At last the day came for our departure and we started on the last lap of our journey. This time there was a whole cavalcade of riders. I had on my full Tibetan regalia. By midday we were on the crest of the hills which overlook the Markham Gartok plain. I hardly knew how to go on, I felt so ill. Walking down the slope, leading our horses, as is the Tibetan custom, nearly finished me. When still one-third up Rapga remounted. This was a signal and so for the last part of the hillside we rode down. Unless this had happened, I think I should have fainted. The whole plain of Markham Gartok, at a height of about 14,000 feet, now opened up before us and we moved steadily towards the garrison a few miles ahead.

As the party of smartly dressed riders neared the town, all the inhabitants came running out to greet us, lining the route into the large Tibetan fort. Once in through the main archway our horses were led away and the General, by rank, military governor of Markham and, by birth, Prince of the old Dege Kingdom in Sikang, came forward to meet us. He stood, a man of magnificent physique dressed in his superb robes, smiling a welcome to us both. "Are you tired?" he asked using the honorific of the Lhasa dialect, "come along in." I staggered through the porchway into his exquisite flower garden, feeling already very much better.

CHAPTER VII

GUEST OF THE NINTH GENERAL

". . visited of the Lord of Hosts . . . with
earthquake and great noise. . ." Isaiah 29.

SITTING around a decorated square table, on the low rug-covered couches, in the Dege Sey's very tastefully furnished living-room we chatted and sipped tea into the sunset. Pangda Rapga and the General talked heart to heart, burdened as they were with the problems of their people. This meeting after many years meant much to both of them. To me, the Dege Sey was a charming host, setting me completely at my ease from the very first. I was expecting to speak in English from the reports I had received, but he persisted in his courteous Lhasa dialect until well on in the evening, when he rather shyly began to use a few phrases. He had apparently heard of Rapga's exhaustive study and was a little hesitant to display what he felt was his own limited knowledge. After the first great desire for conversation had been somewhat satisfied, Rapga withdrew and I was left alone with the Dege Sey. He was a tall man and broad with it. His long black hair had been plaited into a queue about his head. Thoroughly masculine, he was of a most commanding appearance, yet there was a softness about his eye and his smile which was most winsome. He looked what he was, a Khamba Tibetan with a background of culture. He sat on his cushioned dais, arrayed in the gorgeous orange silk robes of his high office. From his right ear hung a long blue turquoise ear-ring and, as he spoke, he poured a small quantity of very finely powdered snuff on to his thumbnail, which he kept poised before him until he had finished what he was saying. Then, with a most adept sniff, he inhaled it and with watering eyes continued to talk with enthusiasm. As he asked question after question, one could see his great hunger for a fuller intellectual life. His appointment to this far eastern sector of Tibet isolated him from the social contacts he had so much enjoyed in Lhasa. "I hope you will be able to stay three months," he said hopefully, "there are so many things to talk about." His unconcealed delight at my coming emboldened me to reveal something of my hopes for the future. He listened very sympathetically, as I told him how I longed to get through to Chamdo and Lhasa and set up contacts for the starting of medical work. "In a way," he said, "I don't hold out much hope but we'll try. I'll write a letter for you to the Governor of Chamdo and, I tell you what, there is a British wireless operator there named Robert Ford, a very good friend of mine, you should get in touch with him because he is personally known to the Governor." He paused a moment and then added, "Still there is time yet and we can think about it." In a little while Pangda Rapga came in. To my surprise he asked if he might smoke opium. Reclining on the couch in the shadows he received the lamp, opium, pipe and instruments from Aku. He went through the process I had seen all too often at Po, of rolling a little ball of opium with the aid of the flame. Then with a deft flick of his hand he stuffed it into the bowl of the pipe over the lamp and began to inhale. In Lhasa-controlled Tibet it is illegal, but the Dege Sey did not question his old friend's indulgence. Years ago Rapga had been wholly given over to this habit but afterwards had in some way reduced it. Recently, no doubt under the increased strain of events, he had been taking more and more. I felt very concerned for him and sensed a look of pity in the gaze of our host. The long journey, my weakness due to a stomach disorder, together with the prolonged conversation, brought me to that demoralised state of mind when all one's energies are devoted to keeping the eyelashes apart. Fighting a losing battle, I felt it would be better to retire than to fall asleep in the presence of the General. I excused myself, and with a clap of his hands a servant appeared to show me to my room. I lay down with a grateful heart. In the fort, "Lights out", a session of lama music followed by the firing of a cannon, had long since sounded, and I was no sooner snuggled down into my sleeping bag than I fell asleep.

Pangda Rapga had announced that he was staying a few days. I, of course, would have to await a permit from Chamdo before proceeding further. This being the case, Kungo Dzong, the Civil

Governor and magistrate of Markham, invited us both, together with his superior, the Dege Sey, to a feast. Expecting this to be something after the Chinese style, I was rather taken aback when told that the feast would last three days. It was quite an experience. Every morning at about half past eight, the head servant of the Kungo Dzong would come across, pay his respects to the Dege Sey and in the language of the orient say, "Come, for all things are now ready." We approached the compound of the Civil Governor, on a series of stepping stones, dotted about in a sea of mud. To see any one of us in our finest gowns slip into such a morass of filth would have given, I am sure, considerable merriment to some of the poorer citizens. In the yard outside the Governor's residence was an outhouse in which about eight people were employed with wooden mallets beating out some kind of dried plant used in paper making. The process was very crude. It was completed at a nearby spring, where a thin watery paste of this powder was allowed to collect on pieces of framed canvas. After drying in the sun, a coarse yellow paper was obtained. For many hours every day, these people, some of them still almost children, pounded away. I found out they received a mere pittance for their pains. On arrival we were welcomed by the Governor, whom I took to be his wife at first, owing to his rather effeminate features. His wife, however, soon appeared on the scene and I was disillusioned. We were now led very sedately through their surprisingly small house into the garden. We were seated in a kind of wooden hut used as a summer house. It was not typically Tibetan and round the walls were numerous rather obscene and cheaply printed Chinese pictures. In addition to the usual low couches and tables, there were one or two foreign chairs and a high table on which lay some National Geographical Magazines. Breakfast was served immediately. It was a pleasure to eat the exceedingly fine tsamba found in the households of the nobility. The coarser varieties bought in the villages, no matter to what extent one might become accustomed to them, always seemed much harder to swallow. Tibetan feasts have little original in them, being a rather poor edition of Chinese tastes. Having been to sumptuous Chinese meals in China proper, I found the things spread before us not particularly tempting. In such a wilderness country it is naturally not easy to furnish a table of note. The first day we had quite interesting conversations, although I found the Kungo Dzong's dialect much more difficult than the Dege Sey's. The second day was tedious. The three Tibetans gambled all day on a game of the domino type, in which I think they found very little diversion. I looked at Geographical Magazines and explored the garden. In my tour of inspection, I found a colony of silversmiths living in a shack in one corner of this walled piece of land. They were employed on making exquisitely engraved silver bowls for the Kungo Dzong. They were artists as well as artisans. I looked at their appalling living conditions. It would be difficult to conceive of more abject poverty. There were also a maimed eagle and a parrot. This latter bird could ask for a nut in the Lhasa dialect, which was quite intriguing. The most vital character in the whole place to me was a small boy of about twelve, an orphan employed in the house on odd jobs but who was obviously a gem. His frank keen spirit, bright eyes and engaging smile put to shame Tibet's feudal and dissipated aristocracy. The third day of the feast was the most wearying of all. The shuffle of the dominoes continued monotonously. The various meals were duly served. Everyone was trying hard to enjoy themselves and failing miserably. At last it was time to go. Everybody said good-bye as if the three days had been the most enjoyable ever spent. Tibetan currency notes printed in Lhasa were slipped into the hands of the servants and, dodging the mud by the light of the flares, we returned to the fort. There was a sense of having fiddled whilst Rome burned.

Constant messages began to come from the "big river". The Chinese armies were massing. Sometimes a patrol boat would be launched out towards the Tibetan bank, or there would be a volley of fire. The skirmishes continued for some weeks. These omens of the coming battle meant that Rapga should not stay too long in Gartok, so on the tenth day from our arrival his newly-formed caravan assembled and moved off towards Chamdo. I was now left alone with the Dege Sey and had a better opportunity to get to know him. He was a widower. His wife had died very tragically following the birth of his third child, now about five years old. His other two children, a boy of seven and a girl of nine, were his constant companions and adored their father. His love towards them, and in fact to all the children around him, was very touching. He had started a school for his own and the soldiers' children. For several hours a day one could hear them chanting their lessons. Sometimes when we sat talking in his big living-room, with the wide lattice windows open to the garden, little figures would peep through the curtain serving as a door, and seeing the General there, tiptoe up to his table with their big wooden slates and, half bowing, display their laboriously written Tibetan letters. A nod of approval from the General—who as founder of the school, was really like their headmaster—and they would scamper off thoroughly delighted, to continue their lessons. The Dege Sey was a man with a thirst for learning and after discussion we decided that as time permitted, we would teach each other things that we wanted to know. He longed to be able to do arithmetic more accurately and to learn the meaning of difficult political phrases he constantly encountered in the different foreign magazines which came his way. He was very ready to teach me the Lhasa Dialect of Tibetan, which I had only started studying a few months back and I soon began to collect pages of useful idioms.

With Rapga's departure, I had an opportunity to send my letter of application to the Governor of Chamdo. I requested in it that, in view of the emergency, permission be given for me to come to Chamdo to organise a medical team to handle casualties. I said that my friend in India was getting together personnel for these purposes and that we were willing to engage in this work, as soon as permission was granted. I also requested, if this were not possible, that facilities be granted to me to travel by Lhasa to India. I enclosed, too, a letter to Robert Ford who corresponded regularly with the Dege Sey, helping him in his study of English. In view of these developments, I had broached the question of medical supplies with the Dege Sey, suggesting that Ga Ga return to Po and bring up the remaining loads of medicine to Gartok, in readiness for the fulfilment of these plans. After Rapga had gone, the Dege Sey took all necessary measures to expedite this proposal. Time was short. The position, on the farther side of the Golden Sand River, was changing every day. On the remote crossing we had used, on our journey into Tibet, Ga Ga might be able to slip through to Po. It was worth trying. With a soldier, especially ordered to act as an escort to the river, Ga Ga went off, riding the grey to fulfil his important errand. When coming into Tibet, I had felt that only as things opened up was I warranted in shifting the whole of our supply of medicines, and now that time had come. In a few weeks I hoped to get sanction from Chamdo to move forward.

The time in Gartok was proving very valuable. I had considerable leisure, as the General was often busy with official mail or arbitrating local disputes. I was able, therefore, to do quite a bit of study in the Tibetan New Testament. Then I was able to do a certain amount of simple dispensary work. The people were allowed to visit me in the General's compound. He was very good about this. I had asked if I could live in the village amongst the people, but he said he feared that something untoward might befall me as a stranger, and insisted that I stay with him in the fort. Nevertheless he gave me full access to those who wished to see me. Injections for syphilis were in great demand and I gave quite a few. Lamas from the local monastery would also visit me and some received Gospels. On occasions I was also able to give a few words of testimony, although I felt the main emphasis should be on the establishing of firm recognition by the powers that be. In moments of relaxation I began to explore the surrounding countryside. I climbed the hills above the town. There were three distinct sectors; the fort; the people's houses, low single storeyed mud-dwellings; and the lamasery. The total population of the entire district could hardly exceed two thousand. Often of a Lord's Day morning, I would walk out in the bright sunshine amidst the crops, which were well forward, breathing in the freshness of God and musing on some theme concerning God's love toward us in Christ Jesus, our Lord. One of my favourite hymns of that period was:

> "Thou my everlasting portion!
> More than friend or life to me.
> All along my pilgrim journey
> Saviour let me walk with Thee!
>   Close to Thee, close to Thee,
>   All along my pilgrim journey
>   Saviour let me walk with Thee.

> Lead me through the vale of shadows
> Bear me o'er life's fitful sea;
> Thro' the gate of life eternal
> I shall enter Lord with Thee.
>> Close to Thee, close to Thee,
>> Then the gate of life eternal
>> I shall enter Lord with Thee.'

It often came to mind later in the days of my captivity.

With the way still open through S.E. Tibet to India, it would have been very easy to contemplate an escape from the almost overwhelming circumstances that faced me in the mounting menace to the east. For long, the Lord had been straitening me to His will. I knew that I must, if I were to truly follow Him, walk to-day, to-morrow and the day following. There could be no returning. By His grace I must stay at all costs in the forefront of the battle line. My meat must, as His disciple, be to do His will and finish His work. On the Indian side, there were many of the Lord's servants. If Tibet was to be penetrated from that side, there were those there to do it. On the China side there were now so few, and in Tibet proper, only myself, as far as I knew. Withdrawal was impossible. I could only advance. Should such a man as I flee? Yet at times I still wondered as to the details of the course I should take.

One night in the middle of August, I was sitting in the subdued light of the General's chamber. The children were peacefully sleeping in the shadows. Although it was only about half past nine, I was thinking of retiring. Outside all was peaceful, the occasional footfall of some servant in the courtyard being the only stir in the silence. Suddenly there was a tremor. We sat stiffly alert for a moment. The movement of the house increased in violence and a few pieces of clay plaster fell from the ceiling, with an ominous crack on the hard polished floor. We still sat rooted to the spot. As the wooden pillars began to crack apart from the mud and stone walls, I suddenly seemed to awake to the situation and said to the Dege Sey: "Shall we go outside?" He literally leapt to action. "We shall!" he cried. With one mad grab he tore his youngest boy naked out of bed, the old nurse wakened the other two kiddies and we fled for our lives, out into the garden.

For how long we crouched low on the ground I do not know. The reeling of the earth went on, it seemed an eternity. I tried to stand but daren't, lest I be flung down. I expected to see the earth open up any minute. The houses took the terrific shaking very well, being mostly of only one storey and with walls between one and three feet thick. They cracked but did not fall, although the fort archway was most severely damaged and had to be repaired. As the earthquake died away, we were at first hesitant to go indoors and the General and his three children sat on a bed in my room with the door open, ready to dash out if there should be further tremors. I kept my eye on a lamp hanging from the roof. It was really a long while before it ceased swaying. At last all was still, but then came a new terror. Out of the cloudless star-filled sky came the most uncanny noises we had ever heard. Not thunder, not gunfire, but a new noise unlike any other. We all felt somewhat unnerved as the great cracklings reverberated through the heavens. I racked my brain for a scientific explanation but the Tibetans in great consternation exclaimed, "The gods are fighting! The gods are fighting!" and hurriedly ascended to the roof top of the school house, to light incense sticks. As I looked up into the majesty of the night sky, I thanked God that I worshipped Him, Who reigns supreme over all the works of His creation. Gradually the noises died away and one by one we crept into bed. Following the earthquake, an old woman in the village began to whisper: "Many years ago when we heard such noises, it meant war with the Chinese." And many took it up as an omen.

Some days later the jingle of the horse bells of the official Lhasa rider told us that the mail from Chamdo was coming in. I was very surprised to see with him Tsering Dorje, whom I found out afterwards to be travelling with all speed to Kangting. There was a letter from Robert Ford. The first item of significance was that reports of the earthquake had come in. The Tibetan-Assam border had suffered most severely. The Bramaputra had been blocked for a time and the route through S.E. Tibet to India destroyed. In places the whole configuration of the earth had been changed. For many it had meant sudden destruction. For me everything was wholly confirmed. That I should stay had now been proved.

I was utterly shut in by God, to endure by His grace to the end, within the borders of Tibet. Yet the letter from the Chamdo Government would not give me permission to proceed. He had only forwarded my application to Lhasa. Soon travellers began to come in telling of deaths caused by the earthquake down country.

CHAPTER VIII

AMBASSADOR TO THE LAMA-KINGDOM

> ". . . I send thee, to open their eyes, and to turn
> them from darkness to light, and from the
> power of satan unto God. . . ." Acts 26.

TOWARDS the end of August, I was overjoyed to see Ga Ga return
from Po. He had quite a story to tell. The first thing was that the
grey had broken up. It developed a big boil and just could not
make the grade. He had had to hire another animal. On the
farther side of the Golden Sand River, he had travelled alone for
a short distance but did not encounter any red troops. Away up
on the passes he had fallen in with some of Pangda Dopgyay's
men but was again delayed, as the river near the two villages
between which we had camped was in flood and a bridge had to
be constructed before they could get over. He had arrived in Po
the night of the earthquake, with the place rocking about him.
Cidenla, although in an invalid condition, had come down from
the third floor of the white house into the courtyard for safety.
The steward had been away inspecting the boundaries of the
estate but on his return had arranged for the loads of medicine
to be sent with Ga Ga back to Gartok. The very evening all was
ready, a detachment of Red troops was expected at Po, so Ga Ga
had taken an hour's ride down the valley to a place from which
he could be up and over the pass the next morning before anything
transpired to detain him. Pangda Dopgyay had gone on his way
to Kangting to talk with the Communists, as planned. Bundi was
particularly glad to see Ga Ga, as he had been fretting over a
rumour, which said that I had been intercepted by the Reds and
taken to Batang. With all our medical supplies now in Gartok,
all we needed was permission. In the letters from Chamdo, one
had been from Pangda Rapga, containing unofficial permission for
me to stay. He also said he would arrange for a visit to Chamdo

if that were possible, whilst my application was being dealt with by the Lhasa Government. Meanwhile I might continue indefinitely where I was. All this the Chamdo Governor could not state in an official capacity but was apparently willing for Pangda Rapga to write and tell me. This was the result of a conversation they had had together. To gain even this permission was an answer to prayer and showed that the Lord was determined that I should stay in my present position. The possibilities of my getting to Chamdo and Lhasa now were greater than perhaps at any time. The opportunity before me was the most wonderful in recent missionary effort amongst the Tibetan people. Partly out of religious conviction concerning a "feast of ablutions" and partly as a holiday, the Dege Sey pitched a tent or two out on a broad island between the streams coursing across the plain. This rather delightful spot he had planted with 800 or more young poplar trees as a kind of park. A portion of the river was suitable for bathing. He suggested that we spend the days out there and return in the evening. The problem of cooking he solved by erecting a nomad tent close by and using it as a kitchen. Gezang Drashi during these days was a very welcome visitor. He was, apparently, handling some of Pangda Tsang's property and lands at Hla Dun. He was a man of about 38 and we had a good time together. Before he left he said to me with an air of mystery: "Do you know why Tsering Dorje, Pangda Dopgyay's head servant, went all the way to Chamdo and then came straight back through here on his way to Kangding?" I let him answer his own question. "There is a possibility of negotiations for a peaceful settlement between the Chinese and the Tibetans," he said in a low voice. There had been a final plot then. Were the brothers playing a master card? During these days, Azung was also a visitor, although what his business was I did not find out. The Dege Sey and I thought of a scheme for damming the river. No sooner said than it was done. He mobilised squads of people and two or three days saw an immense wall of earth supporting a lake of water nearly six feet deep. The schoolboys were delighted with this new swimming pool and I enjoyed some very good swimming too, although a little spartan.

Early acquaintance with the Dege Sey was now forming into a

mutual understanding, preparing him for the Gospel. An un-thought-of opening was given me. Prior to the present festival, the Dege Sey had been away in the mountains to visit his oracle, a very brilliant young lama graduated from one of the three world-famous lamaseries of Lhasa. The perplexing situation baffled the General and he sought guidance and counsel from this particular priest, whom he greatly revered. After spending some days at his hermitage in the hills he had returned. Two or three weeks had passed and now this lama had come with another eminent lama to see the Dege Sey. It was quite an occasion and I kept very much to my room. The day came however, when I was summoned to be introduced to this much-honoured guest. The Dege Sey went to some trouble to explain that I was a preacher of the "Jesus doctrine". The lama immediately showed great interest. Our host, seeing this was the case, then went so far as to say that, his two honourable guests both being devoted to the propagation of doctrine, it was a most suitable apportunity for us to discourse upon the same. The atmosphere was at once somewhat artificial as a result of this remark but the lama after a few moments turned to me and said with great sincerity: "Tell me, what is the content of your doctrine?" I looked at the man before me. He was of an exceptionally intelligent appearance. Although only twenty-nine years of age, he had nevertheless completed the most arduous course of instruction in the Buddhist teaching and way of life in one of the first lamaseries of the land. The discipline of those years, his solitude and constant contem-plation had left a mark of serenity and depth on a young face, and yet in his question he showed that in all his searchings he was not yet satisfied, nor did he count himself as having attained the goal of complete enlightenment. In a way I was not surprised that the Dege Sey had vacated his place of honour and to-day taken the lower seat of a disciple. The other lama, a man of nearly fifty, also a "doctor" in Buddhism, was sitting on another couch. That this opportunity was of the Lord I could not doubt. I must go forward in His strength. The grace and the words were given and I began to speak. It was probably the fullest declaration of the Gospel of Jesus Christ I ever made to the Tibetan people. Full of weakness, I yet stood in the unassailable strength of His changeless truth. The three men listened respectfully and without interruption. When at last I finished speaking, the young lama added no comment and asked no question but simply said, in a way to me, and yet in a way to himself, "How very strange." Yes, God's strange work of judgment on sin, met by His own beloved Son dying on a Roman cross, is unheard of in the cults of Lamaism, and yet "to whom He was not spoken of, they shall see: and they that have not heard shall understand"! The older lama felt he must ask me at least one question. "If God is so Almighty and so incomprehensible to man, how can man then know God?" I remember the answer coming from above. "He can be known, because He has been revealed." They were obviously baffled by the "Way of Salvation" and yet interested. When I offered them a whole Tibetan New Testament each, they willingly accepted them.

After this consultation with his lama, a team of other lamas, no doubt on the advice of the "oracle", were engaged to conduct special ceremonies for the protection of the garrison. The head lama of these incantations was a blind, thick-set cripple, already well on in years. In spite of his infirmities, he was a very astute wily fellow with a quick mind. His colleague, a much younger person, was of the cocksure, smart-aleck type but was held in high repute for his learning. He no doubt was quite a clever man but spoiled himself with his arrogance. The ensuing days were filled with discordant trumpeting and clanging of cymbals. In their spare time they would devote themselves to debate and at times one could hear, emerging from the school house, where they were accommodated, the clap of the hands indicating some point gained in the discussion. When debating, the lamas will stand to speak and then bring their right hand flat down on their extended left palm as an assertion that their point has been gained. These two lamas were certainly a match for each other, and I think viewed themselves as a match also for the foreign preacher, who had intruded into their sphere of influence. One night fairly late, the younger lama came into my room, in an aggressive mood. With him came a whole crowd of servants and soldiers residing in the fort. He stood and began to ply me with ickfire questions on religious matters, chiefly relating to the existence of God and the soul, which doctrines are not asserted in the original doctrine of Buddha, although implied in one form or another in Lamaism as it is practised to-day. The "performance" went on, and I answered him. It was obviously not going to be a fair discussion and smacked of an attempt to make me look small and himself important before the people. It was a difficult situation. Suddenly he came out with a very puerile question which turned the discussion into a farce. I replied to him sharply, saying that I had not come half-way across the world to talk of spiritual things on that level. He cleverly accommodated himself to the new turn in the conversation and switched on to something else. He still maintained a superior attitude and after a very long conversation, finally left. Ga Ga was a little abashed at the summary way in which I had spoken to the lama and said apprehensively, "You know, he is quite renowned in these parts." Next day we went over to the park and the Dege Sey spoke to me. "Last night," he said, "I was listening to your debate with the lama. I was standing outside the window. You became angry, you know. The thing is, you do not yet understand the ideas of Buddhist debate. The question he asked you was quite valid from the standpoint of Buddhism. Even if his question had not been reasonable, yet in the circumstances it should have been taken up reasonably." He was very sincere with me. It was humbling and I realised afresh how much I had to learn. Maybe I had spoken in the flesh. It was, nevertheless, good that the Dege Sey felt free enough with me to point out such things.

Some evenings later I was invited by these two visiting lamas to their own quarters. Both were very congenial. The old fellow welcomed me and the young lama was quite changed, speaking to me respectfully and sincerely. There followed a long session, in which just about all the main points of Christian doctrine were discussed or mentioned. For me it was a wonderful opportunity. The atmosphere was completely different and the enquiry straightforward. God was very gracious to me and marvellously helped me to speak of the Way of Life. Talking with adherents of Lamaism is always fraught with difficulty. The expansion of the Tibetan language came with the growth of Buddhist philosophy; thus words used often represent two distinct concepts.

D

We take up and use a word in Tibetan, unconsciously giving it a Christian content. For them however, it has a Buddhist content. We speak of God. In our minds this word conveys to us the concept of the Supreme and Eternal Spirit, Creator and Sustainer of all things, Whose essence is Love, Whose presence is all holy, and Whose ways are all righteous. For them, the Tibetan word god means nothing of the kind. We speak of prayer, the spiritual communion between God our Father and His children. For them, prayer is a repetition of abstruse formulae and mystic phrases handed down from time immemorial. We speak of sin. For them the main emphasis is in the condemnation of killing animals. When I was at Batang I saw an open-air performance of a buddhist play. One of the chief sins depicted there was the catching of fish. When I asked the special significance of this "transgression", I was told, "Oh, fishes mustn't be killed, they can't speak," meaning, I presume, that they utter no sound. It is a common sight to see a man, when killing a yak, at the same time muttering his "prayers" furiously. Gross immorality is also condemned by the most thoughtful lamas, but rarely publicly. We speak of the Saviour. They think of Buddha or the Dalai Lama. We speak of God being a Trinity. They will say: "Yes, god the Buddha, god the whole canon of Buddhist scripture, and god the whole body of the Buddhist priesthood." We speak of man's spirit being dead in sin and his thus being cut off from God. They cannot understand. A person, they say, is only soul and body. What do you mean by the third concept, a man's spirit? When a man dies, they believe his soul escapes by one of the nine holes in his body; we know nothing of his spirit, they say. We speak of a revelation from God, His own Word which we are commanded to believe, and they know no word but the vast collection of Buddhist sayings, which only one in a thousand even vaguely understands. Those who have studied them believe that only in the exercise of the human intellect, in meditation and contemplation over a very long period, can one begin to enter into the deep things of the "spirit". What "spirit" though, perhaps few of them realise.

We, of course, speak of the Holy Spirit as a gift of God to the believer in Christ. They say, "What nonsense! As if a man could obtain the Holy Spirit as easily as that." Of course, I would point out the other aspect; that it is not so much our possessing the Spirit, as the Spirit possessing us. On acceptance of Christ the believer is born of the Spirit, yet it may be but slowly that He will obtain full sovereignty of the heart and will. This is dismissed as being contrary to the concept of God being a Spirit. We speak of the Almighty power of God and yet of man being responsible to Him, particularly in his acceptance or rejection of His way of salvation. I was told this was a "lower doctrine", cause and effect as a fatalistic law being widely propounded by the lamas. I was surprised how even a man like the Dege Sey really believed in reincarnation. There was rather an amusing incident. He was saying to me how they had to be very careful, for even one of the domestic animals might be his grandmother. I was about to make some mildly humorous comment as to the general treatment of dogs in Tibet, when the words were taken out of my mouth and far more eloquent sounds fell on our ears. From the courtyard came the piercing squeals of some pitiful canine, which had just been either kicked or battered with a brick bat. The Dege Sey, generally quick to see a joke, sat quite unmoved. Incarnation as a doctrine itself is readily accepted by the Tibetans, but when we assert there is but one incarnation of the Living and True God, "The Word made flesh", it is totally unacceptable to them. Resurrection again is not thought a thing incredible. They claim that many of their saints have risen from the dead. We believe the Word of God when it says: "There is no man that hath power over the spirit to retain the spirit: neither hath he power in the day of death," yet they will assert that some of their lamas have power to dismiss their spirit, which we believe belongs to the Son of Man alone. On one occasion I sat with Pangda Rapga. He said: "I would sum up Buddhism in two words, 'Retribution and Reincarnation'." "As for Christianity," he continued, "from what I have read, I would also sum it up in two words, 'Authority and Faith'." "If you wish thus to sum it up," I answered, "I would have to put one more word between those two. You must say, 'Authority, GRACE and Faith'." "There is no argument between the Buddhist and the Christian," he said. "The Christian declares that there is one authoritative revelation of God. There is no ground really for discussion. You must accept that revelation by faith. You must bow to that authority." I felt that in his understanding of this much real progress had been made, and this provided one of those rare occasions when we were in complete agreement.

The evening I spent with the lamas in Gartok covered much of this familiar ground. When I departed they were most courteous; it may be that the younger one even regretted the way he had come into my room some evenings before, and one earnestly hoped that a ray from the Throne of Grace had shined unto them. Their series of ceremonies were now quickly concluded, accompanied by the most childish superstition. A pile of bones, including, I believe, a human skull, were buried in a big hole just outside the village. Having performed this last rite they departed. Whether the General, or the lamas themselves, really believed that such measures would avert disaster is very open to question, and yet it may be that the blind faith of an old woman who once said to me "The communists cannot come into Tibet, for we have very strong gods" was also with them.

A peculiar lull now set in. There was no news from the river. One day a messenger had come to the Dege Sey with a letter. It was, to the General's surprise, from the other side of the river. He opened it in my presence. In bewilderment he began to read. It was from Pu Tso Wanje, head of the Batang communists, written and sent to him secretly. He turned page after page of rather poor Tibetan. The virulent words castigated Britain and America as devils, exposed the plots of the Imperialists and explained the policy of the Communist party towards racial minorities. Tibet was to be autonomous, but all Imperialist influence must be cleared from its borders. He pleaded with the General to stage an uprising and surrender to the People's Liberation Armies. The disgust of the General was difficult to describe. One thing was at least clear from the letter, that the "People's Army" with their "revolutionary" supporters were planning to attack very soon.

Towards the end of September, a man came in from about thirty miles out to the North and pleaded that I might go to their valley, as a man had been shot. When the Dege Sey heard this, he was willing for me to go this thirty miles deeper into Tibet, provided they supplied horses. This was eventually done. It must have been already the first week of October when I set off. We rode hard for several hours, until all habitation was left behind. My escort unslung his rifle and loaded a bullet with deliberation. I knew we were riding through bandit country. Three armed riders were coming in the opposite direction, but passed us quietly. In five hours we were up in great rolling nomad grasslands. We had a meal in a tent, of coarse tsamba and lump cane sugar, before going on over a pass to a distant valley. By about five we reached our destination. It was a well-built village and the barley harvest was in full swing. I was shown up into a low room; from floor to ceiling could only have been five foot six. The only furnishing was a large "bookcase" containing long and thick Buddhist books. This room must have been originally constructed for meditation. The bookcase was really a frame with big pigeon holes, in which the Buddhist books, one in each hole, were placed. The books were of the usual Tibetan kind, a large number of inscribed sheets of parchment, all loose leaf, piled up to a thickness of about four or five inches, each sheet being nearly two feet long by four or five inches wide. The sheets were kept between two ornamented boards and tied together with ribbons. We laid out our bedding by a small window. The host was very courteous and made a very "generous" gesture to me, asking in all sincerity whether I would be requiring one of their young women of the village for the night. I had heard about such an evil practice but this was the first time I had been asked personally. Ga Ga confirmed that the landlord's offer was perfectly genuine. From the Tibetan point of view it indicates a high standard of hospitality. One stands amazed at the almost unbridled promiscuity amongst the Tibetans. One day in Gartok, Ga Ga had pointed out a very striking Tibetan girl, still very young, and had said "Do you know what her name is? It's 'sixty-seven'!" "Whatever do you mean?" I asked incredulously. "Yes," he replied. "She is called sixty-seven because she had lain with sixty-seven men by the time she was seventeen." On one occasion I had asked Ga Ga about his own wife. As far as he knew, she had had about twenty-five men, but this seemed to give him no concern at all, apart from the gonorrhea from which they both suffered. He, like most other Tibetans, found his own alternatives when away from home.

Having assured the obliging host that I should not be requiring any such services, I proceeded to the patient. I was shown into a dark filthy corner of an upstairs room, where a begrimed Tibetan lay grovelling in agony, in a pool of pus. I was told that a month had elapsed since the shooting and that the bullet was still in his body. He had been on horseback and the rider behind him had accidently fired his pistol, with the result that he had been shot in the back of the knee. Owing to the infection, the whole leg from toe to thigh was swollen up like a balloon. With very inadequate medical knowledge or experience, I was cast totally on God. If I did not operate, he would certainly die of gangrene; yet if I did, the chances of doing so properly and successfully were very small. I could only pray. I gave a local anaesthetic and numbed the upper part of the leg. I made a hasty study of the anatomy of that part of the body, which I was horrified to find contained a major artery and vein. Once it was anaesthetized, I was able to straighten out the limb and find the hole, as the Tibetans had said, right behind the knee. Disinfecting the wound and surrounding skin, as best I could, I donned sterilised rubber gloves and went to work with a scalpel. I made two incisions and inserted a pair of forceps. I moved them around inside his leg for some time, when suddenly there was a grating of metal. It was to my indescribable relief, and the absolute dumbfounding of the audience, that I produced the bullet from the hole. I then pushed the forceps right down into the calf of the leg, breaking up all the pockets of pus and thus releasing some of it. The operation finished, I went up the valley for a walk, paddled in a babbling stream and had a quiet time with my Bible. The big step I had taken in opening up the man's leg in such a condition rather appalled me, but strangely enough I opened the Scriptures at these words: "If thou forbear to deliver them that are drawn unto death and those that are ready to be slain, if thou sayest behold we knew it not; doth not he that pondereth the hearts consider it? and he that keepeth thy soul doth not he know it? and shall not he render to every man according to his works?" This word from the Lord convinced me that I had made no mistake. I walked up over a hillock and through a small gully which was most peculiar by reason of its coloured sands. On the hill in the turf were cut the words "Om mani padme hom".

A day or two of poulticing and the man was on the mend. I left strict instructions with the landlord how to proceed in my absence. It was my joy in this remote Tibetan village to distribute a number of Gospels, which were gladly received. The General had given me a time limit of four days so I had to get back. The nights were wonderful. A great harvest moon and the reapers busy labouring in the fields under the pale light. How long would the harvest now be, from the sowing of the Word. Ploughing down the long furrows of language, the preparing of the ground through laborious building of contacts with the people and their rulers, the scattering of the living seed,—O for that day to come rejoicing with the sheaves! "And they came to Bethlehem at the beginning of barley harvest"—Such a precious time in Scripture, and back in Gartok again, as from time to time, I wandered over the plain in meditation (during what were to prove my last days of freedom), my heart burned to enter in to all that the Lord of the Harvest had in store.

CHAPTER IX

THE RED CONQUEST

"Though thou exalt thyself as the eagle, and though
thou set thy nest among the stars, thence will I bring
thee down, saith the Lord." The Prophecy of Obadiah.

NASTURTIUMS, red and gold, blossomed in profusion. The little
schoolchildren carefully picked up the flower pots and carried
them, the blooms dancing on their noses, until they put them
down safely on the school verandah. From the rooftop of the fort
the General's flag fluttered defiantly. It bore the ninth letter of the
Tibetan alphabet, for was he not the ninth general of the Tibetan
Army? On the lawn we had been playing soldiers with the children.
A strange mixture of reality and make-believe. The weather had
been very thundery. "It had a pain in its stomach", as the General
used so often to say. Everything was tense and yet not tense.
No news of moment had recently come through from the river
and no messenger for at least a fortnight from Chamdo. It was all
very baffling. Yet one felt the silence was but the lull before the
storm. Pangda Rapga had written a few weeks back: "The nation
is lost. It may be many years before we shall rise again." He had
seen and judged all the factors and was perhaps one of the few
who could foresee the certainty of the impending doom.

In my little room God poured His word into my heart preparing
me, more than I knew, for the great crisis of my life. I read:
"And of Asher he said, let Asher be blessed with children, let
him be acceptable to his brethren, and let him dip his foot in
oil. Thy shoes shall be iron and brass and as thy days so shall thy
strength be." And again, "Happy are thou, O Israel, who is like
unto thee, O people saved by the Lord, the shield of my help
and who is the sword of my excellency! and thine enemies shall
be found liars unto thee and thou shalt tread upon their high
places."

I was standing talking to the General and his Colonel in the garden, one sunny day. It must have been the 10th October. A messenger galloped into the fort and, hurriedly stepping into the garden, made his way straight toward us. He obsequiously handed a despatch to the General. A pursing of the lips, combined with a flick of the head, indicated dismissal and the courier withdrew, his tongue extended and voicing an occasional "lags so" as all "inferior" Tibetans should in the presence of their superiors. The Dege Sey quickly read the brief contents and turned to the Colonel. Very gravely he said: "A pass has been lost to the advancing Chinese on the southern sector, in the Gunk Lama country." I watched their reaction to this news. There was little doubt they suspected treachery. The Gunka Lama being still a boy, the territory was in the hands of an unscrupulous regent, whose loyalty and obedience were very open to question. The Colonel with professional contempt replied. "Hm, so soon and so easily." It was a severe blow. The Dege Sey had sent many of his men to defend the three vital southern passes; now with one gone, the whole of the south was threatened. News soon came in that one of the Tibetan Government magistrates in the southern area had been captured by the Chinese. "I think you should go to Chamdo," the General said to me, but I could only continue before the Lord. In the face of a full-scale attack, which was probably now the case, it would be fruitless to act on one's own feelings and start chasing around the countryside. God's way would be made plain. The General walked heavily to his room.

The following morning, the jingle of the horse bells of another official rider set the air on edge. It brought a report from the north. It contained evil tidings. "Three hundred communist troops have crossed the Golden Sand River and are advancing inland," read the fateful words. The General smiled sardonically. "It may be exaggerated of course," he soliloquised hopefully, but as a military man he knew he could not ignore it. He immediately ordered one of the centurions to organise a detachment of cavalry to proceed at dawn to engage the enemy. They were supplied with a Bren gun and each man was to be armed with a rifle. Next morning from the peak of the highest mountain dominating the plain a column of white smoke ascended. A pathetic plea to the gods for their favour. Some of the young fellows were destined never to return. We watched them ride off until the sound of the bugles was lost in the stillness of the morning. No sooner had they disappeared up the valley than another government rider came cantering in. We were sitting in the living-room when the note was presented. It came from the main front. One brief glance at the scrawled Tibetan covering the coarse piece of paper was enough. With grief and anger, and yet maintaining great calmness, the General tossed the note to the Colonel. "Finished!" he said. "Eighteen hundred enemy troops are over the Golden Sand River and have broken through the defences. By now they will be at Bom Ting. If they drive fast they can be here to-morrow." The Colonel finished reading the dispatch and sat gloomily awaiting the General to break the silence. "Well, what do we do now?" the General at last questioned us, with a tone of mockery and irony in his voice. If Chamdo were standing it might be possible to effect an ordered retreat, but not a word or an order had been received from the Chamdo command. Were communications cut? The General's hope had been, if possible, to stage a big battle on the plain of Gartok. This prospect now was rapidly becoming fantastic. I had visions of the Tibetans fighting to the death and the fort being burnt down over our heads. Kungo Dzong was ordered by the Dege Sey to flee for his life. His reputation amongst the people for perverting justice meant that anything might befall him if he stayed. On the other hand the General, who was famed far and wide for his beneficent rule, obviously found great comfort now in the knowledge that he was loved by his people.

After a few minutes I thought it wiser to leave the General and his staff, that they might freely confer together. I returned to my room. The stillness, as of approaching death, seemed to grip the air. Time dragged on. Afternoon wore into evening. Darkness fell. I lay down but it was hard to sleep. From time to time I glanced over to the General's quarters and the butter lamps were still burning. I do not think they went to bed. All sorts of documents were being turned out, presumably to be destroyed. Through it all the children slept blissfully, little realising that the Chinese they ridiculed in their boyish songs were so near to them. In the early hours of the morning, I eventually dozed off. It needed much faith to rest quietly in the Hands of my Lord in the face of destruction, but His strength was unfailing. Should I flee from Gartok alone, and leave as the General suggested? In my heart I had absolutely no conviction that this was God's way for me. I could only stand still and see His salvation. I must trust implicitly that His way would be made unmistakably plain as events moved on. Maybe I should be able to stay, even under the new regime, as a witness of the Lord Jesus Christ to the Tibetan people.

Early next morning the General came to my room and announced his decision. He was going to withdraw to the north. He said I was to travel with him, taking with me two boxes, one of clothes and one of medicines, and that he would provide animals for me within the hour. The fall of Gartok was imminent. Absolute confusion now ensued. Servants, acting more on their own instinct than their master's orders, rushed hither and thither thrusting valuables in boxes. As one ran by he said to me: "It's just terrible! We shan't be able to do a thing. There is no time." As soon as news of the proposed withdrawal leaked out, social order began to break down, people prepared to loot and soldiers to desert. The surrounding country went rapidly over to banditry and anarchy. Just about an hour afterwards, the General appeared in my room wearing his most magnificent apparel. Standing there, his strong, proud head held very high, he said with some bitterness, as he eyed the servants in panic, packing up the last things: "Look at these servants. What do any of these paltry things matter now, when we have lost our nation?" There was nothing I could say. Straining every nerve, he controlled his emotion and then declared to me: "All my forces are scattered. There is only one thing I can do. For my men's sake I must go and surrender." So disregarding all the turmoil and preparations for flight, he assembled a select few from his officers and servants and prepared to depart. I knew I was in the presence of a man of immense courage and unswerving principle. Personally he could escape to Chamdo and Lhasa, or ride where he would back westward. He could even make India by some route or other, if he wished to save himself, but for the one hope that he might save his men being cut up any further, he was going to give himself into the hand of the enemy. This then was the end. My course was clearing. It lay straight through the centre of this debacle. I hesitated for a moment and then as he passed towards the courtyard I said to him: "Shall I come with you and act as your interpreter?" He paused, a little taken aback at such a gesture of friendship in so great an hour of crisis. "Come with me," he replied, and we walked towards the horses, being saddled in the yard.

Out from the fort we rode, past a dumbstruck crowd of Tibetans and then southwards across the plain. For quite a while no one spoke, feeling, I suppose, as the human heart does so often in times of tragedy, "How can the sun shine?" Riding abreast of my horse, the General whispered across to me: "I expect they will kill me now." Of course, I did not know, and I could say little to comfort. Along the dusty trail worn in the grass, an old lama came trudging out to us. He came forward and clutched the rein of the Dege Sey's horse. Overcome with grief, he cried out: "You mustn't go! You mustn't go!" The General dealt tenderly with the old man and gently urged his horse onwards. Nothing could deter him from fulfilling his decision now. On we rode in silence. It was a funeral march. Turning into a little valley we came to the bank of a shallow stream and the Colonel suddenly dismounted. I wondered what was the matter. From the folds of his great gown, a place where Tibetans keep half their belongings, he drew out a small bag, opened it and drew out a number of wrapped sweets. Going personally to each rider, he gave one to each. The tenderness of his simple action carried out so naturally, in the face of such tremendous odds, displayed to me a special touch of greatness. We passed on. The frightened inhabitants were fleeing to the hills. Many were dressed in their best gowns and had their meagre possessions strapped to their mules and yak. The country was sadly beautiful. The bells on the horses made a peculiar blend of sound, which with the sustained monotony of one particular note gave the impression, at odd moments, of pipes playing in the distance.

As we drew nearer the enemy's spearhead we met officers and men of the demoralised Tibetan forces. They cried like children to the General, who, I was amazed to see, comforted them like a father. Never did I hear one word of harshness. We sat in an upstairs room of an old deserted house as they poured out their story. We also took this opportunity to have a meal of tsamba and cheese. The General knew all too well that Tibet had nothing that could stand up to so strong a foe. After the meal and the conference with the men, we continued on our journey. We passed through another village and then took a sharp turn into a valley leading up over a pass. From the summit the view of high snow mountain peaks was glorious. I judged the direction, and reckoned the distant range to be beyond the upper reaches of the Mekong and Salween. As we descended the farther slopes we came across more Tibetan soldiers. They had been disarmed. One of them showed us a pamphlet given to him by the Chinese officers, illustrating by cartoon pictures the Communist policy and aims in the "liberation" of Tibet. He said that, when they had been overrun, they had had to give up their guns but the Chinese had given every man a few silver dollars and told him to go home and fight no more. The men we met were all dog-tired and utterly bewildered. We pulled out of the narrow valley coming down from the pass, and saw a small village situated some hundreds of feet below us. We descended slowly until almost level with the houses, at which place the General called a halt. In this, God mercifully overruled. At any time, we were liable to be sniped at and our halt averted what might have been a further tragedy. A man was sent forward alone, to act as a liaison officer if possible and to find out whether the advancing Chinese troops were in the vicinity. Only a very few minutes passed and he returned to say that the advance units were only just round the corner. They were willing that we should go forward and contact them.

The big moment had come. We skirted round the brow of the hill and there they were, just as I had seen them before, in yellow cotton-padded uniforms, the red star badge bearing the Chinese numerals "eight" and "one" pinned to the centre of their peaked caps and, on their feet, nothing but rubber plimsolls. "Eight-one" stands for the first of the eighth month which is the birthday of the Chinese Red Army, now more than twenty years old. A little Batang boy of about fourteen years of age, a diminutive fellow, came up and announced himself as an interpreter. The General with his great height bent over him and talked with him like his own child. We were motioned to sit down on the side of the road and await the arrival of the Red Army officers. They came along in about a quarter of an hour and were delighted to hear of the General's surrender. They of course called it an uprising, which suited their purposes better, as self-styled liberators. With them appeared a most monstrous figure, a man attired in the old lama style costume, with flowing cape and round pointed white hat. He was flitting about all over the place looking quite demented. He came a little nearer and I heard the Dege Sey suddenly remonstrate with him: "Azung, what on earth are you doing?"

It was well on in the afternoon and by the time we were allocated quarters in the village, now under martial law, it was almost nightfall. We walked slowly over some empty fields to one of the houses. We eventually gathered in an upstairs room of a very sturdy dwelling. It was already dark when the negotiations began. The startled host had not, like many of his fellow-countrymen, fled away, so he was present to kindle a few pine chips in the centre of the room. As the flickering light grew stronger and the shadows danced less violently upon the wall, I could discern the faces of our company. There were the General and the Colonel on the Tibetan side. On the Chinese side there were at least one of their commanding officers, a special staff officer, presumably a Communist party man, an English speaking junior officer, who had already introduced himself to me as a Lt. Chang and certain others, whose ranks were unknown to me. The cross-examination of the General began in Chinese, English and Tibetan. I really had to say very little, but I did my best to ensure that a fair interpretation of the General's words was conveyed to those present. Back and forth in the different languages, the officers tried to elucidate why the General had resisted, which to them seemed a most extraordinary thing, although to anyone else the most natural thing in the world. He was very calm. "I acted on the orders of my government," he maintained to the last. "I surrender because I consider that further bloodshed is absolutely useless." Having established, to some extent, that the resistance was on account of the Lhasa Government's order and that his capitulation was his personal decision, they duly accepted his unconditional surrender. Arrangements were made for the Colonel to return through the night to Gartok, to ensure that all resistance would be withdrawn should the Chinese troops attacking from the north arrive first at the garrison. With this the meeting was concluded. There was a medley of voices as the Chinese broke up and went out, but at last we were left alone in the stillness of the room. In the yard below, a guard was placed on duty. The Dege Sey and I exchanged impressions. We both felt that things had gone remarkably smoothly. The Lord indeed had been very gracious to us in such difficult circumstances. I had just laid down my gown and odd clothing for a rough bed on the floor when a Chinese soldier appeared, to escort us over for another conference, this time being held out in one of the bivouacs. It was a very cramped tent. All necessary personnel being present, we were just about to begin, when one of the officers looking at me said: "Who is that man? It is not necessary for him to be here. He had better go back." It was very dark in the fields and it was only after much difficulty that I found my way back with one of the Chinese soldiers. Their Army lay encamped in the open but, apart from the odd flash of torches or a glint of firelight, all was pitch black. The Dege Sey was not long before he returned and again we were left undisturbed. He told me in a low voice that they had discussed the hand-over of between four and five hundred rifles that were stored at the Fort. We were to return to Gartok to-morrow. I slipped out on to the flat roof to make sure we were not being spied on, and then we lay down again. I had no proper place for sleeping, but it did not seem to trouble me; there was so much else to occupy the mind. What would the future now hold for Tibet? What would it hold for me? I knew that I was in God's hands. We occasionally whispered a word or two. The pine chips flickered uneasily. It was very quiet now and the shadows deepening . . . yet "Father with Thee there is no variableness or shadow of turning."

Part II

WAR ON THE SOUL

CHAPTER X

ARRESTED

"Jesus said: 'Lovest thou Me? . . . . Verily,
verily . . . . another shall gird thee and carry
thee whither thou wouldst not.' " John 21.

THE morning dawned bright and frosty. The first thin ice was on
the puddles and crackled under the feet of the horses as we marched
out of the village. The Chinese commander had ordered an
immediate advance to Gartok. The Communist forces walked in
single file carrying their guns and packs. There was not a single
rider among them. The Dege Sey and I were, nevertheless, permitted to ride providing we kept in the centre of the troops.
Before and behind stretched the long yellow snake-like columns
as far as the eye could see. I noticed a heartbroken Tibetan peasant
lovingly sympathise with the General on the roadside. We were
travelling a route I had never seen before. Our way took us along
a narrow valley for two or three hours, after which we turned up
a gully and commenced a gruelling climb. Soon the bugles sounded
and the footworn soldiers lay down in the grass or sat on the
boulders. Each man had a canvas bag of tsamba, looking like an
elongated sausage, curled around his body or over his shoulder.
These were untied and, with a little water or tea from their bottles,
the tsamba was mixed into a paste for eating. Some used chopsticks for this. The sticky uncontrollable mass of barley flour
demonstrated once and for all that tsamba must definitely be
eaten with the fingers. They also had another kind of flour called
"Dai shih fen" which was a mixture of wheat, nuts, egg, salt, etc.
A little more than ten minutes elapsed and the bugles sounded
again. The pace slackened now considerably and the previously
well ordered columns broke up as one and another were unable
to maintain the speed of the leading men. Up and up we climbed.
I was sorry for some of the poor fellows, especially those designated

to carry the loads. Whilst there were whole caravans of mules, yet some of the men were obliged to stagger over the pass with a bamboo pole weighed down with cooking utensils. Their clothes were black with soot and their bodies at the point of exhaustion. I saw one of the comrades, a youth of about eighteen, sitting on a stone coughing up blood. In spite of the arduous demands of the "People's Liberation Army" in their advance into Tibet, yet the morale of the troops was very high. Everyone was a volunteer, they claimed. The greatest secret was obviously in their mental armament. They really believed from the only teaching they knew, or were allowed to know, that they were liberators. They had come to free Tibet from the intrigues of the imperialists and the shackles of feudalism and to bring in the dawn of a new age. The allusion to the "millenial" kingdom of Buddhist mythology was a clever point in their propaganda. According to the lamas, salvation was to come out of the north country, and was not the name of Stalin and the hope of the Communist Era as a beacon shining to all the oppressed peoples of the earth sitting in the shadows of reaction and tyranny? The policies of Mao Tse Tung, faithful disciple of Marx, Engels, Lenin and Stalin, would fulfil the highest aspirations of Buddhism. For the Tibetan people it would mean autonomous government, religious freedom, protection from aggression and a place of equality and honour in the great family of races united in the mighty nation now rising as a peak in Asia, the "People's Republic of China". As bearers and implementers of such an "evangel", "right" was on their side. Invasion becomes liberation, conquest becomes civilization. To resist then becomes treason, to surrender is the first step as a revolutionary—the very first thing that one has done for the good of one's country. Near the summit of the pass we stopped again and for the first time I was able to sit and talk freely with the Communist officers. One fellow was a Batang man who spoke both Chinese and Tibetan fluently. I found he was a relative of the widow who invited me to a feast in Batang. With him and some of his colleagues I had quite a conversation. "We are struggling hard for peace," was one of the first remarks made to me. As yet completely unindoctrinated, and just a raw imperialist needing reform, to be thus addressed by a Chinese officer, engaged in the active invasion of Tibet, was baffling in the extreme. As far as he was concerned this situation presented no difficulty. If he were well up in his "learning", it would be explained by Historical Material-ism and the Law of the Unity of Opposites in the Marxist Dialect. If he were not, then amidst all the hardship he would increase his political consciousness and strengthen himself with one of the "Om mani padme hums" of the Communist Party such as "Under the brilliant leadership of Mao Tse Tung and the Chinese com-munist party we are bound to move forward to final victory. Long live peace! Down with the warmongers! Struggle with the Imperialists to the end!" I found to my amazement that the desires expressed in the west for peace were being repeated in all sincerity by these young fellows. I had my first lesson in the new language.

A few hours brought us down into the Gartok plain. Some half mile or so before the town, everybody stopped and the Chinese Army officers began to arrange for the formal take over of the garrison. Certain others of the Dege Sey's men and myself were told to go ahead as we were not required to take part in the "Victory Display". In the surrounding fields several companies of the Chinese troops, who had attacked from the north, were already bivouacking. They had, as anticipated, arrived first but, operating under the command of the officers who had accepted the surrender, they had not yet entered the fortress. Back in the fort, everything was deathly quiet. The old nurse and the three children were there anxiously awaiting the return of the absent father. Ga Ga was nowhere to be seen. Leaving the horse in the yard, I went back to the big gateway to watch the take-over. The local people, still utterly at a loss to understand events, gathered silently to witness what was now about to happen. Several hundred yards away I could see the General, still looking positively regal and unconquered, walking between the Chinese commanding officers, above whom he towered. He had ridden as Commander of his own forces for the last time, now he must walk as the defeated, back into the surrendered citadel. After the officers with the Dege Sey had entered the fort, the flag of the Ninth General of the Tibetan Army was lowered and the flag of the "People's Republic of China" unfurled in the unfettered breezes of the Tibetan Uplands. In an endless stream the yellow-coated "liberators" filed in to occupy the lamasery, the fort, and all chief points of vantage in and around the town. They carried small cannons and mortars, if I discerned their arms correctly. Some of these were heavy and needed at least three men to carry them. The Tibetans stood awed by the continuous flow of soldiers and equipment. Some said: "Aren't their men small!" Others said: "Aren't the guns big!" But all agreed that never before had they seen the Chinese in such strength.

Eventually Ga Ga turned up. He was full of stories. A man in the confusion of the General's absence had stolen some horses and had nearly been lynched by the villagers who caught him. He described gleefully how even children had put dung in his mouth whilst he was held down on the floor. Then the fleeing magistrate had been attacked by bandits. This he felt to be a just retribution, as he had commandeered some of the poor people's horses without paying for them and had also left his baby behind him. Whether this was all true was difficult to know. Then he said some of the soldiers had run away to Lhasa and last, but not least, he had met somebody from the village we visited to the north, who reported that the man from whom we extracted the bullet was beginning to walk. "Does the man they nearly killed to-day need medical attention?" I asked. "I expect so," Ga Ga replied nonchalantly. We prepared to go, but everywhere being under martial law, it was difficult to reach places even within a hundred yards of our room. I was still at liberty to converse with the General and to go to him in his living-room, but I kept much to my own quarters as Communist Officers were coming and going and, now it was dark, sentries were posted everywhere, challenging even the servants as they went about their duties. Some of them nearly jumped out of their skins as a guard would bark a Chinese "Halt" out of the gloom. The chief steward of the Dege Sey came into my room after some considerable time and produced a few dry bread rolls. This was intended to be a meal. I looked at him, not that I was unthankful, but I was sure that the Dege Sey under the most dire circumstances would never offer his guest dry bread for his supper. "What's the matter?" I asked somewhat taken aback. "Isn't there any jam?" "Oh, yes," he said, lowering his voice, "but I don't think the master would want the Communists to see that jam pot." It was both ludicrous and pathetic. A few minutes later, with the air of having risked great odds, he returned and from the copious folds of his garment produced a half-eaten tin of jam. I suppose in his mind such an article imported from India was a dangerous indication of wealth!

On the morning of the thirteenth of October I was present with the General and the Tibetan-speaking officer of the P.L.A. We were conversing in the big living-room and the Dege Sey was still sitting in his place of honour. "You'll have to take a position now, you know," said the Communist officer. "I don't want to do anything, thank you very much. I shall now become just one of the ordinary people and that will suit me perfectly," the General answered with some definiteness. "Oh, no, we shall fix you up with a job all right. And what do you want to do?" he said, turning to me. "I want to go on to Chamdo, if possible," I answered. "I guess it will be back to Hong Kong for you," he returned pointedly. The conversation lapsed and then the young officer took it up again with increased enthusiasm. "We had a great time when the missionaries left Batang—American imperialists, especially the young one. There is no question as to what he was. He was a proper spy. He went around taking cine films of the lamasery, and somebody definitely saw him get a lot of gold out of the bank down in Kunming. Then when we searched him we found a receiving set. We took it off him, of course, and I gave him such a blow with my fist!" The Dege Sey and I sat dumb and expressionless before such "patriotic zeal". The officer, busy on some errand or other, or concerned over the General not yet having a position, went out and we were left alone for a short period. Making sure that the officer had really gone, the General said to me: "They are pestering me about you. They think you have a gun, but I have told them that I can absolutely guarantee you haven't, and that you have no interest in military affairs— other than the time we played soldiers with my children of course," he added with a smile. As we were talking, the Tibetan Army Colonel came in. He had been the General's right hand man all through the crisis. He was almost weeping. With one great outburst his pent-up feelings poured out in a tirade of grief and rage. "Our own men have looted my property," he sobbed convulsively. "Our own men . . . as if everything that's happened is not enough . . . our own men . . ." and he collapsed on the floor. "Slowly, slowly, Colonel. Don't upset yourself," the General said quietly. It was the hardest blow of all. Some time later a meeting was convened to deal with this breach of discipline. All the disarmed Tibetan troops were assembled and the General had to give a lecture on the present situation. The Tibetan forces would eventually be incorporated into a defence unit under the direction of the Chinese occupying forces. All uniform and all food would be provided by the new military H.Q. There was no need for looting, which could lead to very serious measures being taken against offenders. He tried to explain that what had been done had been done for their good, and sought their co-operation. The numerous "lags so's" and low bowing which followed could have meant anything, although one felt there was still very real esteem for the Dege Sey himself. The ragged crowd of soldiery dispersed. Men without a kingdom and who knew no loyalty now other than to themselves. I returned into the garden. Whilst I was there a Tibetan came up to me. I had seen his face before. In a moment I realised he was from Batang, a nominal Christian. "What are you doing here?" I asked him. "We had to come," he said, "for interpreting with the P.L.A." He was friendly and I felt sorry for him. I asked after some of the folk at Batang and he said that Timothy Hsiao had told him I would have escaped to India by now. "They say that there is a spy at Gartok," he continued in a low voice. "Do you know?" "No," I said, but understood perfectly what he meant. He left talking with me and quietly went his way. It was very kind of him. He no doubt loved the Lord and His people more than I knew.

A couple of days went by. I studied quietly in my room. All around were soldiers and, although I had not been restricted in my movements by anyone yet, it was most unpleasant walking about with guards stationed everywhere. Ga Ga reported that he had attended a meeting for the masses outside. "The Chinese say that America and England are very evil and are taking Tibet away from us," he said, half asking an explanation. "Apart from the people probably not knowing who America or England are, I should think you can judge for yourself," I said laconically. One of the servants came in to tell me that the General wanted to see me. "I have a message from the Commander-in-Chief of the Chinese forces here," he said. "He wants to see you, with your servant, as soon as possible in the Kungo Dzong's summer-house." In compliance with these orders I went straight across. The guard showed me in. "What a change," Ga Ga remarked. It certainly was. The only things that had not altered were the lewd pictures high up on the wall. In a few minutes Lt. Chang, the English speaking officer present on the night of the surrender, came in. I took it for granted that he would be asking a lot of pointed questions, so I stepped in first and gave him a kind of testimony as to my calling and work. He was quite delighted and hurried to record what he could in his little note book. A senior officer came in and said that I would have to move my stuff from the fort and go to stay in a house in the village, which they would designate for the purpose. They wished me to move out immediately. Help would be given to enable me to do so. With that we left.

Once back to my little room I began to pack up. In all, there were six loads of luggage. It took some time. Before we were out, a Chinese soldier was already in sweeping the floor. The room was to accommodate some of their officers apparently. Within half an hour all the boxes were stacked outside. The last I saw of the compound as a free man was the young Chinese soldier throwing the dustpan of refuse he had just swept up over a border of plants and flowers in the garden. By one carrier or another, all my goods and chattels were taken over to one of the low single-storeyed mud houses of the village. I was shown into a room in which several of the comrades were living. They were mostly junior officers. Mr. Chang was one of them. His English really was exceptionally good for a young fellow. He had studied agriculture at a Shanghai university and had spent three years with CNNRA. Earlier I had asked him whether he was a Communist. He had replied: "No," but said he counted himself one of the people and on their side. One of the other officers came in to the new quarters to see me. He said: "This is the front line, we cannot allow you to continue here. It will be better for you to get back to Batang. You have some friends there, haven't you?" I felt very sad. After he had gone Mr. Chang spoke to me. "If you want any food I have some money granted for that purpose. You just say what you want and we'll buy it from the villagers." I told him I could manage my own affairs. I had Tibetan currency and some silk I could barter, but he was very persistent. Later he added: "If you want to go outside at all, you must ask one of the soldiers to go with you; you understand, don't you?" It was now very evident I had lost my freedom. Perhaps it will only be until we get to Batang, I tried to convince myself, and then perhaps not—the disturbing thought came surging in. To think I was a prisoner. It seemed impossible. "Have a read of that," Mr. Chang suggested cheerily. I looked at the pamphlet he handed me, "On Democratic Dictatorship" by Mao Tse Tung. I glanced at a few pages. It was poorly printed and the English unnatural. "The Communists are more intelligent than other people. They understand the laws existing in things," I read.

The arrogance and ungodly spirit of the treatise caused me to put it down in disgust and turn afresh to my Bible for consolation. How I needed that thirty-third chapter of Deuteronomy now, which I read so recently with its great word: "The beloved of the Lord shall dwell in safety by him and the Lord shall cover him all the day long and he shall dwell between his shoulders." "Would you like to help me with this?" Mr. Chang suddenly asked. He was struggling with the translation of a propaganda leaflet. "I am afraid I can't," I replied. "It would be against my conscience to do it!" "Oh!" he said, quite amazed. He did not ask me again. The comrades were in and out all the time. They were thoroughly enjoying themselves for these few days after their rather hard time since the main assault began. They were fortunate because many of the troops had been sent straight on from Gartok without a break, to take part in the attack on Chamdo. They were all very well equipped with U.S.A. revolvers and holsters and would sometimes take them out for cleaning. Towards evening a haggard old woman, whom I had recently treated for an abscess, found her way into the room. Dear old soul, she looked so woebegone. In her hand she held a bowl of milk and with a most sympathising gesture signalled to me to take it. The comrades were quite taken aback. "What ever does she want?" they cried. I explained and then declined, trying to indicate it was not convenient for me to receive it, but she insisted. Such was the love of some of the Tibetan people to me in those last days I was amongst them.

Evening drew on. From the conversation, I could gather that there was some probability that we would leave for Batang on the morrow. The comrades insisted that I should have the only raised part of the floor for my bed. As a prisoner, courtesy cannot exceed orders, so I settled down fairly comfortably to my first night as a captive in the hands of the Communists and yet, in the most real sense, in the hands of the Lord. In His infinite grace He shielded from my eyes the fact that more than another eleven hundred and fifty evenings would yet pass before I slept again in freedom.

CHAPTER XI

CAPTIVE TO BATANG

"He changeth .... the appointed times ...." Daniel 2. /

THE next day was most trying. We were going. Then we were not going. Then we were going. Then the mules had not yet arrived. All day we were on the verge of departure. Yet by evening time we were still "undeparted". I was taken over by Lt. Chang to see the Dege Sey. It was a bitter farewell for us both. Various Communist people were there. Thoughtlessly I spoke to him in English. "Please speak in Tibetan," he asked uneasily. He was virtually a prisoner in his own castle. I wondered what I could give him for a present. With the permission of my captors, I carried George's typewriter over with me and offered it to him as the only recognition I could give of all his kindness to me in the past two and a half months. As I did so, Lt. Chang opened it and examined the machine. The Dege Sey immediately enquired how I was placed for travelling. Had I cash with me? The previous day he had quietly sent over tsamba and dried meat by the hand of the old nurse and now as a last gesture he was determined to see that everything possible was done for me. A servant appeared and handed me two hundred silver rupees. I was loath to take it, but he had grasped the situation perfectly. Loose rupees on the road would be invaluable under my present circumstances. The following days proved how wonderfully the Lord had touched his heart to give me a gift of money rather than anything else. It would be impossible for me to trade my silk and the old Tibetan paper currency would almost certainly be unusable. So we parted. We could show little of our feelings before those watching us. I shall always remember him as one of Tibet's finest sons, a very gallant warrior-gentleman. As darkness fell I was made to stand in the big courtyard of the fort beside my boxes, until the mules arrived. In the twilight the Chinese troops paraded. Once mustered they had a time of community singing. With great enthusiasm and high spirits they sang out their favourite revolutionary song, "Unity is strength . . ." to the night sky. This was followed by a pep-talk given by one of the officers. Political and technical instruction go hand in hand in the P.L.A. No company of the People's Army would be complete without the "Political Committee Member", that is to say a Communist Party indoctrinator with the duties of a watchdog. These fellows are really the "padres" of the Communist-led armies. They preach Marxist sermons, give political lectures, contact the troops in all circumstances, try to solve problems and act as adviser to the Commander. Any bourgeois thinking, lack of enthusiasm, cowardice, un-Marxist outlooks or sub-proletariat behaviour, will receive their immediate attention and be reported regularly. At the time of nationwide political campaigns they will be largely responsible for the handling of mass meetings amongst the troops, accusation meetings, struggle meetings and the routine meetings for criticism and self criticism. They will at all times be also a confessional for any of the officers or men with troubled political consciences. Their duty is to raise and maintain the proletariat political consciousness of the unit at the highest level, at all times relating theory to practice, policy to specific duties and instilling by their example utter devotion to the cause of the revolution. The apparently unselfish and heroic lives lived by some of these men, who are entirely devoted to their ideal, are quite amazing. Yet little do they perhaps realize the agony of mind which they bring to so many of their comrades as they act in persecution of all whose thought is at variance with the thought of their adored leader Mao Tse Tung. They are part of the State machinery of inquisition. Stalin refers to them as a deciding factor in the formation of the Red Army. Their presence is the guarantee of strait-jacketed living along Marxist lines and the death of individual freedom as known in the west.

At long last a number of mules arrived. They were not sufficient but somehow we managed to get all but two boxes loaded on to them and then trailed out from the fort in what was now complete darkness. We were a party of about six. Lt. Chang, three or four other ranks, Ga Ga and myself. During the last day or two, Ga

Ga had been staying with a friend. We passed through a maze of sentries in the dark. It seemed to me that we would be shot at any moment. All around were the tents and camp fires of the troops. We could hardly see the road and as we proceeded further it was inky black. Lt. Chang, after about half a mile, shouted out towards a glimmer of light across the plain and we stumbled over in that direction. The wind was getting up and the thought of pitching a tent was not pleasant. Suddenly Lt. Chang ordered us to dump everything down and unload the mules. We stood where we were. We could not even see each other, but I began to sense somehow that Ga Ga was not present. "Disappeared" would hardly be the word to use. Apparently he had gone running after the horses! I now had to pitch the tent alone. As it was a Tibetan tent the Chinese did very little to help me, as they were not familiar with the ropes. It was a fantastic and utterly exhausting task. Only the Lord's enabling made it possible at all. Apart from the billowing canvas, tent pegs were the main problem. They were lost as soon as they left the hand. After a long while the tent was up. We could see nothing and do nothing. An old torch was of very little use. We just lay down on the ground under the flapping canvas with what rugs and clothes we could lay our hands on and "wished for the day". We awoke from a troubled sleep to a hopeless shambles. The Chinese insisted that I break up two of my boxes and tip the contents into smaller packages of canvas to ensure a more even distribution of the loads. The confusion was even greater. A Tibetan came along and salvaged the two boxes for his own use and we managed to catch on to a caravan of two hundred animals returning to the river. Although up at dawn, we were not away until ten. Ga Ga had been back to the fort and collected the two boxes left behind in the fort on the previous evening. Now there was a total of some thirteen or fourteen mule-loads of medicine, Scriptures and equipment.

We climbed the pass that we had crossed with the troops but a few days previously. Lt. Chang, being short and fat, was sorely put to it. I offered him my horse but he resolutely refused. As we came to the summit my eyes ranged back over the plain. There lay the little city, the fort and the lamasery in the far distance. My heart was nearly breaking. Away on the great skyline I could pick out the ranges and grasslands to the north. I could see the pass in the hills leading on to the Chamdo trail. I had hoped so highly to be treading that road further into Tibet and on to Lhasa. Now I was leaving this immense country and this stricken people, leaving as a prisoner led on into an unknown and unthinkable future. As I gazed out to that lost horizon, I could only cry out in an agony of soul: "Lord, Thou knowest all things, Thou knowest all things." For me it was the greatest disappointment I had ever known. All down the years God had been knocking, knocking at the doors of the Lama-Kingdom. If they had known at least in this their day the things that belonged unto their peace, how often He would have gathered them but they would not, and now their house was left unto them desolate. To me it was stark tragedy. Broken, baffled and amazed, I turned in my saddle and looked down the new valley. Into my saddened spirit the Lord in His own special way poured in His peace and calm. He will not allow His children to be swallowed up with over much sorrow. In His grace He breathed into me the sense of His will transcending all that had transpired and as we descended so great did this reassurance become that I found myself saying almost without thinking to Ga Ga: "It is the will of God, it is the will of God that events should befall us so."

With still a couple of hours of light to go, we arrived at the village where the surrender had been made. Having so much time on our hands, our camp was well ordered. The tent was soon pitched and we bought wood and had a cooked meal. Everyone's spirits revived and Lt. Chang spoke to me very freely, so that the consciousness of being a prisoner was greatly diminished. We had a good night's rest, although some of the comrades had to stand guard, which they did in watches.

Next morning we packed up camp, also in a very orderly manner, and proceeded down the valley, then up over a low wooded pass. In the distance to the east I glimpsed one of the big residences of the Pangda family. It had been built to the order of Pangda Dopgyay although he had never lived there. As we passed through the woods our party straggled out. Lt. Chang ordered me to keep close to him. He was afraid I might try to escape. It would have been dangerous, but not altogether impossible. By midday we filed into Hla Dun. The weather was better than when I saw it before and it looked less of a dung hill. We waited there for the whole caravan of mules to go through. As we passed through the village, who should meet us but Gezang Drashi. I introduced him as a friend of mine to Lt. Chang, who in a moment of weakness consented to our going into his house for a rest. Gezang Drashi talked exceedingly artfully. When the P.L.A. came through he had fled temporarily to the hills to let things pass over before determining any course of action. On returning he had organised a meeting in the village to stabilise the feelings of the local residents. When Lt. Chang questioned him on his political outlook, he astutely went to a back room and produced a copy of one or two Communist pamphlets. Meanwhile, his wife had made us a meal of meat dumplings which was simply delicious. As we left, Gezang Drashi said sympathetically to me in a low voice in Tibetan: "You will have to talk cleverly now." As we went on our way Lt. Chang expressed himself. "Really quite progressive," he said. I could not help but smile to myself. "Who is he? What does he do for his living?" "Farming," I replied non-communicatively. "Funny kind of Tibetan farmer, speaking such good Chinese and really quite well educated." I did not think it necessary to inform him that Gezang Drashi had been educated in a foreign Mission School, was a centurion of Pangda Dopgyay's private army and had handled, at one time, a major share of Pangda Dopgyay's trading in China and India. Further that he was steward of all Pangda Tsang's land and property in the Hla Dun area.

The afternoon brought us up on to the grasslands and back past the "mani" piles. Suddenly Lt. Chang asked me: "Why do all you missionary people have to get linked up with Local Government Authority?" "Do they?" I asked innocently. He was quite indignant over the matter, which he must have been going over in his mind. The subject was not pursued but it helped me to realise what not to reveal to him, that the journey might proceed peacefully. By evening time we dropped down into the vicinity of Bom Ting. Ga Ga went up to the village to buy wood and was away two or three hours drinking. I was thoroughly angry, as we all sat about waiting to light the fire and no one had

had any tea. To crown it all he was nearly torn to shreds on his
return by the company mascot, a great labrador type of hound,
which savagely attacked anyone not clad in a yellow uniform. I
was sorry I got upset afterwards. It was all so futile, especially
in the position I found myself. The strain was beginning to tell
a little but, as days went by, God led me on into a patience that
was destined to see me through an undreamt-of pressure.

The following day we branched out on to a path I had not
traversed previously. It brought us out to another quite large
village overlooking the Golden Sand River some miles below the
Batang crossing. The waters were now blue. We were about three
thousand feet above their surface. Lt. Chang began as time went
by to order the boy about in what I considered a most unjustified
way. Ga Ga was not a prisoner, neither was he employed or paid
to run errands for the Chinese troops, yet Chang's attitude was
thoroughly "imperialistic". It was that of a conqueror to a sub-
jugated people. From the Communist standpoint he was certainly
a very bad advertisement. Years later I realised that, for all his
being in the P.L.A., he was an example of what the Communists
call a "backward particle" or "backward element" in their
midst. They would say that he had drunk in the poison of the
capitalist way of life. He needed to reform himself through
labouring in the cause of the revolution and in living the "Masses'
life". Under the education of the Communist Party he would
eventually become a "keen particle" and a "good citizen".
Many students reformed themselves in this way until they wholly
adopted the proletariat world outlook. Some, however, concealed and clung to their past way of life and were purged as
counter-revolutionaries. Once down to the river we skirted northwards up the west bank, crossed two tributaries with the help of
the horses and came into a village called Gora. Here we passed a
good night on the rooftop of a Tibetan house. It was notable in
as much as I had quite a talk with Lt. Chang along Christian
lines, which ended by his trying to assure me that he was not
anti-Christian. It is almost laughable the lengths to which
Communist officials will go to try to prove this point. The stated
policy of "religious freedom" can never conceal the fact that the
basic nature of their programme is to adopt every conceivable

measure to bring into being, in the shortest possible time, a system of society which is to have as one of its distinctive features the complete absence of Christianity, or any other faith for that matter. The entire scope of their propaganda, by reason of the basis of materialism on which it is asserted, is in essence anti-God. Smart attempts to veil this, which became quite frequent as the days passed by, were wholesale deception and typical of the master-mind of Satan from whom the whole philosphy springs.

The fifth evening out of Gartok we camped at the river-crossing. Here two villages faced each other across swirling waters. This area had been the scene of the fighting. As we passed through the doors of a house Lt. Chang pointed out to me the bullet marks in the wood. We rested in the living-room of a Tibetan family for a time, until arrangements could be made for us to cross to the east bank. The Tibetans were very downcast. I heard an old fellow tell Ga Ga of the day of the battle. He was one of the residents who had refused to leave his home. "When the Chinese came over," he said, "we pleaded with them not to attack us in this house, but they threw their hand grenades up at the windows just the same." In the same room was a Tibetan sitting with us. He had been shot in the leg. "What happened to the 'centurion'?" Ga Ga asked. "Terrible, terrible," was the reply. "He resisted to the end. At the last he was caught in a room. They sent one man in to get him to surrender but the 'centurion' shot him dead. Then they sent in another man. We don't know what happened but the second Chinese got him." "Where is his body now then?" Ga Ga continued to pump his informant. "Out the back of the village. I guess the dogs have eaten half of it already." Ga Ga made a grimace of horror and revulsion. The Hla Dun centurion, who entertained me so well with his young wife just two and a half months ago, had died bravely but in vain. From the battered home of these Tibetans, I was led out toward the river. As we passed by an enclosure, I saw a man lying on the ground amongst the vegetables. He was writhing and groaning in the shade of a roughly made shelter of branches. Someone said he had been badly wounded. All they could do was to let him lie where he was. The thought of the man in agony there, probably at the point of death, constrained me to request Lt. Chang that I

might go over to see him. When he realised it was for a religious
purpose he consented. Having said so much about not being
anti-Christian, I suppose he felt it difficult to say no. Whatever
may be the reason, the Lord graciously overruled, so that I was
given permission. On kneeling at his side, I saw the extent of his
wounds. There were some four gaping sores. He had been shot,
strangely enough, in both arms and legs. He was thus completely
helpless but wholly conscious. The wounds were already festering
terribly and the flies sucking at the pus. He seemed to be in great
pain. All he could whimper was: "Kachrug, Kachrug," the
Tibetan term of entreaty. I had no medicines, all my boxes being
with the mule train. I tried then to speak to him of the Lord Jesus
Christ. Poor man, he was so demented he could hardly listen.
He kept moaning for his son. His son lived some days away.
If he could only get a word to him. I seemed impotent in my
present position to do anything and felt very upset. When I
returned to Lt. Chang he enquired sarcastically: "How are you
getting along with your work?"

At the jetty a lot of loading and unloading was going on. Sixty-
pound yak-hide bales of rice were being ferried across constantly
for forwarding to the front. These were stacked in big piles on
the beach. At last we were ordered on to the ferry, one of the big
wooden boats built by the Chinese especially for the assault.
Slowly we pulled away from the shore. The great chasm yawned
to the skies and the clear October waters of the Golden Sand
River rushed beneath us on their journey to Yünnan, the land
south of the clouds. I watched Tibet receding from me. My last
impression was of that wounded soldier. A man who from the
sole of the foot unto the head had no soundness in him, only
wounds and bruises and putrifying sores. They had not been closed,
neither bound up, neither mollified with ointment. There could
be no more eloquent symbol of the spiritual and moral condition
of the Tibetan people. Thousands of miles away from this tragic
scene many were sitting at ease in Zion, glad to know that they
themselves are complete in Christ. As one of the saints has said:
"Jesus hath now many lovers of His heavenly kingdom, but few
bearers of His Cross. He hath many desirous of consolation, but
few of tribulation. He findeth many companions of His table,

but few of His abstinence. All desire to rejoice with him, few are willing to endure anything for Him or with Him. Many follow Jesus unto the breaking of bread; but few to the drinking of the cup of His Passion." I had professed so much, yet done so little. Now God was going to take me at my word and answer a prayer I had written in my early days amongst the Tibetan people.

> "O Lord, I have not learnt to cry.
> Perhaps I laugh too oft, for true conformity
> To Thee and Thy rough cross, or try
> To love Thee without sorrowing—
> Talk but touch not, thus they heed not.
> What heart, O Lord, moved through the garden?
> I too have slept, but wake me Lord,
> E'en though it be to love with tears."

On disembarking we tramped up into the village of Juba Lung. This had been the springboard for one assault. Over a period of weeks the Chinese had massed here. Lt. Chang pointed out a house. He said: "We used to have a machine gun on that roof." Towards the back of this house we found accommodation on another rooftop. Other troops were stationed around and one young fellow began to ply me with questions. Lt. Chang was annoyed and snapped at him: "What do you think you are doing, asking him questions?" After this hardly anyone dared speak to me and I also thought it best to speak to no one else. The comrades talked amongst themselves. There had apparently been very few casualties when they forced the crossing. One boat holding about seven men capsized and they were swept downstream, but the strategy of attack had on the whole been very successful. On the eve of the offensive, which coincided with attacks to the north on the Chamdo front and to the south in the Gunka Lama country, a small force had been despatched northwards from Jubalung. They had travelled well up the east bank, then crossed the river at dead of night at a most desolate point which was completely unguarded by the Tibetan Army. The entire surprise force arrived on the west bank still undetected. On the Tibetan side they had travelled down through the night over very rough country unintercepted, until just before dawn they were in a position to strike at the Tibetan forces holding the village opposite Jubalung. This was undoubtedly quite an achievement. As the fateful morning of October 7th, 1950, dawned over the mountains they opened fire on the Tibetan village. The Tibetans were stunned by an attack on their own side of the river and diverted forces to meet it. At this juncture the main units of the Chinese army stationed at Juba Lung poured down on to the beaches and in their prepared craft made an all-out frontal assault, straight across the river. The Tibetan bullets could account for but a fraction of the Chinese commando forces. In a matter of minutes the first men were over and charging up the beaches. With hand grenades they cleared the houses of the Tibetan troops who, being attacked from two sides, were very soon overrun, Through this breach torn in the Tibetan defences, many hundreds of Chinese surged up the passes to Bom Ting and on to Gartok.

While the troops chatted over their battle experiences and exchanged news, I was left alone. My heart was heavy. I could not believe that I had been mistaken. From the very first day in September 1941, when God had sealed my call to Central Asia, right up to this present time I had been conscious of His leading. He had provided for all my need. He had done the humanly impossible in bringing us right across China against all odds at this critical time for this key moment when Tibetan doors began to swing open to the Gospel. Everything had been accomplished with such precision. All had moved forward so perfectly and then suddenly in a moment all seemed reversed. What had transpired in the heavenlies? Could he who had fallen as lightning from heaven contend with the One Who "rideth upon the heavens by His Name Jah"? I could find no answer; Satan was striking at the very root of my faith and calling. As I turned the leaves of my Bible my eyes fell upon these sublime words:

"Then Daniel blessed the God of Heaven. Daniel answered and said, Blessed be the name of God for ever and ever, for wisdom and might are his: And he changeth the times and the seasons; he removeth kings and setteth up kings; he giveth wisdom unto the wise, and knowledge to them that know understanding; He revealeth the deep and secret things; He knoweth what is in the darkness, and the light dwelleth with Him."

It was a word from the Throne. I had realised so little in experience before that Our Father is Lord of all His own appointments. He disposes the times and seasons. He changeth even the appointed times. It was His good will. Under His moulding hand and through many a wilderness, I was yet to prove that the same will was both acceptable and perfect, the outworking of His most wondrous kindness and ever in the higher interests of His great kingdom.

The last day of our journey to Batang had now arrived. I estimated the date as the nineteenth of October but was afterwards told that it was the twenty-second. I could never reconcile this in my own mind. Somehow in the course of the catastrophic events of the past two weeks I had lost three days. As we left Juba Lung, Ga Ga came to the end of his patience. Having endured all the indignities of having to serve the invaders and being treated little better than a prisoner, he told Lt. Chang, by means of my interpretation, that he was not prepared to load our horses with any more of the Chinese soldiers' kit. Lt. Chang was livid. "We have been very good to you," he said, "and you won't even carry our odds and ends. Tell your servant that he better be very careful indeed or else I'll not guarantee what will happen to him." It was a nasty situation. At all cost I wanted to get to Batang without incident until I could see the highest authority there. It was useless to argue or antagonise these troops, who were but fulfilling their officers' orders to escort us to the Batang H.Q. The result was that Ga Ga had to walk. "We didn't ask to be brought down here with all our stuff," he said plaintively. I felt sorry for him but knew that there was no other course for us in the circumstances. We passed another village, of fair size. I remembered what the Batang KMT magistrate had said, that there were 33,000 people living in the Batang county. On the river I was surprised to see a newly built junk. The Chinese were finding means to navigate the Golden Sand River in certain stretches. By about two in the afternoon we topped the small pass overlooking Batang. Lt. Chang loaded his pistol. "Can't take any risks," he said. "One of our men lagging behind the main party was sniped at and killed by a bandit here a week or two back." I remarked that a missionary of Batang named Shelton had also been murdered on this pass some years ago. We crossed safely however, and descended to a small stream which was thoroughly appreciated by the soiled and thirsty travellers.

Much refreshed, we moved along the fertile valley now rapidly broadening into a plain. One of the comrades bought some pears at a farmhouse, a luxury in most places in Sikang. He very generously distributed them amongst the comrades, giving both Ga Ga and myself a share.

We came into Batang round a back way, arriving first at the old Mission compound. The rebuilding of one of the ruined Mission houses was in progress, and large numbers of men were employed on carrying timber. I was taken straight over to the main building, now being used as an Army H.Q. It seemed unbelievable to be walking through the compound. I was taken upstairs and into the very room where the church held meetings the few weeks John and I had laboured together in that place. There, where I had preached the Word of Life, I was received by a senior P.L.A. Officer. A comrade brought me a cup of tea. Very little was said to me, as they apparently were not authorised to handle my affairs. After a few minutes, I was escorted through the town to the old Tibetan fort. I felt very self-conscious going through the town as a prisoner. We arrived at the fort again, went in past Pangda Dopgyay's cannons and then upstairs into a room just opposite the hall where I had feasted with the old KMT Commander, now of course, nowhere to be seen. I waited quite a long time, sitting at a table, while Lt. Chang reported to his Commander-in-Chief. At long last a man appeared. He was a sharp featured young fellow, about my own age, with rather merciless eyes but obviously very intelligent and, I should think, ruthless in decision. I was much taken aback at his youth and could hardly believe he was the chief officer in Batang, but I was quite wrong in my judgment. He was the highest officer, in charge of the garrison, and in fact almost certainly directing the entire offensive on that sector of the front. He was dressed just the same as the ordinary ranks except that he wore a greatcoat, which the other ranks were generally too busy to wear. He was a man of few words. Lt. Chang had no doubt primed him as to my main data. I took the opportunity to request him that I now be per-

mitted to lodge with my Christian friends in the town. The reason
for my being brought in custody to Batang, I told him, had been
stated by the officers at Gartok to be that they could not permit
of my free movement in the front line area. Now, here at the rear,
I could see no further reason for my being held. He replied that
I would have to stay with the P.L.A. in the fort. I looked round
at the room, which was fairly spacious, trying to picture myself
making my living quarters there. We talked a little of the Sino-
Tibetan conflict now in progress. In my ignorance I referred to
China and Tibet as two distinct nations. This was a fatal error.
"What do you mean?" he questioned me indignantly. "Tibet a
nation indeed! China and Tibet two nations! Whoever heard of
such a thing? Tell me," he said, "who told you that?" He might
as well have asked me who told me the earth was round. I was
appalled at my mistake. He had apparently found out all that he
wanted for the present. He stood up and walked out, giving orders
to a guard as to how I was to be housed. I did not hear what he
said but just followed where I was told. I was taken downstairs
to the centre of the great fort. Lt. Chang came to a room. It had
one lattice window but was so distant from the light, which came
down a kind of well in the midst of the building, that it was
almost pitch dark inside. Lt. Chang took one look. "Too dark,"
he said. My heart sank. Surely they were not going to accommodate me in one of these dungeons. They moved to the next room
and thrust open the thick wooden door. It was dark but a sufficent
glimmer of light made it possible to discern the outline of the
interior. "Put him there, that will do," Lt. Chang ordered. I
stepped in and immediately the door was padlocked.

CHAPTER XII

TIBETAN DUNGEON

Could we with ink the ocean fill,
And were the skies of parchment made;
Were every stalk on earth a quill,
And ev'ry man a scribe by trade;
To write the love of God above
Would drain the ocean dry;
Nor could the scroll contain the whole,
Though stretched from sky to sky.

*Pencilled on the wall of a narrow room of an
asylum by a man said to have been demented.
The profound lines were discovered after his
death.*

I PAUSED a moment and then groped my way across the cell. The floor was loose dust beneath my feet. About a yard from the door I brushed against some wooden object just above my knees. It proved to be a derelict door lying on its side. A little investigation and I found it was resting on a couple of disused mule saddles. This, I presumed, was to be my bed. I slumped down upon it and sat silent and motionless in the darkness. I was too stunned to pray. As my eyes became accustomed to the gloom, the size of the room became apparent. It was about seven feet wide and twelve feet long. Sitting on the door that had been torn off its hinges, I peered through the ragged gaps in a sheet of torn dirty yellow paper pasted on a latticed window just in front of me. I could see the guard with his gun and fixed bayonet. He was standing in a kind of passage-way leading into an inner courtyard of the fort, where stood another guard. Soldiers and officers were walking to and fro going about their duties. In the far corner of the room, on the same side as my "bed", was another small latticed aperture covered with filthy paper which let in practically no light at all. The walls had probably been white at one time but were now thick with dust and cobwebs. Gradually I realised the location of my prison. It was situated under the central buildings of the fort in a narrow corridor joining two courtyards. It was already well on in the afternoon and the interior of the cell grew darker. I knew not what to think. It was not fear in the ordinary sense. The only emotion I can recall to parallel it, in any way, was when our house was bombed in London during the war. Something catastrophic had happened and I dared not move. In a moment one becomes transfixed. Then follows an eternity and eventually a reawakening. There is a consciousness of being under a Mighty Hand, that awes one to complete submissiveness. I felt like some hunted animal crouching low and still in the grasp of an unknown captor, not daring to rise lest fresh disaster befall me.

As the awfulness of my predicament began to dawn upon me and take shape in the form of more normal thought, all sorts of terrors began to haunt my mind. Will I ever get out? How can they do it? Just to shut me up in here and leave me! What have I done? Alone here in this terrific country! How could I let them take me like this? My health will break down here in this filth and with no exercise. Oh, when shall I ever be free again? When shall I ever be free again? The first flood of reaction began to recede and in its place came that calm resolution of will that God gives to those who trust Him, so that I said to myself: "Geoff be still, you are under the hand of the Lord!"

There was a shuffle outside the door, the rattle of the guard's gun and the twisting of a key in the padlock. It seemed an age but the door at last opened. "Come and get your bedding," Lt. Chang ordered. From amongst a small quantity of my baggage, which had arrived, I picked out my sleeping roll, a rug and my saddle-bags and was returned immediately to the gloom of my cell. The guard hastened to replace the padlock. I spread out the rug on the old door and sat down again. Whatever would I do if I had just to sit and sit day after day like this? It was too terrible to think about. Again there was somebody at the door. Who could it be this time? The guard broke in and slung a bamboo basket of warm rice on my bed. In his other hand he had a billy-can which he passed to me and then immediately withdrew. I bowed my head in thankfulness. I was very hungry and fairly

wolfed down the tough yak's meat and rice. Afterwards the guard
brought in a billy-can of tea made in the usual Chinese way
without milk or sugar. I felt better for the meal. It was now
becoming quite dark. A red wax candle used in temples was
brought and stuck by the lattice window and in its flickering
light I knelt in prayer, committing myself into the hands of my
Father whose love we need never question.

My guard had apparently received instructions, for at daybreak I was brought a bowl of water for washing. Some mornings
they would forget, but this was only occasionally. A visit to the
toilet at various intervals through the day was always a looked-
for break. It meant a few moments of precious privacy and also
an extra view of the outside world. From the narrow slit of a
window in the upstairs chamber, I could see into the fields between
the city and the big lamasery. Sometimes I saw people walking
freely through the cut barley stalks. It would give me a sense of
great exhilaration. I would somehow project myself into them
and live a moment or two of their liberty. Yet its last result was
often sadness. Tragedy, it seemed, had befallen me, and yet the
world went on. They had their business and I was left to my
solitude shut away in the dungeon. Hour after hour, the first day
dragged slowly by. Nobody came. The troops ate once in the
morning, then again at four in the afternoon. The meals were
identical, being comprised of rice and tough yak's meat. I ate
much the same as they did, except that mine was often nearly
cold by the time it was brought to me. I found the rice hard to
stomach and the poor meat hurt my teeth and was most in-
digestible, but I was determined to receive it as the Lord's
providing. In such circumstances to receive anything at all was
a blessing and evidence of His restraining hand. I passed the
second night. I was glad of my Tibetan gown as the evenings were
getting cold, even in Batang situated at only 10,500 feet. I noticed
it particularly because my room was situated in the stream of a
draught. Guards constantly changed. One young comrade looked
in. He was full of sympathy. "How very bitter," he said. I found
the dust very trying. If I walked about much it was easily stirred
up and settled on everything, impregnating my rug and clothes.
Because of this, even darkness had its advantages. It made the

dirt become less irksome. The third day dawned, still nobody came. With me I had a few books. By bringing my saddle-bags into the cell the first evening, I had procured a Bible, also a Chinese and Tibetan dictionary. It was only between eleven and one o'clock each day that there was sufficient light to read in my prison room, and then only if the weather were good. This undoubtedly increased the suffering of solitary confinement, at that time still so new to me.

These first days, left so utterly alone in such dark and filthy confinement; subjected to it so suddenly and without reason; cut off from the outside world by immense distances and hedged in by a foe, who as yet did not deign even to speak sensibly to me; together with the absolute shattering of my highest expectation of years, my work amongst the Tibetans cruelly snatched from me, my position of opportunity in Tibet destroyed and myself brought back to Batang a helpless prisoner, now sinking lower and lower in a mire of fateful circumstance in this dismal dungeon out at the back of beyond; all this created an unbearable pressure weighing down upon me, crushing my spirit and rending my soul. The spiritual poverty of my life and service suddenly came before me. All my Christian life seemed just to crumble away. So much of all that I had said and done, ostensibly for His Kingdom, was now, under His rebuke, revealed to be nothing but wood, hay and stubble. With tears, I broke down and knelt trembling on the dusty floor. My mind in a turmoil and overcome by a sense of sin and unworthiness, I wept my way afresh to Calvary. There God met me again. His love to me was wonderful. I thought of the way behind as the way of a prodigal but now, as I knelt in the dust, the Father came running out to meet me where I was. There was no rebuke. I had come to where I had found Him at the first. I tried to blurt out: "I have sinned . . . I am not worthy . . . I am not worthy," but was only conscious of His great arms around me and His kiss of pardon on my dirty cheeks. And there I knelt and knelt until I heard those matchless words: "Bring forth the best robe . . . Bring forth the best and put it on him." It will live with me for ever. Into my heart came a peace and a joy in God's grace and forgiveness, in a measure I had never known before. My mind returned to the other dimly

lighted room on that evening when we had boarded the Yangtse
River steamer at Shanghai on our first journey inland. I could
hear again dear Con Baehr singing in the cabin: "King of my
life I crown Thee now . . ." As the words surged back into my
mind, I could only stand up and, pulling my Tibetan gown
around me, sing out in renewed consecration to my Lord and
Saviour:

> King of my life I crown Thee now,
> Thine may the glory be,
> Lest I forget Thy thorn crowned brow,
> Lead me to Calvary.

About the fifth day, Lt. Chang appeared. He was bright and
breezy. He looked in through the lattice window. "Not much of
a place," he said, "but I guess you can stick it for a few days."
How my heart leapt at that phrase "a few days". What did he
mean? "Would it be possible for me to have some daily exercise,
do you think?" I asked him. "I will make your request known
at our officers' meeting," he replied. "Maybe we can do something for you." Shortly afterwards the door was unlocked and I
was taken upstairs. The guard led me into the very room in the
fort where I had sat as a guest at the KMT Commander's feast.
On the floor were a pile of my books, letters and papers, together
with tracts and other odds and ends. Lt. Chang with a group of
soldiers and officers surrounded me. Only about two of them
could understand English and all the others were filled with the
most childish unconcealed curiosity to see all that they could of
the foreigner's belongings. The search and examination now
began. That which was considered of doubtful character or
viewed as possible evidence was placed in one pile. A map of
China or a book on Tibet with a map of racial groupings at the
back of it was handed immediately to Lt. Chang, as a suspicious
object. All letters were collected and placed carefully on one side.

To my horror I saw some rough notes of a preface I had
written for the glossary of political words I had compiled for the
Dege Sey. I managed surreptitiously to purloin this sheet and
destroy it later. I had not yet learned how futile are such attempts
to try and conceal one's moments of folly. God will have every

icta out with us in His time. After about half an hour of humiliating perusal of all my private documents, a great pile of possibly incriminating material, comprising certain books and letters and my passport, was carried off and I was ordered back to my cell. Lt. Chang informed me that I must be thinking over in my mind my past life and all the things I had done against the people. In a few days I would be required to write out my life's history from the age of eight. Contrary to his expectations perhaps, I was very pleased to do this and looked forward to writing such a statement very much. I felt it was a step forward in clarifying my position as a missionary and an opportunity to tell the authorities what the Lord Jesus Christ had done for me. Late one afternoon soon afterwards, Lt. Chang produced pen and paper. By the time I had had my meal it was nearly dark. I scribbled by candlelight and managed to complete three pages of tightly written foolscap.

Once these had been handed in, I constantly expected things to move for the better, but days went by and again I was left alone. I began to realise that my solitary confinement would quite probably be prolonged, so I decided to plan my day. This was helped by permission being granted for me to have exercise under escort every morning. In this God was very gracious to me, as some of the guards liked being out in the open too, so were not in a hurry to come back into the precincts of the fort. My routine, with various modifications according to circumstances, was as follows. At the sound of the reveille bugle, rise and pray. About 8 a.m. the guard would bring the water. Wash, then repeat and memorise Scripture. (This was because reading whole passages at that time in the morning was often quite impossible and at the best of times a very severe eyestrain). Sing hymns and choruses. First meal. Exercise. Return to cell. Commence reading of the Scriptures as soon as light permitted. Reading straight through, I could get through a book like Matthew in good time before it was too dark again. I found this reading long passages at one sitting most helpful. Many a day, though, I was denied reading through bad weather which meant poor light. In the afternoon I would walk to and fro in the cell, letting the mind range freely or composing poems. The second meal followed at about 4 p.m. In the evening I would sit and think quietly or meditate and then, after prayer, retire early to bed. In this way my solitary confinement moved on into a new stage. In the first period, it had mastered me; now I was in a way master. I could plan. I had a programme. I was increasing my knowledge, I was maintaining my powers of intellect. In all this I do believe God gave me wisdom and fortitude.

On about the thirteenth day I was led out of the cell to the big room where my papers had been scrutinised. The commanding officer was there, seated at a table. At his side was another officer. Lt. Chang was seated on a chair just before the table. They motioned me to sit down on a chair provided. The C.O. questioned me in steely tones. We spoke half Chinese and half English, Lt. Chang interpreting when necessary. "What are you doing out here in Tibet, a lone foreigner like you?" "Missionary work." "Who sent you?" "I came here in answer to a call from God, Who also sent me." I wondered whether I should use such spiritual language, yet after a moment's thought I was convinced that I should. "Yes, but who sent you? All missionaries in China have a Society? What is your Society?" "I do not belong to any Missionary Society." "But you must. There is not a single missionary in China who has not been sent by a Society. What is your Church?" "I came out to China from a local Church on the edge of London in England." They were somewhat exasperated. Lt. Chang, looking as I had never seen him look before, glared fiercely and then raved at me: "Your passport is out of order. Do you know that? This is a very unusual passport." I pleaded the absurdity of such an assertion. My passport was perfectly valid, having been issued in Chungking in May, 1948. There followed a long interrogation on all the British passports I had held and when, where they had been issued, and where they had been renewed. They were not satisfied and Lt. Chang summed up the point with a great flourish by saying: "Anyway your British passport doesn't mean any more than a scrap of paper to us!" This diversion on the passport had apparently taken up more time than the C.O. wished and, being a man of conciseness, he summed up the findings of this first interrogation. "The first point, you are a British subject moving independently in Tibet. The second point, you are in touch with important Tibetan personages and yet have no clarified motives or recognised H.Q. or Society. The third, there is the question of your passport. If you could lead people to believe what you say, they would believe you, but I consider you are a British Imperialist spy." With that I was dismissed and the guard took me back to my cell.

To be branded as a spy was very serious. Whatever would happen if I was unable to convince them that I was a missionary? After the interview, Lt. Chang on occasions would talk with me, sometimes out in the big square before the fort or when they were examining my belongings. All my medicines and general baggage now had to be unpacked and almost every single bottle and packet scrutinised. I was called upon to do the packing and unpacking in the centre of a large crowd of laughing inquisitive soldiers. Often I would be questioned about this and that. Certain drugs and medicines, for instance glycerine, excited suspicion immediately. A number of things were taken away for laboratory tests. I think they suspected me of using some of the chemicals for explosives. "They can be used for more things than one," Lt. Chang said, looking at me accusingly. It all greatly saddened my heart and I found this constant badgering and suspicion very wearing. One day as we were doing this work, Lt. Chang said to me very ominously: "In Malaya your Government has killed or deported five hundred thousand Chinese people. You just think how we treat you!" "I didn't know there were five hundred thousand Chinese in Malaya," I said. "There are two million," he replied curtly, appalled at my ignorance. "I suppose I am an enemy alien by now?" I ventured. I wondered really how far the war in Korea was going. "Just about," he said significantly. In due course he told me that Robert Ford of the Chamdo Radio Station had been captured and that we were both to be sent down country. He announced to me jubilantly, "We have broadcast to the world that two British nationals and two Indians have been captured in our liberation of Tibet." One day soon after, I was taking my exercise under the eye of the guards when Lt. Chang came up and spoke to me. "We had expected to send you down country to-day but the mules were required for other purposes. At Chungking there are several foreigners. Some of them will be sentenced to three years, others to ten years and some will be shot," he said with great definiteness. "But whatever for?" I asked, absolutely dumbfounded. "For doing things they should not have done," he said relentlessly. "Chungking is my H.Q.," he continued. "When I was down there, there were six Italians being dealt with."

A combination of factors in my solitary confinement now began to play on my mind. In the loneliness the spectre of execution dominated my thoughts. There commenced that psychological build-up of fear. All that I had ever heard about Communists was sufficient to warrant the worst of terrors, the international situation was tense, Britain and China must be at war, alleged British atrocities in Malaya would bring retaliations, and now I was being sent to Chungking where the shooting of foreigners was going to take place. The whole thing seemed inevitable. Satan used to the full every factor to bring me into the bondage of fear. For two days I was in an agony of mind. I clung to life. I could not bear to think of disappearing out in the Tibetan hills, never to be heard of again. "Died Abner as a fool dieth", the words rang through my mind. "Thy hands were not bound nor thy feet put into fetters, as a man falleth before wicked men, so falleth thou." I felt I had thrown my life away. Only twenty-nine and to go out like a candle, nothing accomplished, chances missed, just one more tragedy of the Tibetan hinterland. After two days' struggle in prayer, my tightly clenched hand relaxed. It was His triumph, I simply let go of my poverty-stricken life, let it go to Jesus and His peace came again. "He that loveth his life shall lose it." Should I spurn to die, derided and alone? He proved Himself my Resurrection and I could only sing:

> "Out there amongst the hills my Saviour died.
> Pierced by those cruel nails
> Was crucified.
> Lord Jesus Thou hast done all this for me:
> Henceforward I would be
> Only for Thee."

The reality of His triumph over this attack of the devil was proved in later days. Although threats against my life increased to very great intensity and the real possibility of execution was constantly before me, yet Satan was never again able to bring me into bondage to the fear of death.

At this time of temptation or shortly afterwards, I considered very seriously the possibilities of escape. In the mountains I had excellent Tibetan contacts. There was the Linka She country, strongly anti-Communist and headed by the Linka Jabon, whom I had met at Po prior to George's departure. He had invited us to his country. I toyed with the idea. If at nightfall, when taken to the toilet, I could slip down over the rail into the lower court-yard, it would bring me out very near to the wall at the back of the fort. This looked out into the open fields and up the valley to Linka She country. Although I might be discovered, I could with ease mount the wall at that place and, once in the fields under the cover of darkness, make a clean getaway. Once away on the hills, a whole army searching for somebody in the night would be more or less useless. For food, I thought that over a period of days I could store up a certain amount from my daily fare. It could be bound up in some rag and concealed in the folds of my Tibetan gown, which I was wearing every day on account of the increasing cold. I planned also to take my Bible and two diaries I had with me, still undetected in my saddlebags. This could all be carried on my person. Once in the Linka She country I could with the help of the Linka Jabon get a man to take me through to Lhasa. Travelling by night along unfrequented mountain trails, I reckoned it could be managed. At Kalimpong I could pay back everything and give a suitable reward. It was a mad scheme but not wholly unfeasible. The thoughts of execu-tion were no doubt one cause behind it. I prayed and read the Scriptures, wondering what God's course for me would be. Satan would be very willing for me to hazard my life. If the guards shot at me, as they almost certainly would, or I lost my way or ran out of food in the mountains, or ran into unfriendly brigands, who mistook me for Chinese, all would be finished. One day, as I continued perplexed over the whole matter, I came to that Scripture in Jeremiah: "Thus saith the Lord, the God of hosts, the God of Israel; if thou wilt assuredly go forth unto the king of Babylon's princes, then thy soul shall live, and this city shall

not be burned with fire and thou shalt live and thine house: . . .
Obey I beseech thee the voice of the Lord, which I speak unto
thee; so it shall be well unto thee, and thy soul shall live." In
face of so direct a command I could only set my face to go to
Chungking, believing that my life would be spared. The thought
however, of being tried for espionage by a people's court was a
terrifying prospect. My mind was nevertheless diverted from
taking the risk of escape. Sometimes I went to the other extreme.
I thought of the miraculous deliverance of Peter. Was not Peter's
God, my God? Some evenings I would place my boots and
clothes especially neatly, believing that maybe in some special
way I should be delivered from my cell. To have everything ready
was the least I could do.

Some six weeks had now slipped by. The leaves of the young
saplings on the hillsides turned to red and gold. Although I was
still in the very dark prison room, yet my lot had improved a
little. My captors had relented. I had been permitted to buy
about four ounces of sugar to help me eat the rice, for I had
already lost weight considerably. I could feel that my cheeks were
quite hollow. On one or two occasions I had been given a little
egg and better quality meat. Every morning now, I had a thin
gruel of some kind of milky liquid. Most days I was also allowed
between two or three hours out in the big square or on the roof
of the fort. As the settled autumn weather had commenced, it
was glorious to get a breath of fresh air in the sunshine. Out on
the square I used to enjoy myself immensely. On the south side
of this big open space was a thoroughfare. Although I had to keep
well away from the public and pace slowly up and down between
my two guards, yet it was good just to view the people passing
by. Sometimes I would catch glimpses of those I knew. Mrs. Ren
went by one day and some of the orphanage children. Up on the
rooftops I could occasionally catch sight of the long thrasher-
sticks swinging in time, as the women beat out the ears of barley.
Then once a whole line of horses and mules were on sale to the
P.L.A. On the north side the comrades sometimes played basket
ball. One fellow even asked me in fun if I would join in. Quite
a lot of building was in progress. Sawing of timber and pounding
of mud provided a scene of constant activity. Then the surround-

ing country was superb. The mighty ridges to the south received their first sprinkling of snow while I was there. It was all so much more precious to me now.

The sight of my fellow human beings living and working around me made me realise how infinitely wonderful are the common blessings of life. Just to be free to do those ordinary things, to work and play, to walk down the road, or to go climbing in the crisp mountain air. Once, whilst walking back and forth, I saw a hawk pursuing a sparrow. Like lightning the pair of birds swooped across the square, the hawk within an ace of tearing the sparrow to pieces. Down they went right to the ground and then with one deft twist upwards the sparrow escaped into the eaves of the schoolroom near to the new army quarters. I was overjoyed at the outcome of this brief drama. He escaped from certain death. All my feelings seemed pent up in that tiny bird. I have thought since: "Ye are of more value than many sparrows." It was on the square also, when the guards were rather slack, that some of the comrades spoke to me and, by reason of their numerous questions, I was able to witness to the Lord Jesus Christ. Back in the fort, by means of the more obscured lattice window, some of them even talked to me there and received odd tracts I still had on my person, but this was soon discovered and stopped and opportunities became very few. One day on the square whilst the work of building was in full swing, to my joy I saw dear old Pastor Li stumping along with his stick. He looked out across the yard to the buildings, but I sensed he had already seen me. Disregarding the sentries standing some distance away, he began to walk across the square. He reached the other side and looked at the buildings for a moment or two, then came back. He came deliberately near me and, in a voice I could clearly hear, he whispered in Tibetan: "Don't be cast down, don't be cast down." Before the guards could realise that the old man had spoken to me, he had stumped off in another direction. In Paul's day he would have been known as Onesiphorus. "He was not ashamed of my chain."

My other form of recreation was to be allowed to walk about on the roof of the fort. A guard would accompany me. Generally speaking, the guards never conversed with me, but one day I was surprised to find one who was willing to talk. He had served previously in the KMT. Army. "None of us really wanted to come to these parts," he murmured. His loyalties were obviously elsewhere. He even went on to speak favourably of the KMT Air Force. From the Communist point of view he was obviously still in very serious need of reform. But even this kind of conversation I found diverting, as the days went past without speaking to anyone. Once I saw one of the Christians from the rooftop away in the distance. He was holding his baby. I did not think he could see me but I raised my hand and waved slightly and to my joy he waved back. Fortunately the attention of the guard had not been attracted. A wave from a brother in Christ in such circumstances was a veritable feast of fellowship. On the rooftop was a big stack of hay and sometimes, when the sun was really warm, I would sit amongst it and study. Over a period I was able to go over the passages relating to the Tabernacle in some detail, and I fondly imagined that, if I had a long while of reading my Bible in solitary confinement and did eventually get free, I would be quite an authority on things scriptural. This thought was, I am sure, of great displeasure to the Lord, and was to be utterly smashed by succeeding trials. Whilst pacing back and forth on that very special day, December the second, in the morning sunshine, I was reading Joshua, Chapter One. I came to the words: "Pass through the host, and command the people, saying, Prepare you victuals; for within three days ye shall pass over this Jordan, to go in to possess the land which the Lord your God giveth you to possess it." Then in Chapter Two the phrase "three days" occurred twice. Then again in Chapter Three. I was generally very cautious about taking odd phrases of the Bible and making them fit circumstances, but I was arrested by the thought that in three days God was going to do something. Then the question of interpretation came to mind and I felt that perhaps the three days were a divine indication to me of three years. I remember distinctly pacing up and down, struggling in my mind against such a suggestion. How could I bear it, three long years in prison? This time it was not merely some aberration of human thought but truly a most remarkable revelation. Quite the most remarkable, in some ways, that I have ever had. The vision was for an appointed time to be fulfilled in both days and years, precisely as stated. Meanwhile the preparing of victuals was in hand. My present Bible reading was to last me a long while. The deathly waters of Jordan were yet to be passed over and the land possessed.

The next three days were days of excitement. I myself was busy packing. The long planned trip to Chungking was soon to be undertaken but just when we would leave was still uncertain. I pleaded with Lt. Chang to allow me to leave the medical supplies and Tibetan Scriptures with the local Christians, but he would not hear of it. The Batang H.Q. almost certainly had orders from higher up because he said to me: "No! Everything must travel with you wherever you go." By the time broken medicine bottles and damaged materials had been thrown out and my things neatly packed again, there was a total of thirteen loads to go the 1,100 miles to Szechwan. They said I was going to Hsinching, but after all had been said I could not help but feel it was Chungking. My tent was still to be used and the P.L.A. provided fresh poles and iron pegs to go with it. We were to travel at the very coldest time of the year across the Sikang plateau, at an average height of between 12 and 15 thousand feet. Lt. Chang, who had been in charge of my affairs since my capture, looked at me. My hair had not been cut for months and I had not bathed since September. My beard was long and unkempt and my clothes filthy from the dust of the cell. "I think you had better have a bath," he said and "I'll arrange for one of the comrades to cut your hair." This was a noble suggestion. One memorable day I went with Lt. Chang and several of the comrades to the hot springs about half an hour's walk from the town. It was like being in heaven to walk up through the fields to see the stream laughing its way down the mountain side, to feel the rough mountain path under foot again. Nobody spoke to me but it did not matter. There was a voice in everything. I soaked and soaked in the great wooden tank of steaming sulphur water. The comrades all crowded together in the other tank and left me to wash alone. Whether this was out of consideration, or for the simple reason they did not want to be contaminated, I was never quite sure. It was wretched having to return to my cell and to live even a day again in that filth and darkness, but I knew now it could not be long.

On the morning of December 5th I was taken out of the dungeon for the last time. Lt. Chang said that the day of my arrival at the Batang fort was October 22nd, thus my first period of solitary confinement had lasted forty-five days. Although the conditions were really very deplorable, yet through it all the Lord's great goodness was clearly visible. Amongst the personnel of the P.L.A. there had been those who were considerate within the limits of their duty, and at no time had anyone struck me or wantonly illtreated me. The Commander spoke to me more humanly as we prepared to leave. He took a signed guarantee from me to the effect that they had not damaged or pilfered my baggage and told me I was to be escorted to Hsing Ching in Szechwan, by Staff Officer Chien and Staff Officer Wang, to whom he introduced me. My horses were brought in. I hardly recognised the grey, like myself he had grown thin under the new living conditions. I was annoyed to see that both animals had sores on their backs. They had obviously been worked hard these few weeks. What they would look like by the time we arrived at Kangting did not bear thinking about. It would be an agonising trip for them, because whatever their condition I would have to ride them. At last all was set. A herd of donkeys had been hired by the P.L.A. to transport everything to the village of Jabo Ting where the yak trails began. The command to depart was given, the darkness of the old Tibetan fort slipped behind and my mind filled again with visions of the open grasslands and far horizons.

CHAPTER XIII

UNDER ESCORT THROUGH SIKANG

"Is the wilderness before thee?
Desert lands where drought abides?
Heavenly springs shall there restore thee,
Fresh from God's exhaustless tides."

J. N. Darby.

AT Batang all my diaries were discovered and confiscated but, as certain important dates remain clear in the mind, it has been possible by recalling the different camping places to reconstruct the dates with almost complete accuracy. The journey between Batang and Kangting under armed guard will therefore be narrated in diary form.

1950, *December* 5th. As we moved towards the city gate of old Batang, I asked Chien and Wang to allow me to bid farewell to my Christian friends. How God exceeds our expectation of Him. Wang said he would take me over. We called at Pastor Li's house. He was out. Went across to Hsiao's place. It was a miracle. Just at that moment on that day, the majority of the true believers in the town were gathered there for a meeting. Chien and Wang went in with me. There were about eight present. Before anything could be said to stop us, we were having prayer together. Three of us took part. It was my last prayer in Tibetan. As I left, Hsiao gave me his Chinese hymn-book to take with me. I noticed that their baby, John, was plump and bonny. Old Pastor Li whispered to me as I passed out of the door, "My girl has a lovely baby boy! I have called him 'Yung Ch'uan', 'Eternal Spring'."* God had greatly triumphed. There was yet a testimony to His Name in old Batang. In three hours we made Jumbating. Our tent was pitched on an open space in the centre of the village, now important as the Kangting-Batang yak terminus. Large numbers of yak-hided rice bags lay stacked against the houses for transport to Batang and the river. We took our meals in a Tibetan house. A

* i.e. "fountain"—or "well of water", as in John 4.

Shensi Chinese with us made "mien" (flour strips like macaroni). I felt simply ravenous. The Chinese officers were astonished at my appetite, but it was my first square meal for weeks. The escort of about ten armed soldiers stood guard at the tent flap in watches during the night. Just to be out of the cell filled me with joy all day, although apprehension of the future was difficult to quell at night. I slept with the officers. When I knelt in prayer in the tent, Chien explained to Wang what I was doing, in a very audible undertone.

December, 6th & 7th. Still at Jumbating. No yak arrived yet to take us on. A lot of wind, and the dust blowing everywhere most unpleasantly. One of the escorting N.C.O's was displeased when he found out that I disapproved of the P.L.A's advance into Tibet. Up till then he had been very helpful. Learning all the colloquial Chinese possible. In the evenings sat late with the officers in a Tibetan's house. Each sang a song. I did a folk dance with the Tibetan family, dressed in my Tibetan gown. A poor Chinese, who said he was doing "public work" there, sang a lot of Shensi songs which much delighted Chien, as that was his home Province. All this was a great break after the solitary confinement.

December 8th. Broke camp about 8 a.m. and reached a spot just this side of the first pass by about one. Stopped for the day as the cattle and mules needed grazing time. Weather fine but much colder as altitude already nearly fourteen thousand feet. A yak train, on the road up, was in pretty bad shape, broken saddles and loads strewn on the trail. Several yak must have run amok. Given a certain amount of freedom. Allowed to draw water from a stream, which I appreciated very much.

December 9th. Grey horse very vicious but Wang handled him just like a tough Tibetan. I asked him the secret. He said he was from North China, where they also used horses a great deal. Crossed the pass at midday. About 16,000 feet. Very cold atmosphere and some snow. Noticed a peculiar red rock formation looking like a group of lamas to the right of the pass. Camped in a dell about a thousand feet down but still above the tree line. Permitted to gather fuel which consisted mostly of roots of scrub and dry yak's dung.

December 10th. Descended into wooded valley and advanced

along it, camping in the early afternoon in an open stretch of pasture land. A fair sized river already well frozen along trail. Dangerous riding across it as ice tended to break up into big floes under the horse's weight.

December 11th. Cold very intense. Continued riding along the same valley. Legs numbed like blocks of ice. Forced to walk to prevent frostbite. Chien and I stopped, being well ahead. He lit a match and ignited a very dry bush. It flared up and gave us about three minutes' warmth. Unlike its predecessor it was only too easily consumed. Clambered to within about two miles of the summit of the second pass, when a party of troops hove in sight. They proved to be an escort sent out from Litang to relieve the escort sent with me from Batang. Chien and Wang continued but the Batang troops returned. The new escort had brought mules with them carrying fodder, owing to lack of pasture at this time of year. The last part of the pass was very exacting. I struck at the grey but he was too weak to carry me. I had to walk. It was about all I could do to make the top. The past weeks had affected me more than I realised. At between fifteen and sixteen thousand feet and with the low temperature any weakness soon becomes apparent. Chien and Wang both had horses but the escort had to march day after day. Some of them said the first month nearly killed them but after that they became more hardened to it. Physically, altitude rarely affected me, but I often used to feel bad tempered in the heights, when called upon to make an effort. Camped very high. Colder than ever. Very difficult to get any water. Some small streams to be found but these frozen almost to the ground—only a muddy trickle after ice broken up. Iron tent pegs bent when driven into the earth. Continued reading in 2 Samuel. Lived David's rejection in my own thought in a new way. "If I shall find favour in the eyes of the Lord He will bring me again. . . ." I found great comfort in the loving kindness of God to David. At times the conflicts of mind concerning the future almost over-whelming. The more I thought the more I realised how in so many things I might be compromised politically. Yet grace was given to continue with a cheerful spirit. Chien sometimes unconsciously encouraged me by saying: "This man is very able to 'eat bitterness'."

December 12th. Moved down into broad wilderness valley. Encountered a huge caravan of twelve hundred yak moving forward in droves of fifty carrying rice for front line troops. Nomads in control. Nomad women scraping up some kind of salt deposit in the gulleys. Reached the open grasslands about eleven and, finding a nomad encampment by a broad stream, Chien decided to pitch camp. The afternoon was marked by a gale which swept the great open flats like a hurricane. The tent was all but blown away. We held it down with big boulders out of the river.

December 13th. Continued into the most tremendous grassland country I have ever seen. A vast plain stretching as far as the eye could see with just low hills on the horizon. All over it roamed big herds of antelope. Chien and Wang were captivated at the sight. We camped about two and then they took me hunting. Our strategy was to enclose a herd in a triangle and then, as they tried to jump out, shoot. I was not allowed a gun, needless to say. It was a miracle Wang did not shoot me in his reckless attempts. He fired in all fifteen times but failed to bring one down. I was amazed Chien trusted me as he did, although I suppose the possibility of escaping in such open desolate country was practically nil. I greatly enjoyed the break. God in His dealings with us will not permit us to be sad all the day.

December 14th. Travelled still on across the plain. Came to a place where warm sulphur water ran from the earth in good quantity. The troops called a long halt for washing. Came to the end of the plain and camped in the early afternoon at the entrance of a new valley. A valuable talk with Chien under the stars. He seemed greatly to respect my faith in Christ. He was one of the few amongst all the Communists I met who seemed to possess a richer and warmer personality. He had studied history and being a man in his forties, had a maturity born of experience. He had been in close contact with the famous General Liu Be Cheng, responsible for the Tibetan campaign. It was interesting to realise that he was the intelligence officer who had first been sent in to Pangda Dopgyay. He must have been in that first detachment I had met on the pass between Batang and Po, although I could not recall him. He told me not to worry over things and that all could be settled once I arrived at Chunking. Although my escorting officer, yet he was the kindest man I met in the P.L.A. That God had placed us together I have no doubt—perhaps for his help as well as mine.

December 15th. We travelled most of the day, still in grassland country. By evening time we came to the first houses we had seen in eight days, a village and a small lamasery around a few hot springs. The place had been hit by an earthquake some time before and the accommodation was deplorable. All along the way we had eaten wheat cakes, mien on occasions and minced pork carried from Batang. Although we were now in a village there was nothing much procurable. Dried yak dung was still the fuel, there being no trees for many miles around. Had a delicious bath in a hot sulphur spring at night.

December 16th. Reached Litang, one of the highest cities in the world at 14,500 feet. The lama city holds about 4,000 lamas and the civil city about two thousand people, I should imagine. I was taken to the local Government buildings but, to my great relief, not placed in prison. I had to sit about being stared at most of the day but, at last, Chien arranged for a room to accommodate Wang, himself and me and also his batman, one of the comrades. I did not know they had batmen in the P.L.A., but apparently they do. The cold, intensified by an arctic wind, was about the severest I have ever known in all my travels. We sat frozen to the bone in the ramshackle place provided for us, until we were given the use of a small brazier. From morning till night we clung around it, imbibing the carbon monoxide fumes, and risking scorching our boots and clothes. Eventually an arrangement was made for yak to be provided on the 20th. One day the Garrison Commander invited us to a meal. He looked at me and asked Chien: "Is there any question about him?" "No," said Chien. "Well, he might as well come along, then." It was quite a simple affair but I began to realise that Chien must be a very high ranking Intelligence Officer, as he was held in great respect. Locally they were having quite a time with the Tibetans, who, under the policy of the People's Government towards racial minorities, had to be paid fairly for all transport facilities provided to the Army. Some of them were extracting the rice from the bags and replacing it with earth. Yet at this stage the Chinese were not allowed to punish them. The Commander was finding it a real headache.

December 20th. Within the first two miles we lost a whole basket of meat which must have fallen off our yak. Crossed small pass and camped by deep stream in a valley where the only fuel was the dead stalks of giant sorrel. It took us an age to boil the tea. The horses too were exasperating—had to chase them up and down till well after dark before we could tether them properly. The frost was cruel. How the comrades stood on guard I do not know.

December 21st. Prior to leaving, the Tibetans crossed over the frozen stream and hunted musk deer all over the opposite hillside. We could see them running about but they failed to get a kill. We climbed up on to small pass through magnificent yak-herding country. To the S.E. we were confronted with mighty snow peaks, no doubt the Minya Gonka range. The simple grandeur of the landscape caused me to exclaim to Chien: "Isn't it wonderful and to think God made it all!" He smiled derisively: "China is very great," he replied. We camped with the nomads on their winter pasture grounds. At night there was an awful rumpus. Wang was swearing at a Tibetan at a nearby campfire in the most bloodcurdling Chinese. Chien sat listening to him in our tent. "That man," he said, referring to Wang, "is devoid of intelligence." I gathered Wang was acting contrary to policy. A minute or two afterwards Wang appeared half-grinning, half-angry. "I've just found a fellow with our basket of meat. The very one we lost. Believe it or not! He swears that somebody sold it to him on the road and that he didn't know it was ours!" Whether Chien reprimanded Wang or not I do not know but, later on, Wang brought the Tibetan in and gave him a cigarette and tried to smooth things over. I could not help smiling to myself when the Tibetan seeing the turn of events—with the cigarette in between his fingers and the smoke coiling languidly to the top of the tent, said—"Oh, that's nothing, we Tibetans and Chinese are all one family!" Whether this excused his own eating of the Chinese meat, or was a sheer satirical comment on present Sino-Tibetan relations, it was hard to tell. Wang as a Chinese, probably little realised that the Tibetan, who appeared so readily to forgive him on the ground of a cigarette, would no doubt take his life with not so much as a thought, if the occasion demanded it!

December 22nd. Over another small pass into a valley, where the

stream was not frozen although full of ice. It seemed a little less
cold and the sky clouded over. We camped in a clearing amongst
the trees. Chien retired early but I sat with Wang by the fire. We
had a long discussion on spiritual things. He was a very frank
fellow and said what he thought. He obviously really believed the
materialism he had been taught.

December 23rd. A short stage to-day. Passed through a beautiful
pine forest. Came out into Hsi Golog village, like so many
Tibetan villages stretching all down a valley with houses every
few hundred yards. The horses were in a deplorable condition,
the sores were dreadful on their backs. Even Chien was alarmed
and allowed me to mix up some sulphur ointment and apply
dressings. The grey was very fractious and the whole process
dangerous. There were a good number of Tibetans in the main
part of the village and I thought how grand it would be to be
preaching the Gospel to them rather than be a prisoner, but His
ways are not ours, His pleasure is inscrutable. "It pleased the
Lord to bruise Him." "It is the way the Master went, should not
the servant tread it still?" I must learn that there is no resurrection
without crucifixion and no way to the Throne of His glory but
through His Cross of shame.

December 24th. A long tiring day. We crossed the famous Ra Ma La,
a three-headed pass. We brewed tea at the top midday. As we
descended the wind was very strong. Down and down we stumbled
until, very exhausted, we arrived at a small group of houses about
4.30. A Tibetan landlord had swept out an upstairs room. Rarely
have I seen cleaner accommodation in Central Asian country.
Chien, Wang and myself installed ourselves and we were given
a charcoal brazier, which was quite a luxury. After a meal, and
when it was already dark, it was necessary for me to go downstairs to give more hay to the horses. Chien permitted my going
and I clambered down the notched tree trunk to the lower floor,
which was given over in the usual manner to stabling. Below,
it was absolutely pitch black. My boots squelched in the manure
and straw on the floor and the fetid smell of the animals was
nauseating. I felt my way amongst the mules and horses, expecting
to be kicked any moment. What a place, I thought. Then as I
continued to grope my way in the darkness towards the grey it

suddenly flashed into my mind. "What's to-day?" I thought for a moment. In travelling, the days had become a little muddled in my mind. Then it came to me. "It's Christmas Eve." I stood suddenly still in that oriental manger. To think that my Saviour was born in a place like this. To think that He came all the way from heaven to some wretched eastern stable, and what is more, to think that He came for me. How men beautify the cross and the crib, as if to hide the fact that at birth we resigned Him to the stench of beasts and at death exposed Him to the shame of rogues. God forgive us.

> "Love to the uttermost, love to the uttermost
> Love past all measuring His love must be;
> From Heaven's highest glory to earth's deepest shame,
> This is the love of my Saviour to me."

I returned to the warm clean room, which I enjoyed even as a prisoner, bowed to thankfulness and worship.

December 25th. Continued down valley, a kind of gorge and a region of the earth's surface never shined upon by the sun. It was icy cold and very still. Before noon we reached the shores of the river Yalung, a big tributary of the Yangtse. It was about two to three hundred yards wide. Enormous stacks of yak-hided rice bags lined the beach. We crossed by a small wooden ferry. Horses were restless and shifting about dangerously. I was afraid they might capsize us but God preserved our lives. Ya Chiang village, our destination for the day, lay on the farther bank. Chien obtained a room for us in the local doctor's house. He was a real medical man, at one time in charge of the Sikang Provincial Hospital, until Liu Wen Hui, the Governor, took a dislike to him and banished him to Ya Chiang. It was very small and could sleep only four of us on the floor, when all the furniture was pushed back. Different folk came in, including the new Batang magistrate on his way into Batang. Conversations overheard were quite interesting. One man told Chien that twenty-seven thousand loads had already been sent in to the Batang front of the P.L.A. offensive against Tibet. From what I had seen I could quite believe it. "There is a preacher here," Chien told me, "probably a friend of yours." I tried hard to think who it might be. I wondered too, what they would be doing at home in England to-day, my first Christmas in captivity.

December 26th. Assembled in the road outside by about ten. Chien said: "Wait there," and disappeared. About five minutes later he appeared and with him to my absolute joy and amazement were dear John Ting and two other men. There followed five minutes of indescribable happiness and fellowship. Chien acted like a gentleman, letting us talk freely. I told John of the way of the Lord with me in all that had befallen me. As for himself, he was there in Yachiang living with a Christian family and preaching the Gospel. He introduced me to the two with him. They were local Christians witnessing there for the Lord Jesus Christ. What an oasis in the desert. The marvellous loving kindness of God our Father in all His dealings with us is too wonderful for words. Our parting emphasis was on prayer for the work of God in the interior.

A very dangerous pathway up another gorge. At times one slip would have plunged both horse and rider into the roaring torrent below. At about four in the afternoon the grey was so weak that it could hardly stand. Chien and I conferred as to whether to abandon it on the road side or stop for the night. Our escort and mules were pressing on and the ironical situation now arose, whereby Chien and I were left alone in the open country. Wang had to be sent on to tell them to return. At that moment a Tibetan came along and said he would buy the grey on the spot. How clever they are. Although it was in such a bad condition, he must have judged the horse to be a superior animal, which good feeding would soon restore to health. Then he could sell it at a fabulous profit. After some talking, the Tibetan told us that it was not disease but just fatigue that was troubling our animal. I realized, that as I had not been permitted to handle the horses myself at Yachiang, they had probably not been fed, although I had given money for hay. The Tibetan took us to his house and we spent the night there with his family. They were obviously fairly wealthy and gave us a good time. They fed the grey with maize, to which it most ungratefully replied by all but kicking the son of the household in the chest.

December 27th. Rose at 1 a.m. Chien by arrangement with the muleteers was determined to make Dung Golog. It was going to be a forced march. By 3 a.m. the whole caravan was ready and we moved off. The moon rose pale and clear, shedding an unearthly light on the trail. About 4.30 a.m. we lit a bonfire and warmed ourselves, then moved on again up a long valley. I jogged along in the saddle, kept awake by the chill air of the early morning. Gradually over the high ridges before us to the east the darkness began to pale to blue, and I moved forward, my eyes fixed on the ever brightening sky. The slow and certain growth of light was fascinating. First a glimmer turning to a brightness, then brightness increasing to a radiancy, until with one piercing shaft of splendour, the morning sun burst over the ridges to flood the cold and misty valley with its healing rays. As I rode on into the dawning, I remembered the words: "The path of the just is as the shining light that shineth more and more unto the perfect day." Later, as I journeyed on through all the night of imprisonment, this experience was to be turned to a triumphant symbol in His hand. It was 7 p.m. before we were over the pass and in Dung Golog. The escort were just about in need of escorting. It was the longest journey in one day I ever made in Sikang. We were accommodated in very cramped quarters in an exceptionally dark room of a Tibetan house.

December 28th. Reached Ra Nga Ka about ten. The road to Gantze, restored for the offensive, passed through here and lorries were still transporting supplies. It was quite astonishing to see these trucks in the grasslands still several days' riding out of Kangting. Chien made enquiries and it was decided that we would travel in by lorry to Kangting. All the loads would be brought on later by mule. This would mean New Year in town, a great compensation to my escorting officers for all hardships of the road. I dressed the horses' wounds for their journey to Kangting. Chien even gave orders that the grey was to travel load-free. In the evening a lorry drove into the village and who should alight but Pangda Dopgyay. Chien immediately went to see him and in a few minutes I was invited over to their night lodging place. Dopgyay was just the same to me and as friendly as ever. I found out afterwards he was on his way as a big representative to negotiate the peaceful liberation of Tibet. No wonder Tsering

F

Dorje was sent to Chamdo and returned so soon. He was there with him now and offered me tea.

December 29th. Boarded an open lorry going to Kangting for repair. We could only proceed slowly. We crossed the derelict airstrip at Yun Kuan Tsai, then up past a village often visited by the Kangting missionaries called Na Wa Shi, until we finally began the climb of the Jedo pass. We were within a reasonable distance of the top. I happened to be standing, so saw what happened. All the others were sitting. Without warning, either the engine defaulted, the gear jumped out or the brake gave way, because we began to roll backwards down the incline. It was quite frightening. In a moment we had left the road, bounced over a patch of rough ground and, gathering momentum, plunged down the hillside. At this juncture I leapt for my life, landing on my feet on the edge of the immediate drop. The lorry, with a sickening lurch, went over the top down the slope and providentially came to rest on a narrow shelf of land about eight feet below. It had been kept upright and no one on the lorry had been injured. By a devious route of rough riding it was possible in the end to get the vehicle back on the road. After a terrible struggle, climbing at a snail's pace, the top was at last reached. The descent was perhaps even more hair raising, as the hairpin bends were so numerous. Some of the bends had not been straightened out sufficiently, thus needing two or three reversings to get round them. At one turn the driver thought he could get round and took the risk. One of the troops was standing at the time. Suddenly he made a flying leap from the truck. We came to a jolt of a stop and we all got out. The truck was hanging on the edge of a precipice, a single boulder having jammed the front wheel and prevented us crashing to what, this time, would have been almost certainly a fatal crash for some of us. We had to descend 6,000 feet to Kangting. The road was continuously downhill. Within about ten miles of the town the driver ran out of petrol and tried coasting downhill on his brakes. This in the end was too much even for his hardened nerves and we came to a final standstill. We were stranded in the pitch darkness on the side of the mountain. The night was spent sleeping on the earthen floor of a small house nearby.

December 30th. Chien and Wang escorted me on foot into Kangting. I had arrived; safe, fit and standing in His strength. Not one good thing had failed of all that He had promised. As He had said: "The beloved of the Lord shall dwell in safety by Him." "And as thy days, so shall they strength be."

CHAPTER XIV

TO THE PEOPLE'S COURT

"Thy way, not mine, O Lord,
However dark it be!
Lead me by Thine own hand,
Choose out the path for me."

Horatio Bonar.

It was more than fourteen months since I had left the city of
Kangting. Then, thousands of Tibetans had lined the streets as
their beloved leader Pangda Dopgyay had gone with his family
into the interior. I had been one of the riders in the great cavalcade, that had clattered up out of the town over the very stones
on which I was now walking as a prisoner with my escort. In
the main street we halted amidst the crowds of people. They were
almost one hundred per cent Chinese now, with hardly a Tibetan
to be seen. Previously the population had been equally divided.
Before us was a big house with a comparatively small courtyard.
It backed on to the hillside and, above it, an old temple stood
perched precariously among the rocks. We went in through the
narrow doorway to a building full of troops. This never failed to
bring over me a sense of desolation. Within about ten minutes
the two officers, batman and myself were accommodated in a
small room, devoid of furniture and littered with all manner of
refuse. A cold wind was blowing dismally through the tattered
paper windows. There was nevertheless one luxury not to be
despised, the electric light. After a general spring clean, we settled
in. For me it was a new prison. I was not permitted to go out of
the premises, yet with good light all other discomforts were as
nothing and I settled down to read my Bible, study Chinese and
write an account of the trip. Chien and Wang were out and about
much of the time but continued to be very considerate on the
whole. I thought therefore that I would venture to ask for per-

mission to see my friends in Kangting. From one or two odd remarks of the troops, constantly coming in and out of our room, I had found out that some foreigners were still in residence. Chien waited some time before replying to my request, and then he said with great certainty: "You don't want to meet your friends!" This refusal by crude "auto suggestion" I considered very unsatisfactory. I was naturally disappointed. I had not yet realised that I must first learn to find all my consolation in Christ Himself. God was aware of all that lay ahead and was graciously schooling me to the discipline of loneliness.

Before New Year's Day, Chien and Wang took me out for a short break. We had a meal in a café, of some delicious mien, and then we went to the Hot Springs at Er Dao Chiao, about three-quarters of an hour's walk outside the north gate. The journey through Sikang had really been quite arduous and I think they felt they were justified in spending a little of the "people's" money on themselves and their imperialist prisoner. The only extravagance in their lives, which were otherwise very frugal, was an unlimited allowance of cigarettes. The hot springs' apartments and hotel had been thoroughly revolutionised and was now in the service of the people. It was thronged with army men and government workers, these latter, both men and women, being dressed in blue Sun Yat Sen suits. It was interesting to see the walls flaming with heart-stirring challenges of the revolution. I was quite taken aback by some of them but Wang explained them to me. Whether they were really understood by the masses was very doubtful at that time but the pasting up of such slogans was an easy demonstration of loyalty and patriotism and thus recklessly indulged in by the people. Here is the kind of thing. "Overthrow feudalism, bureaucratic capitalism and imperialism! Resist America and aid Korea! Down with the Imperialists! Save the country and protect our homes! Oppose the principle of selfish freedom! Maintain the discipline of daily living! Increase production and economise! Long live our great leader Mao Tse Tung! Long live Stalin, leader and teacher of the peoples! Long live world peace!" Such startling injunctions, all so new to me, seemed already to have become the accepted substitutes for the old Confucianist and Buddhist sayings with which the Chinese so delighted to adorn their walls and lintels. For the next eight or nine days I was confined to our one room. On one occasion only did I go outside, and that was to receive my loads into the courtyard. At that moment it happened that a Kangting girl, who had been servant to one of the missionaries, recognised me on the road. I have little doubt that it was through this means that news of my safe arrival in Kangting filtered through to the outside world.

New Year's Day I was permitted to eat with the troops, who had a spread of numerous dishes of pork and vegetables to celebrate the occasion. Most of them were young boys and enjoyed themselves like children at a party. There was also wine which, though limited, still proved too much for one young fellow, to whom I afterwards had to give some aspirins to relieve his splitting headache. These young comrades were mostly very open hearted towards me and were quite ready to converse. During these days I had talks with Wang. He told me how he had joined the revolution. He related how, under the old regime, he had been put in prison because his father would not pay the extortionate tax asked by the KMT. Then after seven days in gaol, during which time the family kept him alive, his father managed to raise money and he was released. He said that to become a staff officer in the People's Army was not easy. He loved his country dearly and felt the only way to clear out the rottenness and corruption of the old system was to destroy it by armed revolution. He was devoted to the cause and obviously willing to sacrifice everything for it. When I asked him: "Will you ever go home again, get married and settle down?" he said: "That means nothing to me. There is nothing for me to do back home." "Why are you so dead against the missionaries?" I went on. "We are not really," he said, "but so many of them are secret agents employed by their governments." "But," I said, "it is not true. For instance, in this town there are several missionaries whom I know personally. Not one of them is a secret agent." "That is by no means certain," he replied. "What will happen to them? Will they be taken down to Chungking?" "I expect so," he said, "but not necessarily." On the steps leading to the latrines, I could see out over the town to the China Inland Mission House. On the upstairs veranda of Mr. and Mrs. Kraft's home, I could glimpse some washing on the line and I thought of them and their little baby daughter. I wondered if anybody would come out to take it in, but although I often looked, nobody came. Chien came in one day. "I saw some of your friends in town," he said. "I told them you were here and would have come to see them but, owing to our waiting for transport to take us down country, you couldn't manage it!" Then turning to Wang he said: "You know, there was a foreign baby with the folk I met to-day. It really was a very beautiful child!" It seemed unnecessarily cruel of him not to let me go, but I suppose it was more than he dared.

One day two little Chinese children came in. They must have lived on the premises prior to its being requisitioned. They were full of mischief. They had been to the Gospel Hall but, instead of taking in the great stories of the Bible in simplicity and trust, their tongues chattered on in mockery and blasphemy. This was heartbreaking to hear and was no doubt due to the influence of the troops, with whom they were constantly in contact. When Chien saw that, even from children, I would not tolerate such speaking of the Lord Jesus Christ, he turned to them and said: "Get outside, you two little devils!" It makes one tremble for the children of the "People's Democratic Republics". I saw one of the "comics" that the younger generation are now reading. It was just a mass of political picture strips. One was entitled "Lenin is our Sun." This is the spirit of anti-Christ that John tells us is already in the world. They ascribe to a man that which pertains to Christ alone, for "Unto you that fear My Name shall the Sun of Righteousness arise with healing in His wings."

About the seventh of January an open lorry was placed at our disposal. We piled all the baggage on board and drove off at around ten o'clock. We dropped some two thousand feet, winding our way downwards through two immense walls of rock sloping up steeply to snowcapped heights, more than ten thousand feet above us. After an hour or two's driving we came to the broad deep placid water of the Tung Ho, and by about half-past two we had crossed the ferry and had reached Luting Chiao. It was a hive of activity. A big bridge was being constructed across the river. Soldiers, like ants, swarmed round the pile drivers, crowds thronged the streets, and the small traders with stalls of fruit, cigarettes, peanuts, rock salt, bamboo hats, rice sugar balls and a thousand and one other things were doing a brisk trade. Our lorry nosed its way through and Chien quickly gained accommodation in a shop permanently rented to the P.L.A. We slept in the attic, a poky little place looking out over the street, which I found enthralling after the solitudes of the grasslands. The next morning a number of wounded comrades were assembled and lifted into our truck and another, which was to accompany us. It was interesting to hear them talk of the fighting on the Chamdo front and of the surrender or capture of other Tibetan Generals. It took us about five hours to climb the six thousand feet from Luting Chiao to the top of Er Lang Shan pass. We came into heavy snow at the summit but until then the view had been breathtaking, as we looked straight across to the 24,900 feet peak of Minya Gonka only a few miles away. Descending the east side, the road was dangerous by reason of the snow, but new huts built by the P.L.A. right across the mountain ensured sufficient personnel on the route to clear it as it fell, so although we moved slowly to avoid skidding into the abyss, we were undelayed. We proceeded in falling snow right to Tien Chuan, a further sixty or seventy miles, where we stayed the night. It was half past nine and quite dark when we got in, but the streets were deserted and all the shutters of the shops closed fast. Chien dismounted and hammered violently on the door of one shop. After some while the good man of the house bade us welcome, as any true son of the people should do to the People's Army in such circumstances, and provided us with the floor of his shop for our bedroom. We slept with our heads dodging the chair legs and counter. Next morning we proceeded into Yaan, the new Provincial capital.

Here I was safely housed in an Army barracks. The troops were very free with me and we had good talks exchanging our outlooks on life. It was a time of opportunity and testimony in various ways to Christ as my Saviour. One young fellow was most astonished to find that death is the result of sin and talked alone with me for a long while. Chien acted quite thoughtfully towards me and managed to get me a bath in a nearby Army establishment.

The great plateau was now behind us and the Szechwan plains began. It was refreshing to see green vegetables again and the freshness of an unfrozen and rainsoaked countryside. After Yaan we moved on to Chunglai. We arrived in the afternoon and found a room in a Co-operative Society. There was a staff of about a dozen fellows and I suppose as many girls. What actual work they did I do not know, but they seemed to do nothing while we were there. They gave us a number of polished boards on some trestles for a bed, and yarned with Chien and Wang around a charcoal brazier. The wounded were taken into the Chunglai Military Hospital. It must have been a fearful trip for them, lying in the lorries on stretchers for several days. In the morning we took breakfast in a teashop. The currency was already stable. This had been achieved largely by flooding the market with the huge stocks of rice taken over from the Kuomintang, thus compelling hoarders to sell. This caused the general level of prices to fall, for all commodities are linked to rice in China. The other factor was that the Government insisted that all taxes be paid in the new People's currency. This immediately gave the people confidence in it and basically the battle against inflation was won, at least for the moment. Whilst we were drinking our tea, a beggar came up and began to pester me. Chien immediately brushed him aside. "There is work for everybody," he said, "there is absolutely no need for anyone to beg." I could well believe this, considering the number of people I had seen all along the road, sitting hammer in hand, breaking up stones for the maintenance of the road's gravel surface. This was hardly a beggar's idea of a livelihood, needless to say, yet beggars were certainly much reduced in number since the take-over. From Chunglai we made our last stage with our present vehicle, reaching Hsin Ching well before noon. We drove up to an old Buddhist hermitage on the outskirts of the town. As we passed a big walled house and compound, Chien said to Wang: "Do you remember when we came through here the first time, the old rascal living there wouldn't put us up for the night?" The lorry drew to a stop and several comrades came running forward. We unloaded everything and were plied with a barrage of questions. We had come from Tibet so were rather special arrivals. I found out that the monastery we were now entering was the Intelligence H.Q. of the P.L.A. forces engaged in the "Liberation" of Tibet. One of the comrades told me that another Englishman with two Indians and a Tibetan woman had passed through their unit but a few days previously. Ford must be ahead of me, I thought. In the monastery all was quiet. Apart from the occasional appearance of the yellow uniformed troops, it might still have been the haunt of hermits and monks. Much of the tranquillity of the old religious atmosphere remained, and intrusions by the soldiers into the precincts of the place were few. The grounds were very spacious. There were ornate halls of idols, beautiful trees and specimens of sculpture in the gardens and courtyards. I was taken to a distant room of new timber. Chien said: "This will be a good opportunity for you to rest." The batman was overjoyed at being in a place where he could escape the eye of his officers for most of the day. He immediately applied for his own liberation, namely, to be transferred to another unit. I was left alone in the new quarters and guards placed outside. It was certainly pleasant to put out my camp bed and relax. "What is going to happen now?" I thought. There was a big airfield at Hsin Ching. Would I be flown to Peking or was the destination still Chungking? After some while Chien came in. As soon as he saw Wang he said: "Do you know they have already executed forty people here, including that old fellow who wouldn't take us in to his place. Quite a few, isn't it!" "Not so many!" Wang replied with some bitterness. He turned to me and said: "These people who have been executed are landlords and rogues, who have exploited and illtreated the peasants." The news was not very reassuring to me.

I was only one night at Hsin Ching as Chien urged me to take the opportunity of a lorry going to Chungking, although he could not yet leave. It was amusing the way he put it, as though I was on holiday and had power to choose. I replied in the same casual way, that I might as well go, so as to get my affairs settled more quickly. Getting things together, I went outside. My new escort was waiting. He was a young officer, presumably of the same unit. By the afternoon, we were in Chengtu. I was taken into a transit camp and placed in a room which had been used as a coal shed. With straw on the ground we made it more or less habitable and I shared it with several of the comrades. I noticed that new girl comrades were being recruited there. They were still in their early teens and I felt they should have been at school or at home helping their mothers, rather than chasing around China in a revolution. What particularly impressed me, though, was the high standard of moral behaviour between the sexes. Young fellows and girls thrown together so closely in the work and fighting of the revolution, from all I saw of them, put to shame the conduct I witnessed in the forces during the war in England. When under indoctrination, I learned something of the reason for this. It is because, in the Red Army, immorality becomes of political significance.

According to Marxism the standard of morality arises from our political standpoint, which in turn is determined by our economic condition. Thus if I have no money to buy bread I will take the political stand of siding with the oppressed masses. This means that to steal from the landlord becomes right; I am not guilty of theft. I am only taking back what he has exploited from my class. From the landlord's viewpoint I am guilty of theft and ought to be punished by the law which his class, as rulers, have brought into being. Adultery and prostitution are said to be the vices of the moneyed classes, the sin of the reactionary ruling classes, such as the capitalists and landlords. It is only they who have the time and money to indulge in such things. The peasantry and workers are too busy slaving for their meagre livelihood under the oppression of such persons. Thus if a comrade in the Red Army is found guilty of immorality, his class standing is immediately brought into question. He is exhibiting traits of the reactionaries in his conduct. He has succumbed to feudal and capitalist influences and needs reform. He will have to be publicly exposed and make a thorough self-criticism before his comrades, who will also voice their criticism of such a "backward element in their midst". This will mean such mental torment and so influence his future, that the restraint on conduct between the sexes is tremendous. The soldier knows that the slightest flirting will be brought up at the next meeting. It will mean interviews with the Party Member, it will mean public disgrace in a way unthought of in the west. In our society, the freedom of the individual is so greatly prized, that sometimes the abuse of that freedom is allowed to pass uncensured. To interfere with the problem of loose living in the west is only too often to be told: "Mind your own . . . business!" So many facets of western life exhibit a corruption that the fire of revolution finds as straw to burn up in its onward march, and few perhaps realise, in their abuse of the very considerable freedom we enjoy, that they are becoming the faithful servants of a force that is encroaching on the rights of the individual in many nations.

Whilst at Chengtu I stood and talked with a boy and girl comrade of about 18 years of age. They conversed with me quite freely about spiritual and social things. They were very open about each other. "She is not my sweetheart," he said, "we just work together." The girl told me: "We must get the country straight first, before I think of marriage."

My eyes were being opened to the fact that the Communistic Revolution was run on principles. That it was not just hordes of rebels overrunning everything but was attracting the finest youth of China into its ranks, who were being filled with enthusiasm to devote their all that their nation might become strong and free. They had seen a form of tyranny in the old regime with its privileges for the few and its starvation, floods, disease, and sheer ruin for the millions. They demanded liberation from that form of government, from the oppression of those classes and individuals who held power. The Communist Party, well organised, armed with a clear-cut philosophy and sworn to the betterment of the workers and peasants, had gained the leadership and nearly all young China, in the flush of their high aspirations, had followed, braving hardship and privation for the emancipation and reconstruction of their nation. They had not yet understood that the idea of tyranny and liberation goes deeper than governments and material progress, or even classes. They had not yet awakened to the new and more sinister spiritual bondage that had begun to engulf them. I was their prisoner, yet I knew that through God's grace in Christ I was freer than them all. "For if the Son shall make you free you shall be free indeed." In the utimate sense there is but one who enslaves and but One who frees. There is only the bondage of Satan or the liberty of the sons of God.

The journey to Chungking from Chengtu passed off very well. We stayed two nights on the road and during the day drove straight through. It was on January 17th, just forty-four days after leaving Batang, that I was handed over to the People's Military and Political Committee of S.W. China at one of their Chungking Detention Centres.

I was taken up under guard to a big long barn of a house, situated in a part of Chungking I could not recall to mind. I was taken into a room at the far end of the building. It was quite large, being about twenty feet by fourteen. There were glass windows backing straight on to a cliff. A few panes were broken but the glass was not too dirty. There was a rough bed, a table and chair and also, in another corner, collapsible tables stacked in a big pile. A disreputable looking fellow in dishevelled uniform was immediately placed on guard. My bedding was brought in. I had arrived. Within a few minutes I was called into the office-cum-bedroom of the senior officers of the establishment. They interviewed me casually, sitting around a table. They asked one or two particulars and then said: "You know your status, don't you?" What that might mean I did not know, but I somehow mumbled "Yes." "It will be necessary for us to place a soldier at your door. You must realise this is for your protection!" they said in all seriousness. They showed me back into my new prison room. These two men I was to get to know much more intimately. The senior one, a fellow of about 34, was called Yang. He had very sharp features and gave one the impression of being very hard-bitten. The younger one, about 28 I suppose, was also a hard looking character with one eye that refused to focus in the same direction as the other. This at first I found quite a distraction when conversing with him. That evening they both came in and I was searched. As I saw them lift up my Bible and prepare to take it away I pleaded with them: "That is my Bible, surely I am permitted to have my Bible." "All these must be taken away for examination purposes," was the only answer I received. "They will be returned to you when we have finished with them." Little did I realise it would be nearly three years before I held that precious volume in my hands again.

CHAPTER XV

"DESPAIRING EVEN OF LIFE"

"Lord grant us calm, if calm can set forth Thee;
  Or tempest, if a tempest set Thee forth;
Wind from the east or west or south or north,
  Or congelation of a silent sea,
With stillness of each tremulous aspen tree.

Still let fruit fall, or hang upon the tree;
  Still let the east and west, the south and north,
Curb in their winds, or plough a thundering sea;
  Still let the earth abide to set Thee forth,
Or vanish like a smoke to set forth Thee."
                      Christina Georgina Rossetti.

LATE in the afternoon a guard brought me quite a good meal of steamed bread and fish. I sat up to the table, pushing the food disconsolately into my mouth, with my mind far away. Yang looked in: "Is the food enough? We want you to eat well you know!" he said, smiling all over his face. As evening drew on, I switched out the electric light and the guard's figure stood out against the light of the corridor. I knelt in prayer at the bedside. Almost immediately there was a roar from the doorway. It was horribly distorted Chinese but presumably was an expression of irritation or even, perhaps, a question as to what I was doing. I ignored it and, in the end, the guard did not persist. The second day I sat cross-legged on my bed and began to read a Tibetan tract containing parts of St. John's Gospel. This had been overlooked by those responsible for searching me and I was thrilled to be able to continue Bible study, even after they had taken my Bible away. During the day, as at Batang at the beginning, I was left alone. At night Yang came in. His face looked like thunder. I guessed the reason. He had probably, by now, read the report from Batang on all my letters and diaries. Whilst journeying towards Chunking, I had gone over everything in my mind and realised that I had several indiscreet comments on the Communists in my diaries, and also, in the copy of my letter to Chamdo, there was a reference to the British Government which could be most embarrassing. Things to which I had hardly given a thought at the time now loomed before me as catastrophic. "That every idle word that men shall speak, they shall give account thereof in the day of judgment," was being proved to me in a most unimagined way. "There are plenty of points for us to get along with," he glowered. "What do you think of that Chamdo letter?" "It would have been better if I had not worded it like that," I said quietly. "You say that now!" he mocked. "That's only one item, there are many many more, just you think! You will have to make a clear statement of everything before we can let you go." "Should everything be satisfactorily settled, would it be possible to return and preach the Gospel to the Tibetans," I asked on another occasion, when things were a little calmer. "Even that would not necessarily be impossible," he said and my hope rose again.

After a day or two Yang issued me a piece of soap. I had washed no clothes since I had been captured at Gartok. On one of the collapsible tables, I scrubbed furiously and then hung each grey coloured article up to dry in a spare corner of ground, outside the back of the building. The guard brought me several buckets of water, which he did quite good naturedly. He then asked me, "Could you let me have a vest or shirt?" I thought for a moment. If I gave him anything and the authorities found out, it might be interpreted as a bribe of some kind. "Don't your army issue you with clothing?" I questioned him. I remembered how well equipped the troops were, on the whole, in Sikang. "No," he grumbled, "they don't issue us anything like that." "Well, wait a couple of weeks and maybe my question will be settled by then and it will be all right." "Two weeks!" he exclaimed. "Some Italians were here six months." The words sank down into my heart like a stone. Six months! Slowly I learned to steel my emotions to almost any situation and in face of almost any announcement. Hope in the human word resulted too often in fresh anguish of soul. When all the years had gone by it was found that only His promise had stood the test of time.

After some days a small neatly dressed officer, of educated appearance, came into my room. He extended a hand and greeted me in faultless English with "How do you do?" We sat down and he began to talk to me in my native tongue. "I have come to tell you that you must put all worries on one side. Everything will be all right. Tell me, have you a father and mother alive . . . ?" We talked generally of my background and conversed freely on nothing in particular. He left with the same extreme politeness. Several days later I had another visitor. He came in so silently that I did not notice him until he was right up to me. I looked at him, somewhat startled. He was a man of nearly 50, very short and terribly emaciated. His high cheekbones stuck out between his hollow cheeks and eyes. His skin was exceptionally sallow. He held a cigarette in fingers stained to dark amber with tobacco fumes. He sat down at the table and began to talk very slowly, puffing at his cigarette as chain smokers do. He asked numerous questions concerning my education and background. "Have you been to a theological seminary?" he asked. "No," was all I could answer. "What then is your sphere of work?" "All Central Asia and Tibet in particular," I replied truthfully. He began to talk about "liberation". I took the opportunity to stress that often man's real bondage is in connection with some habit. Another day Yang ran over briefly with me the ground covered by my statement at Batang.

These preliminary and nebulous questionings, I realised afterwards, are the "dialectical" approach to interrogation. It is necessary to find out the whole course of development of a person's life from earliest days. The dominant influences and conflicts. His social position and class background, the nature of his environment and social contacts and relationships at various stages of his growth. The type of education, his early political loyalties and the big crises of his life. Only after this ground is fairly clear, can the attitude of the Government be determined in regard to interrogation and "brain-washing". The first indication I had of the so-called "thought reform" was when Yang said: "Of course we do not really blame you for anything you have done against the people. Your government and Society must bear most of the guilt, although naturally you must bear some too. Before, you did not know the truth about Communism but now you begin to know, you must gradually change your social outlook. The whole Capitalist structure is based on exploitation. I am sure you cannot agree with such an evil. Then, of course, your nation's imperialist aggression, involving the occupation and plunder of other people's land and resources, you must freely admit is quite insupportable."

Towards the end of the second week a young fellow came in and, sitting down, said to me: "You have lied already in what you have told us. "Do you realise," I said, "that to say that to a Britisher is the grossest insult possible?" Yang joined in, "Yes, and it is to a Chinese too! We have all your data, you must understand that. Long before we caught you we had your particulars. It is no good your lying to us." God gave me patience. My mind filled with conflicts. I had decided that I had no need to tell them of many things I knew. This meant endless fencing as they questioned me. I just did not know what to do. From their standpoint, omission would be considered less than the truth, yet why should I be subjected to their inquisition? The ensuing days were an agony of mind. It was obvious that they were going to go into every facet of my activity in China and Tibet, and not mine only, but that of everybody with whom I was associated. In relation to the Tibetan question, this could be very difficult.

The long days passed one by one. At night I was only too glad to sleep through sheer exhaustion. The tenseness of the past months, solitary confinement, poor food, long travelling and now the new pressure made me feel thoroughly tired. That I could sleep, sometimes twelve hours at a stretch, was of the Lord's mercy. In the daytime I would study my Tibetan tract, or go over my Chinese and Tibetan dictionaries. At times I would just sit still. Outside on the concrete passage way, there was a sound of much coming and going. The medley of footsteps sounded strangely like the shuffle of mahjong pieces. I thought of Ford and wondered where he was. One day at the toilet I saw another foreigner standing by the banana palms. As I passed him, his eye farthest away from the guard gave me a very strong wink and his mouth curled to half a smile. I could see his spirit was unconquered. Another day the guard who wanted to have some of my clothes and who proved to be an ex-KMT fellow showed me a scrap of torn paper. It looked as if it had been torn from a larger piece, perhaps from a statement. On one side was an English word which the guard asked me to read for him. On the back were the words: "I translated a letter of Bull's to the Chamdo Governor. I should not have done this. He should have asked permission of the People's Government of China." Was this a deliberate message from Ford showing me what he had said and the line he was taking? If so, it was a step of considerable courage and thoughtfulness. It seemed impossible for it to be a coincidence.

Days passed and nothing happened. Sometimes I would stand at the door and talk to a friendly guard. I found that several Chinese civilians were also housed in the same building. They were not prisoners in the usual sense, but having a course of "learning". One old chap looked into my room and seeing me there under armed guard said: "Isn't he young? Still, our Chairman Mao is very lenient." "Yes," commented the young ex-KMT guard, "all the Italians went home in the end." At the beginning of February, I was suddenly taken out of my prison room and taken on a truck across the city to a big foreign house overlooking the Jarlin River. This proved to be another detention centre, although some of the staff remained the same.

The first room in which I was placed was a large one, with a trestle bed as the only furniture. All the windows were covered with rice paper. On examination, I found a few minute holes and often used to peer through them to the outside world. From one window looking westwards, I could sometimes glimpse through a peephole a glorious sunset. I shall never forget seeing the great red ball of fire pass slowly down behind the distant hills. It always seemed to beckon me on to God, waiting for me at the end of the road.

> "Though like the wanderer,
> The sun gone down,
> Darkness be over me,
> My rest a stone.
> Yet in my dreams I'd be
> Nearer my God to Thee!
> Nearer to Thee."

Day by day I walked to and fro from corner to corner until my studded boots had worn a cross of marks on the wooden floor. The emaciated officer came and talked again. One of his leading questions was: "What do you think is the message of Macbeth?" I suppose he wanted me to reply: "Ambition, and its disastrous results," but it never occurred to me at the time. This was the last preliminary interview.

Full interrogation on an ever-increasing scale now began. George's movements and mine were investigated step by step, all causes and motives being ruthlessly ferreted out. I was in a quandary. To refuse to speak would invite suspicion, yet to speak all, I knew, would be incriminating myself and others. They began to preach to me their policy towards counter-revolutionaries. They had apparently already judged me to be a spy. Now it was a question of confession. The almost daily line of approach began like this: "If you tell us everything, all will be well, but if you hold anything back, then you will be the enemy of the people by your own choice and will be dealt with accordingly. Our policy is clemency for the repentant, and unmitigated suppression for the impenitent. One is a road of life, one is a road of death. You are still a young man, you must think of your future." As day after day went by and I was questioned and re-questioned by different officials, I could see that something would have to be done. They dealt with the spreading of rumours, a crime of which I was found guilty. In my conversations with Pangda Dupgyay I had expressed certain "imperialistic" views on Russia and also read parts of a letter to him, which I had received from a friend, giving somewhat unreliable reports of events in China. This being deemed as counter-revolutionary activity, they went on to other points. The photographs I had taken were also a serious breaking of the law because they proved to be, according to the People's Court, of "military importance". These snapshots sent home to my parents they presumed to have been sent to the British Government. When these matters had been thrashed out, they reduced everything down to the searching question: "Why did Patterson go to India?" There were several reasons in a way, but none of these satisfied them. Whether the Pangda brothers or the Dege Sey had disclosed anything, I did not know, but there it was, they insisted that I make a clear statement on that point. I was thrown into a turmoil of mind because of the conflicting loyalties involved. How long I knelt in prayer in the solitude of my room I do not know.

What was the Lord's will for me now? He knew George's heart and mine. He knew how we had been prepared to go to all lengths to advance with the Gospel into Central Asia. Surely it was He Who had disposed the hearts of the chieftains towards us? In their dilemma, George had offered to acquaint the British Government with their position when he visited India, in the hope of obtaining favourable conditions for the Gospel in Central Asia, should Tibet's independence be established. I had felt that this was something I did not feel free to do but had agreed that George should go, if he himself believed it the right thing. Thus he had left. If this was now known by the Communists, as looked very likely, and I concealed it, it would mean almost certain execution. They would have no compunction in such matters. Yet if I disclosed that there had been such an intention, then I broke faith with George and endangered our Tibetan friends, who had helped us so much in our entering Tibet. With increased pressure everything came to a head one night. If I was going to die, then I would die for Christ, not for some loyalty to a well-intentioned but possibly mistaken course of action. George was in India and the Pangda brothers, being Tibetans, would no doubt be protected by the policy governing relations with racial minorities. Pangda Dopgyay, too, had not hesitated to serve the new regime. I remembered that even a bandit murderer in Batang had not been shot, lest Tibetan resentment against the Chinese be unnecessarily increased. Before the Lord, in a deep distress of soul, I came to the decision that in the circumstances He would have me be straight-forward with the Communists about everything and everybody. The issue would then be completely in His hands. Looking back I marvel at the wisdom and courage He gave me at that early stage. The fact that I took that step, I do believe, was a very real cause for my confinement being so short and my life being spared. In the ensuing months it was hard to see, but eventually I knew He had led me by the skilfulness of His own hands.

The night of my decision I slept poorly, tossing back and forth on the hard boards. The next day when I was interrogated I gave a straightforward account to the officials of the whole position as we knew it in Sikang and all that had transpired. They were delighted and said to me: "Now, like Mr. Ford, you will have to begin 'learning'. As soon as your question is clear we will send you away to another place for 'education' and then, after a few months there, maybe there will be an opportunity for you to go home." This kind of talking lasted precisely two days. They obviously imagined that they now had me on the run and that I knew a very great deal about many matters. They asked me openly what Government Department had sent me to China and what was my briefing. All this was just ridiculous and I maintained with great definiteness that I was a *bona fide* missionary, come to China and Tibet with the sole purpose of preaching the Gospel. I considered I had been fair to them in telling them the truth, but they now became adamant and I entered one of the most terrible periods of my life.

Day after day I endured constant interrogation. Sometimes four times a day I was hauled out before different officers and tribunals. A special senior officer interviewed me twice. Military and civil officials were called in. They had me standing, sitting, they used court methods and conversational sessions. They covered the same ground over and over again, documenting the slightest contradictions. The Lord gave me the ability to remember a considerable amount of detail, but the great thing was that my heart was now at rest. I personally had nothing to hide and was clear before the Lord through His precious blood. In a sense it was nothing to me to be judged of "man's day". To my own Lord I stood or fell. Back in my prison room I would pace the floor. I remember crying out to God: "Dear Father, if it takes twenty years to make me the man you want me to be, then keep me here if that is Thy will." He lifted me above the agony of my soul in all the pressure. He fought back for me the fear of death and overcame. I was now openly threatened with execution by shooting. "If you do not tell us your British Government connections we shall send you to another place where you will 'suffer bitterness'. If this fails then you will be shot without the slightest doubt." "I wish you could only see what was in my mind," I said once to

Yang. "When we put a bullet through it we shall see soon enough," was the retort. Their torture became more vile. "Just you think," one fellow said, "your father and mother and sister are thinking of you every day. All the time they are waiting for your news, but you won't give in. We would like you to write to them but how can we permit you, when you carry on like this?" Day after day the taunts continued. "You are interested in astronomy, aren't you? Do you want to see the stars again? There is only one way for you; otherwise your life is ruined. Why should you be so crazy as to ruin yourself like this?" One day Yang called me out: "We have a gift for you from one of your friends," he said very congenially. I wondered whoever could have sent me anything and thought it might be from one of the Christians. "What do you think it is?" he said gleefully "It has U.S.A. stamped on it." I was completely at a loss to understand such a riddle. "A pair of handcuffs!" he said, triumphantly. "Your imperialist friend America sent them over here to put on our young people, so I think it is most fitting that they should be clapped on you. I give you two days to make further confessions and then we will put you in irons and place you in the little dark room under the stairs." He let me see past the door, where, sure enough, there was a large cupboard all swept and ready. It is amazing in such circumstances how things work on the mind. As the threats of death and torture came at me daily, I would sometimes look through my peepholes, seeking comfort from the view outside. One day I looked out and what should I see but two men carrying a coffin. After about two hours I looked out again and just at that moment, passing the house, were another two men carrying a coffin. It seemed such a certain omen of death but "if we believe not, yet God abideth faithful." Then, often, I would hear the wireless playing. I remember once the whole of Beethoven's Emperor Concerto came over clearly. I lay on my bed and listened. It sounded like a beautiful waterfall on a summer's afternoon.

At the end of April, I was taken out of my big room and placed in another room, this time very small. It had a floor space about eight or nine feet square. It was, I suppose, a semi-punitive measure as a reprisal against my "stubbornness". At this time, also, my Tibetan tract was discovered and removed with my dictionaries and pencils, and my wrist watch was also taken away. Yang called me into his dormitory. There were beautiful wide windows, with commanding views of the Jarlin valley and I simply wanted to stand and look out over the river and forget the real reason that kept me standing there. "Sit down!" he said. "Now tell me, what is it that you really preach." I began to tell him how Christ died for our sins and that through faith in Him we could obtain salvation. He listened impatiently and with something of a leer on his face. I felt disinclined to go on but he spared me the thought. "We don't like listening to that stuff," he summarily interrupted and then started his routine probing and indoctrination. I was glad to return to my solitude.

Through the gauze openings up above the main windows, I could see the leaves of the trees bursting into green. Autumn, winter and now spring. The warm sunshine began to heat my little room and at long last I started to shed my pullovers and vests. Through the rice paper, here and there I could still glimpse the road. One day I saw a line of six ragged prisoners being escorted by armed guards. This was China's most terrible moment. In the Spring of 1951 the nationwide campaign for the suppression of counter-revolutionaries began. The masses were mobilised and agitated to frenzy by vast schemes of propaganda up and down the country. Huge accusation and struggle meetings were organised and everywhere the people were encouraged to expose anyone with KMT connections or sympathies. A date line was given for the voluntary registration of past links with KMT organisations, after which began a witch hunt for agents, spies, bandits, tyrants, secret society personalities and rumour-mongers, on a scale unprecedented in human history. In Chunking alone, four thousand arrests were made in one night, filling the prisons and flooding detention centres to overflowing. In the reign of terror, father exposed son and son exposed father, mothers and daughters exposed their husbands and brothers. Tens of thousands of allegations poured into the hands of the Government. The counterfeit "evangel", the "gospel" of Mao Tse Tung, offering mercy to the penitent but annihilation to all who resist, was preached in every nook and cranny of China, from the schoolboy to Cabinet Minister. Later on I met many of those caught in this fanatical purge. I talked to a fellow-prisoner and he told me personally how the executions followed. He himself attended one mass meeting, where sixty-eight people were massacred in cold blood, before a great mob who demanded that such enemies of the people be swept from the earth. In those days a man only had to be put up to the crowd with a "crime" on his head and there would go forth the cry of "Shoot him! Shoot him!" The comments of national leaders showed complete satisfaction. "The reactionary forces have received a death blow," they said, "and the masses have been instructed."

It was at such a time that the first "trial" of my case proceeded. Day after day the threat of execution continued. Yet, to God be the glory, these were the days of His greatest triumph in my heart. I would think little of all that they were requiring of me and devote the time to communion with the Lord. He brought a richness of thought to me and simple poems would flow into my mind. At the time of supreme crisis and during the following days He gave me:

Thou art my resurrection, Lord!
My soul, begotten through Thy Word,
Shall rise with glorious body found
To greet Thee at the trumpet sound.

Adoption must o'erride our fear,
We erstwhile slaves as sons appear.
Redeemed the body shall be free,
Thy saints be glorified with Thee.

Now through a darkened glass we peer
Yet can dispense with sage and seer
For we believe the end of grace
Is then to see Him face to face.

So Lord when e'er shall break Thy day
And all earth's shadows flee away,
Alive, asleep, t'will be the same
We rise triumphant in Thy Name.

During this period I was called out by Yang into a room and told to listen to a blaring commentary on the radio. I stood before him, straining at the confused sound. It was the relay of a vast mass meeting, for the public announcement of judgment on a number of counter-revolutionaries. "In China to-day there are tens of thousands going to be executed," he roared, "foreigners included. We'll arrange a meeting like that for you one day. Think over your future well. Fancy dying, cursed by all the peoples of the world!" Another time it was, "Patterson has been arrested in India because the Indian people have now risen up to take over their country. He has confessed his crimes and yet you here imagine you can get away with it. I tell you that if your body ever leaves Chinese soil you'll be a lucky man!" I was taken before an English-speaking officer of about sixty years of age. He spoke the most colloquial English I have ever heard any Chinese speak. He attacked missionaries. "I've known foreign missionaries for sixty years," he said. "The majority are sheer 'washouts'." I stood aghast at his grasp of the language. "They live like kings and queens and all they do is thrust their doctrine down the throats of the ignorant masses. Look at you! You make friends with the upper classes, the very persons whom Christ condemned." I kept silence before his bitter attack. "The whole thing is an instrument of imperialism. From British Imperialism all the other capitalist nations learnt their evil ways. I suppose there are possibly some decent English people but it's hard to say; they nearly all seem tainted with the imperialist outlook. From the opium war to slave traffic, every kind of aggression, military, political, economic and cultural, they have tried them all and you are just one of their lackeys." As he finished Yang took up the cudgels. "Our friend here has spoken very mildly to you to-day, but let me tell you, that there is only one issue. You either yield, relinquish your imperialist standpoint and confess all, or we send you to the firing squad." It was all agonising. Under the barrage of accusation I began at times to feel guilty as an imperialist. I felt as if I was not suffering for Christ at all. Then it would have been easier to bear, yet in the quietness of solitary confinement God continued His loving support and drew forth these lines from my heart:

> "My life is in Thy hands, O Lord,
>   Not theirs. This waiting prisoner, Thine,
> Not any man's to put to sword
>   But kept 'til Thou Thyself refine.

This crucible and flaming heat
Consuming all but gold of God,
Must purge corruption and defeat,
Bring forth the lustre of the good.

So discipline of sons precedes
The power and joy of heirs mature.
Faint not my soul, the hurt recedes.
Thy Father and His love endure!"

My interrogations took on a new turn. Night after night I was wakened up and interrogated into the early hours of the morning. This was most fatiguing. About 7 a.m. one of the officials would come in, peer at my face and then say in most knowing tones: "Ah! I see you have not been sleeping well! You have something on your mind." These night sessions were fearful. They were conducted by Yang with two other officials generally present, and were very stormy. He would sit me down, stand me up, shout at me and carry on alarmingly. In the day they would talk to me. "You are waiting then for death. So young too. We are doing our best to save you, but if you choose death there is nothing we can do." For about three months I walked daily in the valley of the shadow. Every morning I used to wake up and the first thought would be, I am due to be shot. It used to come over me like a dream or a flashback from some adventure story. It seemed impossible that I was one of the characters to be sentenced to death. At this time Satan began to tempt me most subtlely. "Was the promise to Jeremiah that you read in the Batang fort really for you?" I believed the Lord's Word was sure, yet now I wondered whether I had clutched at a straw. Was the verse really meant for me? Wasn't I taking it out of its context? Yet even in this, Satan failed. Never had the Lord proved Himself so strong to me. If I was to die then I died under His own hand. He enabled me to sit in the small confines of my room and coolly contemplate the manner of my departure. One of the thoughts He had given me in confinement was that individually all is unto "the departure", universally all is unto "the consummation". The Lord Jesus walked unto the third day, the day of a finished work, and He would take me through. I pictured in my mind's eye that last morning as I was led out to die. Should I preach, should I pray or should I sing? I

decided I would sing. I went over in my mind some of the songs of
Zion and then chose this great chorus, determined that by His
grace these would be my last words before I saw Him face to face.

"Some golden daybreak Jesus will come;
Some golden daybreak, battles all won,
He'll shout the victory, break through the blue
Some golden daybreak for me, for you."

God marched on to victory in those dark days. How many
were praying for me I little realised. He began to show me something of what He was doing. I recall with great clarity sitting down
in the corner of my room and following Jacob over the brook
Jabbok in my mind's eye.* The struggle of the angel with Jacob
as a man walking in the flesh portrayed my state so perfectly.
He had touched me in the seat of my natural strength and now,
broken and shattered through solitary confinement with everything gone, my work, my liberty, my Bible, and now it seemed
life itself, I could only cling to Him for His blessing. I would no
doubt never be the same again. Then like a shaft of light in the
mind, the relevance of Jacob's act of faith in Hebrews, where he
is seen leaning on his staff in worship, to the conflict with the
representative of the Camp of God, flashed into my mind. What
does it matter if I come up from the waters limping? What does it
matter if I am never the same again, provided my name is Israel?
Then as a prince with God, having no confidence in the flesh,
will I lean on my staff for my lameness and worship 'til the day
dawn and the shadows flee away. Let that be my highest and final
act of faith towards God my Strength and my Redeemer, and I
remembered that God's Word said that, as Jacob passed over
Penuel, the sun rose upon him. So after this I viewed everything
as walking into the dawning, going on into the golden daybreak
and the morning without a cloud.

By now it was already June. The threats to life grew less. The
first offensive petered out and I was left much alone. During the
past months, whilst the emphasis was on interrogation, I nevertheless had had constant instruction and individual lecturing on
anti-Imperialism. There was no text-book. The only reading matter
was a few "People's China" Magazines and some English editions

* See Genesis 32.

of the Russian publication "New Times", also reports of the big meetings for "Peace" convened in places like Stockholm and Paris. I read all these with some eagerness, as it was my only way of gleaning anything of what was happening in the outside world. Officials who handled my "education" would constantly talk with me and seek to get me to express my views. They also went to some pains to help me prepare a criticism of British aggression against China and Tibet. They would hardly believe my ignorance on many historical matters. When I made such a hopeless hash of the task they said: "You ought to be able to tell us about aggression. After all you yourself are an expert in these things, specially trained to infiltrate into other people's countries. We are raw hands. It seems absurd for us to have to tell you the nature of Imperialism." One day Yang looked particularly thoughtful. "Really," he grinned, "I have been at fault in my conversations with you. I have omitted a very important point. The trouble with you, is that you don't understand the nature of real patriotism. You think loyalty to the British Nation as it exists to-day is true patriotism. You are quite wrong. At the present time you are being loyal to Capitalist and Imperialist Britain, the Britain of the moneyed classes. The Britain of the working classes is yet to emerge. It is to the establishing of that Britain that you should give your loyalty." I later realised that this is the line of thought that leads a man to view the greatest loyalty to his country and people as being adherence to the "camp of peace" headed by the Soviet Union, hailed as "champion" of the down trodden masses throughout the world. In fact, in China, the "worship" of things Russian, in politics, art, science and every branch of reconstruction, has become almost a criterion of Chinese patriotism! For their authority they quote not only Mao, but also the last will and testament of Sun Yat Sen, who expressed the desire that China should co-operate with Russia. Once I was told: "You are afraid to tell us your facts, because you are afraid of what the British Government will do to your parents. That is not good enough however, the Communist Party in England is very strong now, and the British Government cannot do just as it pleases. Britain now is in a terrible condition. Food and clothing themselves are becoming a major problem. They are just a tool in America's hand, who herself is facing economic ruin. You must stand on the side of the British 'people'. We are friends of all the hardworking and peace-loving British people. Our only enemies are warmongers like Churchill, and pirates like Truman, who represent the ruling classes of Britain and America."

Towards the end of June the day came when the results of this five months' interrogation and preliminary indoctrination were to be weighed. They handed me a sheaf of duplicated sheets, a book of between twelve and fifteen pages. It was entitled, "Registration of Aliens". If this were a document used for the registration of aliens resident in China, not under arrest, it was a most outrageous document. It covered every detail of one's personal history going back, so far as I can recall, to the age of eight. It was a long series of questions. The entire purpose of this written inquisition was to test the person's loyalty to the new regime and their attitude to the Communist viewpoint. I had already answered everything orally many times, except for the last part, which was headed "Thought Reformation". Here I was to fill in the changes of thought and outlook I had undergone, since being in contact with the new regime and its teaching. I decided to state truthfully what I thought, giving emphasis to the evils of aggression and tyranny. I finished the document with, "Imperialism may well be a monster which devours other nations, but if Communism uses the power of the new state to lead millions away from God and down to hell, then it is more than a monster, it is a virus wreaking death in the souls of men and is more terrible than any imperialism that has yet arisen." I handed it in to one of the officials. A few days later Yang came back. "That statement you wrote", he said, "was nothing more than another libel against us!" I expected him to rave at me but he was quiet. If I had known all that lay ahead I would not have been surprised.

Days passed again. All was silent; I could not think what they were going to do with me. The full summer heat beat into my room through the rice paper until I was almost suffocated. My energy began to fade away. My whole body broke out in prickly heat until my skin was a mass of red blotches and little white heads. All I could do was to sit on the floor with my back against the wall, from early morning until sundown. An official came in to say that as a very magnanimous gesture I could have one window open, in addition to the shutters, providing I promised not to look through it. He said that this was for my own sake, as the feelings of the people was running very high against Imperialist agents like myself. This constant emphasis on the magnanimity of the People's Government became very aggravating at times. I was forever being reminded that I was being given meat every day, or that I had received a hand towel or a bar of soap. For these little comforts I was very thankful and appreciative, yet to use them as an endless spur to the confession of some guilt robbed the gift of any goodwill it might seem to possess.

June scorched its way into July. I continued alone and in great exhaustion. I was supplied with a mosquito net and the last two days allowed to bath in cold water. Then, on the morning of the 7th very early, I was served with breakfast and immediately ordered on to a waiting truck, which drove straight out of Chunking up the south bank of the Jarlin River. My eyes drank in greedily the wide expanse of country but whether our journey was for life or death, who could tell?

CHAPTER XVI

PRISON FOR COUNTER-REVOLUTIONARIES

> "And a light shined in the cell
> And there was not any wall
> And there was no dark at all
> Only Thou, Immanuel.
>
> Light of love shined in the cell
> Turned to gold the iron bars,
> Opened windows to the stars,
> Peace stood there as sentinel.
>
> Dearest Lord, how can it be
> That Thou art so kind to me?
> Love is shining in my cell,
> Jesus, my Immanuel."
>
> Amy Carmichael.

WE drove about ten miles and then turned off on to a gravel track, running up into a range of hills. We were a mixed cargo. I was in the back, wedged in under a great pile of files, envelopes and office material. Yang was on the other side, half sitting on the running board. In the front was a driver of the P.L.A., who was not sure where he was going, and next to him was a young woman. She was obviously not Chinese. "Where are you from?" the driver asked her. "Sikang," she said. I pieced things together in my mind. A Tibetan woman had passed through Hsin Ching with Ford and the Indians. In the house we had just left, I had glimpsed once or twice persons I reckoned to be Indians, and also on one occasion the back of someone in a Tibetan gown. There was little question that the Chamdo party of captives had been housed in the same quarters as I, at Chungking, and that now we were being moved to the same place. We stopped at a village and Yang asked the way to somewhere. I could not catch what was said. We drove on, climbing about two hundred feet

up a winding road, until we suddenly came out to a place where
building was in progress. The jeep jerked to a stop, and we all
clambered out. Two things immediately arrested my gaze. One
was that the young Sikang woman was about to give birth to a
child. She stood there in a cheap looking blouse of bright green
cloth, perspiring profusely in the intense heat. I thought of the
jolty journey she had just endured and how wretched she must
feel. The second was one of the saddest sights I had ever seen.
On the path before us there was a youth with tortured features
making his way with painful slowness towards a small house up
the hill. He wore just a thin vest and shorts, that looked dirty
with poor washing. On his feet were heavy manacles and a
thick chain composed of iron links, each about two inches long.
His two hands were handcuffed with a crudely made Chinese
steel instrument, which bound the two wrists together in one
circle of iron. I looked on with sympathy and horror, yet having
been under prolonged stress, instinctively tried hard to betray
no feelings, whether of pity or apprehension. With the unfortunate
prisoner was an armed guard leading him on to whatever may
have lain before him. Behind the two men, in a deep cutting in
the mountain, lay a large newly-built brick building. The light
grey brick and tiles stood out in striking contrast against green
young conifers covering the hillside beyond. One glance and I
guessed the truth. The windows were small and barred. It was a
prison.

Yang led me down a short incline to the big doorway, bristling
with soldiers armed with rifles and tommy-guns. We passed
through into the darkened interior. One felt "Abandon all hope
all ye who enter here". I was determined to show no fear. Yang
sat me down in a room which obviously had only just been
vacated by the builders. All the floors and windows were still
covered with whitewash and plaster. A few tables and chairs lay
about in confusion and a rough bookcase full of paper-backed
books rested on its side. The administrative staff were only just
moving in. Yang soon appeared with the Governor of the prison.
He looked like a factory foreman, was very burly and may have
been quite a jovial type outside of his duty. Yang spoke first,
saying that at the detention centre he had told me what would

happen if I did not solve my problem, and now it had. I had
been brought here to make a proper confession. He hoped that I
would hurry up and settle my question. He also said that, in
accordance with his warning, my food at this place would be on
a lower scale. The Governor was stern but not unkind in his
manner. He endorsed what Yang had said and then told me that
for the time being there were only two regulations for me to
observe. One, if I required anything, I was to report to a warder.
This was done by standing at attention with the right fist clenched
and raised above the head. I must shout, "Bao Gao", which
literally means "report", whereupon a warder would attend to
my need. The second, I was not to speak under any circumstances
to any of the other prisoners working or moving about the prison.

Following these instructions, a warder came in and led me off
to a designated cell. In the passage-way between the Administra-
tional Block and the main building of cells, I could see a long line
of men stripped to the waist, wearing only shorts and plimsolls,
waiting to collect water. They each had a pan and one after
another shouted, "Bao Gao!" then, receiving permission from the
warder on duty, moved forward to the tap or tub. No two were
allowed to draw water together. I followed the warder, a P.L.A.
soldier, but with one difference. He had a GUNG AN badge on
his arm. "Gung An" really means "Public Security" and is the
term used for the police in New China. Although it had been
"liberated" in 1949, yet the S.W. China Military and Political
Committee was still the governing body in that area, so the prison
was under military control. On the ground floor, long corridors
ran off along both wings of the building, with cells on either side.
In the centre was a long concreted courtyard. My escort now took
me upstairs and along the whole length of one of these corridors.
The entire building must have been about sixty yards long and
thirty yards wide. Upstairs was almost the same as downstairs
except that the cells were bigger. Through the big doors, carrying
heavy Chinese manufactured bolts, I could glimpse prisoners'
bedding, laid out on the floor in neat rows along the walls of the
cells. At the corners of the corridors were pillboxes in which
warders stood with tommy-guns. I was taken to cell No. 9, situated
in the very S.W. corner of the prison. I stepped into the empty

room, but the door was not locked behind me. I realised afterwards that in the daytime the doors were kept open, owing to the work of cleaning, the serving of meals, and the necessary access of officials to the prisoners. Order was ensured by constant patrolling of warders and the armed pillboxes which covered the entire system of corridors encircling the building. The electric light all over the prison was never put off except in broadest daylight.

The cell into which I now entered was a room of twelve feet by nine with an extra square yard by the door. Left alone, I went and sat down in a corner. There were two windows of two feet by about fifteen inches. These were each filled with seven iron bars and a cross piece. There was no glass in any of the prison windows but two wooden flaps of gauze, which could be shut at night to restrict the entry of mosquitoes. The door was two inches thick, made of wood and heavily bolted. In the centre of it, about five feet from the floor, was a small square hole with a little trapdoor, through which the warders could peer at the prisoners when the door was closed. The floor was of varnished boards and the walls of brick covered with whitewashed plaster. In the ceiling there was an electric light bulb surrounded by wire netting, but there was no switch in the cell. As a prison, I have little doubt it ranked as high as any in China. I sat and took stock of my surroundings and thought heavily on the new development of my case. No doubt this was the place where I was to be subjected to "special bitterness". Failure to secure the desired result would mean almost certain execution. I looked up at the iron bars. In the cooler air of the hills and the lower temperature of my brick cell, I felt my prickly heat less troublesome. A little while here and perhaps my energy would return. My bedding was trundled in. I spread the Tibetan rug on the floor in a corner and prepared a place to sleep. Whether I dozed or not I do not know, but before I knew what was happening the afternoon meal was being served. I was not allowed to eat the food served to the other "criminals". Two Japanese prisoners appeared at my door carrying a bucket of thin soup, a bowl of pork and tomatoes and a bamboo basket of "manto".* This was a rather better meal than I generally received later, my diet settling down to two or three meals of rice

* i.e. steamed bread rolls.

and vegetables a day, with a meat dish at intervals of three or four days. Apart from occasional tea, my drink was hot water. After some confusion, owing to lack of bowls and chopsticks, some were at last obtained from another cell and I had my rations doled out to me. I sat down on the floor, gave thanks to God who had kept me to that hour, and began my prison life in earnest.

During my first few hours in the prison, a young official, he could have been little more than twenty years of age, came into my cell. His name was Liu. He had a round boyish face, spoke softly and seemed much more refined in character and manner than most officials I had yet seen. He spoke to me of some of the main features of world politics. He gave special emphasis to the growth of the Communist Party in countries like France. He gave me some books which he encouraged me to study. These were to be my textbooks in the first period of my "learning". Later I was to understand that this period in the prison was viewed as an opportunity for "self conscious" reflection and "thought reform". If in the "self conscious" period one could willingly embrace Marxism and enter into the policies of the new regime, it might lessen one's crime. The sooner one came to the realisation of what was the people's standpoint and, from that standpoint, was prepared to judge all one's past life and determine ones' future outlook, then the sooner could one make a declaration of one's crimes against the people, who would, through the vehicle of the People's Government, deal leniently with one. Thus this first period was an indicator of the prisoner's attitude; whether he was actively and willingly seeking reform, or whether he was apathetic and just "waiting".

My state of mind on entering the prison was not only apathetic but hostile to any suggestion of "thought reform". This meant I was a particularly serious case and no doubt this was one of the reasons for the continuation of solitary confinement. They would not apply other measures until "the ojective facts of my state of mind" had been duly analysed by the committees dealing with "thought reform" of reactionaries at the prison. The communists view such institutions as "hospitals". The prisoners are "men maimed in mind" by poisonous reactionary philosophies and false social concepts. They are "cared" for by officials, who are viewed as "doctors". The symptoms of the "patients", some of whom are in a very serious condition and may eventually have to be destroyed as being unfit for social life, are collected by warders, cell leaders and officials. These are analysed and the "medicines", such as suitable books, special conversations, struggle meetings, further solitary confinement, chains and handcuffs, a "reform through labour camp", etc., applied as the groups of "doctors" decree. The books of reference are the works of Marx, Engels, Lenin, Stalin and Mao Tse Tung. Their authority, the inherent laws existent in nature and society as propounded by the Father of Communism, Karl Marx.

Mr. Liu (we always addressed such officials as Mr.), in view of all this, handed me six publications. The first philosophical work was Ai Tze Chi's *Da Tsung Tze Hsioh*; I suppose in English we would call it "Popular Philosophy" or "The Philosophy of the Masses". Ai Tze Chi is one of new China's leading philosophers. This was a treatise written by him in very simple language and using everyday examples, in an attempt to enunciate the basic principles of "Dialectical Materialism". Another was a pamphlet of some sixty or so pages; the Chinese character was printed very indistinctly on crude brown paper. It was called *A Brief History of the Development of Human Society*. This was a hotch-potch of Marx' principles of Historical Materialism. Published in the form it was, it was really rather an insult to human intelligence. When one thinks that this book is used as the major text-book for the Party-led indoctrination of the millions of Chinese people, is proclaimed as Gospel Truth, quoted as supreme authority and carried by many as a pocket testament, one really wonders what has become of independent thought in China to-day. It commenced with a hoary illustration of how a young teacher in America was alleged to have been punished by law for proclaiming evolution. The writer then paraded evolutionary theory as fact under the superficial discussion of the grandiose phrases of "Labour created man", "Labour created the world", and "The Labouring masses created history". From here the reader was hustled on through the sequence of Primitive Communism, Slavery, Feudalism, Capitalism, and Socialism viewed as the reflection of an irresistible law of progress, resulting from the conflict between the relations of production

and the capacity of production at each stage of history. It ended
with the doctrine of the inevitability of a communist state, in
which contradictions between mental and manual labour, town
and country living, were for ever solved, classes eliminated and
religious faith non-existent. This having been accomplished, it
blandly announced that humanity would then move on to a
higher plane of existence. The third one was in English, a better
version of Mao Tse Tung's *Concerning New Democracy*. This fairly
well known document, brimming with materialistic arrogance
and that assumed authority of a man who believes himself a figure
of destiny moving on in the irresistible laws of the universe,
demonstrates categorically the class structure of the New Chinese
State. It is in fact a blue-print. New China is a Democratic
Dictatorship. This contradiction in terms is conclusively explained
by the fact that democracy is for "the people" and dictatorship
for "the reactionaries". The people include at this present stage
four classes. The national capitalists (that is capitalists who are
not involved in monopoly and have no connections with foreign
capital), the petty bourgeoisie (that is small traders, professional
people, intellectuals, etc.), the peasants and the workers. With
the working class, headed by the Communist Party, as leaders of
the revolution, with the alliance of workers and peasants as the
backbone of the revolution and with the other "progressive"
classes falling in line, the democratic united front had been set
up. This was to act as a dictatorship against the three reactionary
classes, the bureaucratic capitalists, the feudal landlord class and
all imperialists operating in China, of which the Chiang Kai
Shek clique were the mere running dogs. From this I gathered
that I, apparently, was one of the latter, thus subject to the
people's dictatorship. There was one book on history, entitled
A brief history on American Aggression in China. There was one on
current affairs giving various speeches and articles on the Korean
War from the Red standpoint. There was a series of articles
lampooning the American White Paper on China and, finally, a
book on *New China and her New Women Workers*, giving moving
accounts of the betterment of women workers in factories.

After seeing that I had a big earthen pot with a lid for night
use, Mr. Liu retired. I sat against the wall. I could hear the

prisoners in the next cell talking. The books lay on the floor. "They are going to shoot me," an agonised voice cried in the cell adjoining. Another prisoner spoke, "Don't give up hope. Don't give up hope!" As the sun went down the mosquitoes swarmed in; I did not realise I was allowed to shut the windows that first night. I was terribly bitten that summer, but God marvellously kept me from malaria. About six, the doors of the cells were all bolted and padlocked. On retiring for the night I decided, that although in the prison, I would kneel to pray. I had only been on my knees a minute or two, when the guard spotted it. I ignored his protesting voice, which came shouting through the peephole. Minutes passed and then I heard the key being put into the padlock. Two men entered and insisted that I lie down immediately. There was nothing I could do. After this I used to pray either sitting or lying down.

The next fortnight I was left alone in my cell. Only the warders looked in, on their regular patrol every few minutes. I found it hard at first to "bao gao" to the guards but soon became accustomed to it, until it became a natural part of my life. "Bao gao, may I have some drinking water?" "Bao gao, may I go to the toilet?" "Bao gao, I have been called for interrogation," etc. All over the prison during the day the word "Bao gao" would echo through the corridors. One day I made a bad mistake. An official called me from the cell and took me down into the court-yard, where I had a photograph taken for record purposes. When I arrived back in my cell I was confronted with a warder mad with rage. He had not noticed me slip out across the corridor. He had thus come and found my cell empty. "Why didn't you 'bao gao'?" he blared, his eyes nearly popping out of his head. "The official called me so I didn't think it was necessary," I excused myself. He gave me a heated lecture. I had committed a grave offence but I was excused this time. All movement must be sanctioned by the warder, whatever official there might be coming to collect the prisoner. I found the days passed better than at the detention centre. This was because the prison had a routine, which was rigidly observed. All prisoners would rise and retire to blasts of a whistle, blown at 6 a.m. and 10 p.m. For half an hour every morning, there was organised "thought reform", singing and physical jerks. Twelve to two each day was a compulsory siesta. There were two meals a day at appointed times. The rest of the prisoners also had appointed periods for study and discussion and quite a number had set hours for labour. Orders for the various events were shouted through the corridors which meant that I now had a kind of clock.

Having nothing to do, and knowing it was useless to mope on my circumstances, I continued systematically to go over the Scriptures in my mind. The past six months I had been very busy. Beginning at Genesis, I had recalled each incident and story as best I could, first concentrating on content and then musing on certain points, seeking light in prayer. Gradually I had worked through the Bible until I had covered all I could remember. With the passing of time, whole sections were beginning to fade, but God still brought much to mind and now I went through the Word of God in this way for the second time. The strength received through this ordered meditation was, I believe, a vital factor in bringing me through, kept in the faith to the very end. Sometimes I craned my neck and looked out of the windows, which were situated about six feet above the floor. I could see the building going on. As the construction progressed, several big chimneys were erected. Why such big chimneys should be necessary next door to a prison puzzled me immensely. Stories of the second world war came to mind and I began to think they must be for the burning of the corpses of those executed. I could also see, at about half a mile distant, a solitary palm tree. I called it "the victor's palm". I should see it on my way out, if that should ever be.

I used to sit at times and distinguish sounds. At any time our ears are registering far more than we ever realise. One day I heard an unusual noise. It was very slight at first, but it persisted and increased with clarity until I could hear it was someone singing. I stood dead still. The tune was difficult to distinguish but I could tell the melody was not Chinese. I turned this way and that but could not make out from where it was coming. Then, when the guard was not looking and his footsteps had died away, I put my ear to the floor. I discovered a man was singing softly but clearly in a room below. I knelt listening with great excitement. My heart leapt at the words. "Onward, Christian soldiers, marching as to war, with the Cross of Jesus going on before." I jumped quickly to my feet lest the guard should discover me. The Name of Jesus in English! O praise the Lord! Shut up so long alone without fellowship, cut off completely from all who loved the Saviour's Name, it was the sweetest sound I heard in all my captivity. Little wonder that His Name shall thrill and entrance us for ever and ever. I fell to wondering who it might be. Was it Ford, or was it a missionary? I had no means of telling, but whoever it might be, we now had a means of communication. I also began to sing well-known hymns. I knew that he heard me because he would repeat a tune that I had just sung. Gradually we collected quite a repertoire of well-known English hymns. Sometimes we would sing in unison and at other times separately. Some of our favourites were, "When I survey the wondrous Cross", "Praise to the Holiest in the heights", "Eternal Father strong to save" and many others. Then we launched out on to other music. This determined our nationality. English folk songs proved predominant, thus I knew my fellow-prisoner was an Englishman. We also hummed classical pieces, and at evening time the beautiful melody of "Just a song at twilight" often proved a form of good-night between us. With the evidence I had gained on coming to the gaol, together with what I now knew, I concluded it was Ford. It was no doubt harder for him on the ground floor, as on this side half the building was below ground level and thus his quarters would be a little dark and damp. The encouragement of our singing together, coupled with the beneficial effect of the cooler temperature on my prickly heat, meant that some of my old vitality returned. I began to compose poetry, again committing each stanza to memory as it came, since I had no pencil or paper. Psalm two was my strong answer to all the verbiage of the indoctrination on imperialism and the people. To the now especially precious tune of "Eternal Father strong to save", I made up a little poem part of which is here recalled.

> Beyond the rage of heathen kings,
> The people's vain imaginings;
> Beyond the cast-off cords and strands,
> Beyond the proudly sundered bands;
> I see O God, Thy holy hill
> And know Thy King is reigning still.

Beyond each travesty of law,
The people's wrath, the tyrant's claw,
Beyond man's power of command,
Beyond his limit to withstand;
To Christ God's mighty verdict sounds,
"I give to Thee earth's utmost bounds."

So Christ shall lift His rod on high,
Earth's brittle powers in fragments lie.
O kiss the Son, ye kings be wise
Lest grace recede and anger rise.
Meanwhile God whispers tenderly,
"Blest be all they that trust in Me."

Often I would stand at my doorway in the daytime and study the faces of other prisoners as they went about the prison on various duties or lined up for the toilet at the prescribed times. One wondered what they had done, that they should be there. Some were old men and yet there were youths of eighteen. Were they all political prisoners? I had no means of finding out. One day the Governor came in to talk to me. He said: "You are very obstinate, just like many other prisoners!" He spoke at some length encouraging me to confession. "When we have dealt with your whole question (by that I presumed he meant when the Government had passed sentence), you will still have to confess your facts!" I was appalled with the idea that I would be held forever to confess certain facts which did not exist. I did not know which was worse, constant threat of execution or to live in solitary confinement with no hope of release. After this the Government opened their second offensive against me. This took the form of a series of carefully planned interrogations, conducted by Fan Ko Chang.* Mr. Fan, I found out later, was the chief of the Interrogation Corps at this, the No. 1 prison for counter-revolutionaries of the S.W. Military and Political Committee. This new prison and its growing administration constituted the highest court in the whole of S.W. China, and was especially employed at this time on the settlement of political cases and the reform of reactionary criminals. Both Fan and the Governor struck me as among the better type of men in the Communist Party. Fan's manner of interrogation and the Governor's speeches were more

* "Ko Chang" is a Chinese Govt. rank of fair responsibility.

studied than Yang's and the other officials'. Over several weeks Fan covered my main history in China. I was set "examination" papers which I had to write in my cell.

There were leading questions such as "What do you think are your crimes against the Chinese People?" The distinctive character of the Communist judicial system is that a prisoner is never charged with a specific crime on arrest. The awful thing is that what he may think "subjectively" as to his guilt or innocence, or even know to be his real conduct, is ultimately of no consequence. If a man is arrested, it is because, according to the assertion of the Government, there is sufficiently clear evidence to prove him guilty, that is to say that as soon as he arrives he is "objectively" guilty and, in New China, that is sufficient. The mind of the masses is forever preferred above the mind of the individual. The immense strain on the prisoner is therefore that on entrance to the prison he is acquainted with the news that he is a criminal and that the Government have confined him there as guilty of counter-revolutionary activity. He is told that he is an "agent" or "spy" and must recognise that fact with due submission. The tantalising part is that the proofs are generally the written exposures which friend or foe have placed in the hands of the Government unbeknown to the prisoner. His task in the prison is first to reflect on his past life, to find in what way he has offended against the people, or what circumstances might be so interpreted. Some prisoners have no idea at all what they have done, so they go on for months and months just pouring out every detail of their past lives to the officials, who may one day say: "That's it! That is why you came here." I later had one cell leader whose case was a perfect example of this. Being guilty already, it is then a question of confession. Self-vindication is viewed as resistance. The crime is never told to the prisoner until he himself has stated it, except perhaps in the case of executed prisoners, but even in these cases an indictment prior to sentence would be most unlikely. At the settlement of the court a prisoner will be expected to sign that his crime sheet is completely according to the facts, although this may result in his execution or life imprisonment. If he does not confess his crime, the future is unthinkable. For such there is only a life of endless mental torment and perhaps death at the last. If he does confess, then he has hope of a lenient sentence. This magnanimity, however, by any normal standard is only the lesser side of severity. Very few criminals, even the lightest ones, are released under three years.

According to the pattern, my interrogation now presumed my guilt. Piece by piece the whole system began to dawn upon me. I noticed now that the emphasis was not on the death penalty but on indefinite confinement. How often it was said to me in the prison, I do not know. "China has plenty of rice, she is quite able to feed a few prisoners. The prison is newly built; you won't outlive it." Then an official said to me: "Do you want to be here twenty years, your case dragging on one year, two years, or even three years?" There was a prisoner whom I eventually met whose case had already gone on for four years without settlement. In all this time the suspense of mind continues. Week after week my new series of interrogations dragged on. We were obviously getting nowhere. They were held in huts on the hillside. Every time I was escorted there by an armed warder. On these occasions the warders were very fierce and one dared not look right or left. Once in the court room, I had to sit very still on a tiny little stool a few inches high. The slightest movement and the guard would shout me to stillness. In front of me was always a big black table about four feet high and ten to twelve feet long. Behind this, three or four officials sat like sphinxes. There would be one or two who would do the actual interrogating, which was carried on in an icy atmosphere, whilst others would do the recording. These recordings were afterwards read out and I had to put the left thumb in some red substance and leave a thumb-print on the paper. On the wall behind the officials were placed huge pictures of Chairman Mao Tse Tung and Chu De, Commander-in-Chief of the P.L.A. They were made to look particularly overbearing. On either side were pasted slogans outlining the policy of the Government towards the prisoner. "Confess your crime and live! Hide it and you die! Suppression and leniency combined! Acknowledge your sin, reform your thoughts and strive for new life in the service of the people!"

Time slipped by, the heat of the summer passed, Mr. Fan

grew weary of the useless questioning and I was left alone with my thoughts once more. The solitary confinement became increasingly oppressive. I was beginning to taste the other weapon which the Government used, the weapon of time. Interrogation meant hope. It meant, I was told, that the People were striving to save me from my doom and win me back into their ranks. If the prisoner will not "strive" to gain pardon by frank and thorough confession then he must be left until he "awakes", until he becomes "conscious". He needs more reading and more time to realise his hopeless position as a reactionary in the People's State. I was now being "left". A prisoner might be "left" eight months in the prison without any approach being made towards him by any Government official. This would bring men to despair and they would ask for interrogation again or confess some other aspect of their crime.

For almost one year I had been a lone prisoner. Seven weeks had been spent in travelling but all the rest within four walls alone. At times the pressure of solitude was almost unbearable. In the days of my freedom, away in the mountains, George and I had once visited a hermit monk. This man, a brother of one of our older teachers, had already spent five years in isolation. Day after day he sat alone, before a rough hewn idol in the wall, his only reading the Buddhist scriptures, his only companions the coloured prayer-flags hung from the beams. Above his head were a series of black pictures that seemed to portray intercourse with the dead. We were permitted to see him on medical grounds. When we entered with his brother, he began to weep and, when he spoke to us, it was obvious that he was already a nervous wreck. George handed him portions of the Christian Bible in Tibetan, which he willingly received. I, too, was beginning to taste something of the indescribable oppression of unbroken loneliness but, thank God, the terrors need never be mine for God was ever with me and I could talk with Him.

I went over in my mind every official I could remember and prayed that God would save their souls. This was a blessing to me, I am sure, safeguarding against any bitterness of heart that might arise. Then I prayed for many Tibetans by name, especially for my teacher, Gun Ga. God had spoken to him in a remarkable way. One day when our lesson had finished, he sat reading on in a Tibetan Mark's Gospel. He reached the portion describing the Lord Jesus Christ in agony in Gethsemane. What thoughts ran through his mind I do not know but suddenly he put his head in his hands and began to weep bitterly, crying out "Nga sim pam", which means literally "My soul is defeated", that is to say "I am very castdown". Without saying a word he rose and walked out of the room. He accepted a New Testament and, with help received from one and another, professed faith in Christ and willingness to turn from his idols. After I left Kangting, John brought me news that he had turned to the Lord.

These times of prayer and meditation were of vital help and occupied many hours. In the evenings I would sit and pray until my eyelids drooped—but there was still so much time to spare. Each day had sixteen waking hours to fill. I devised all kinds of methods to overcome this trial and gain some relaxation for the mind. I would give myself wholly to vivid imagination, reliving past holidays on the continent or visits to other pleasant places. Sometimes I would be away back amongst the Tibetans. I would study the mosquitoes. I found at least six types in my cell. At the detention centre my speciality was spiders, but here spiders were too few. Then sometimes I would gaze at the floor and make out figures in the grain of the wood or try the old game of turning black into white by changing one letter at a time. Washing clothes was a happy pastime once a fortnight and even the sweeping of the floor had its own satisfaction. I would pace up and down, then stop to listen. If fortunate I would hear the birds singing in the woods nearby, or even catch a glimpse of one through the bars. Often when the wind was blowing outside I would lie perfectly still and listen to that loveliest of all voices, the sighing of the pine trees in the breeze. The soothing sound would calm my tired mind. It took me back to the time when, as a little boy, I was ill and mother would come and stroke my fevered forehead. Truly there is no land where His voice is not heard and how manifold are His ministries. I began to cry out with greater intensity to my Redeemer. My last poem before the new and dreadful stages of the conflict began expressed something of the heart's anguish and desire, during those final days of solitude.

> "Let not Thy face grow dim, dear God,
> Nor sense of Thee depart.
> Let not the memory of Thy Word
> Burn low within my heart.
>
> Let not my spirit Lord, grow numb
> Through loneliness or fears.
> Let not my heart to doubt succumb
> And keep my eyes from tears.
>
> Let not the distance come between
> As months and years increase.
> Let not the darkness close me in
> Let me not lose Thy peace.
>
> Let not the pressure of the foe
> Crush out my love for Thee.
> Let not the tiredness and the woe
> Eclipse Thy victory.
>
> For Thy Joy is my joy
> And my hope, Thy day.
> And Thy Kingdom, gracious God,
> Shall never pass away.

CHAPTER XVII

THE SNAKE-PIT

"Woe unto them that call evil good and good evil; that put darkness for light, and light for darkness; that put bitter for sweet and sweet for bitter." Isaiah 5.

MR. HU, one of the young officials, spoke to me the second week in October 1951, in another empty cell. "What do you think of your question now?" he asked. For the first time since my arrest I cast everything to the winds. Rightly or wrongly I blurted out, "Do whatever you like! Settle my case just as you please!"

A few days later I was sitting alone in my cell, when a man with a blue silk coat, an angular face and big goggly eyes peering through large spectacles, paused in the doorway. He was struggling with an unwieldy roll of bedding and clothes. Behind him came Mr. Hu. With a wave of his hand he said: "You sleep here!" A warder looked in to see what was going on. "May we talk to one another?" the new arrival courteously addressed the guard. "No!" was the sharp reply. He stood helplessly in the middle of the cell. He was obviously in a very distraught state of mind. With a woebegone look he turned the palms of his hand upwards, indicating to me by this gesture that his case was hopeless. In return I placed my hands together and pointed heavenwards, hoping that he would understand that I was a Christian and one who prayed to God. He sorted out his bits and pieces and we sat down together in stony silence. About an hour later another man was hustled in. He was an older fellow with rather gaunt features and a very tanned skin. There being three of us, we were now permitted to speak when occasion demanded it. We were to call each other "Tung Hsioh", which means "fellow-student", but never forgetting that our status was a "fan jen", which means a "criminal". At the instruction of an official, we introduced ourselves to each other. The first arrival was Chang Li, a wireless expert. The second man had presumably been a member of the old diplomatic staff. He knew German. "I have served in the KMT Government twenty years", he said. "That is why I am here." In the next few days we were joined by other "Tung Hsiohs". There was a university lecturer in economics and a Lt.-Col. of the KMT, who had been both a civil detective and a secret agent of the KMT intelligence organisation, known as Chun Tung. This latter strangely enough gave me news of Chao Hsun. He had met him in another prison where Chao Hsun was being tried as a Japanese spy. There was also a boatman, and later a General of the KMT guerrillas. A captain of a Yangtse river steamer also joined us eventually.

Our small cell now became crammed to capacity. Different Tung Hsiohs came and went but a complement of six prisoners was generally maintained. This meant that there was no room in which to walk about, so we just had to sit all day where we were. The first six weeks our cell leader, also a "criminal", was a man about my own age. He was a journalist and had even written progressive and pro-Communist articles. On "liberation" he had gone to a People's Revolutionary University, where he had excelled himself in debate and discussion. Shortly before he was going to graduate, he was sent up river under rather peculiar circumstances. The result was that he ended in the gaol. He had apparently failed to make a full confession of his past connections with the Sino-American Co-operative Organisation, which he joined in the war against the Japanese. After a seven-hour inter-rogation, this question had been settled and now he was doing an indefinite period of "thought reform". His main task was to gain merit by "helping" others to confess their crimes. As a personality he was one of the "lovable rogue" type, although a positive terror at times. "I have just come from two cells downstairs where I have made people confess. I was just like a little dictator there", he boasted unashamedly.

One of his first tasks was to help me learn the prison regulations which were now rigidly in force in our cell. It was very obvious that the Government's tactics towards me had completely changed. Mr. Hu said I must memorise them in Chinese, although Diao, the cell leader, could speak to me in English if he wished. The prison regulations consisted of twenty rules to be obeyed implicitly.

They covered in principle every aspect of routine and "reform". A rough translation will give the reader some idea of how our lives were governed.

No. 1.   All orders of the Governor, officials and warders must be obeyed implicitly. All suggestions as to improving the daily life in the prison must be addressed to the Governor and not scandalously discussed in secret.

No. 2.   On admittance criminals must submit to a search and, apart from bedding and toilet articles, all possessions must be placed in the custody of the prison authorities. On release these will be returned to the owner.

No. 3.   Silence must be rigidly maintained. It is strictly forbidden to peer round corners, gaze through the windows, speak loudly, sing, quarrel, spread rumours, whisper, converse in twos, or soliloquize. Requests and applications must be addressed to warders by means of a "bao gao".* A distance of between three and five paces must be maintained between a criminal and the warder. At no time must the criminal touch warders and he must only move after he has been authorised to do so.

No. 4.   Observe the daily routine. Rise and retire at the appointed times. It is forbidden to exchange sleeping positions.

No. 5.   It is forbidden to tell other prisoners, or agree together, to deceive the authorities, also to make voluntary confession of a spurious nature. No criminal is allowed to discuss his case or divulge the nature and progress of his trial or the content of conversations with officials.

No. 6.   Carry out your "learning" with diligence. Reform yourself and thoroughly reflect upon your past crime.

No. 7.   Observe the discipline of prison work.

No. 8.   Give attention to communal and personal hygiene. Keep your cell and the prison clean. No one must spit or urinate other than in the places provided.

No. 9.   Do not damage tools or any public property. It is forbidden to move anything without permission.

* report.

No. 10. All illness must be reported immediately and application made for treatment.

No. 11. Secret meetings of any kind are absolutely prohibited. Apart from the prescribed meetings for "learning and the review of the life of criminals in the prison", no meetings of any kind are to be held.

No. 12. Personal correspondence is not permitted except under exceptional circumstances, when application should be made.

No. 13. Government officials must be addressed with courtesy.

No. 14. Communication between cells is forbidden.

No. 15. It is forbidden to smoke, drink intoxicants or gamble.

No. 16. On admission, no outside news is to be published in the prison and, on release, no circumstances of the prison are to be published outside. Offenders will be punished according to law.

No. 17. It is forbidden to shield another criminal, conceal any matter, or conspire together. Offenders will be punished according to law.

No. 18. Criminals have the mutual responsibility of watching over each other's actions and of reporting secretly to the Government authorities. Anything of an irregular nature should be immediately reported. Failure to report will lead to involvement in the guilt of the offence.

No. 19. These regulations are liable to alteration at any time as circumstances may require it.

No. 20. These regulations come in force from the day of issue.

As I talked with Diao I began to see how these regulations were applied. The first evening, when the door was shut and Diao had been officially installed, a routine meeting was held for the discussion of the "daily life". Diao presided. Everyone was expected to take part. We were learning to live the communal life. Resolutions were passed regarding where to place the night urn in the one square yard available. Who would empty it in the morning. Who would be responsible for the washing up. Who would fetch the rice. Who would mop the floor, etc. In some cells, these proceedings, by the time everybody had expressed his opinion and the mind of the "masses" had been obtained, would last almost an evening. Different prisoners would "strive" to get an opportunity to do these little tasks as this showed a willingness for labour, a very progressive sign in a reactionary undergoing reform. The first step on the road to release in addition to confessing his crime, was for the prisoner to attain a sufficiently high standard of reform in his own thought and display such a willingness for labour in the prison itself, that the authorities would draft him to a "reform through labour camp". These camps were looked upon as a most desired goal and a progressive attainment. Generally speaking, it would be quite impossible for a "backward" prisoner to be sent there. From the camps, it was presumed that a return to normal "people's" status would be reasonably speedy. Responsibility in these minor duties in the cell nevertheless cut both ways, as the manner in which these tasks were carried out was always linked with the prisoner's condition of "thought reform" and his whole conduct brought weekly under review by a meeting for "criticism and self-criticism". These could be very nasty occasions and weeks of "striving" were easily demolished by an adverse report to the authorities by the cell leader.

At first I was not permitted to do anything. I would have liked to have done something as a matter of help but mocked the idea of striving for "progress". Diao, strangely enough, was very amused at my attitude and warned me gently: "You know, you must try." He covered his remarks in English. A few days together revealed that he was really only a half-converted opportunist, as far as Communism was concerned. He was a most ambitious person and I have little doubt he thought he could have gone to the top in the new regime. I was surprised to find that he knew C.I.M. missionaries in Chengtu. He knew some of the evangelical choruses and we hummed: "In my heart there rings a melody". "You see", he said, "you are a true man. Whatever are you doing here?" "According to my circumstances I suppose they have sufficient evidence to convict me and shoot me," I said. He became very friendly. His knowledge of Communist affairs was far greater than that of any of us. I asked him about the staff of the prison. "They do not seem very educated," I commented. "No," he replied, "their standard of education may not be very high; the main thing is, that their political history is very pure from the proletaria[n] standpoint." "What do you think about my case?" I asked. He looked me straight in the eye. "If you are really speaking the truth, in the end it will be all right, but you must be patient."

The next day "learning" started. The "classic" indoctrination text-book which I had now read, "A Brief History of the Development of Human Society", was taken up seriously. The first week resulted in a major clash with all the members of the cell. Each day, for three hours in the morning and two in the afternoon, we read and discussed the book, paragraph by paragraph. When I say discussion, do not let it be imagined that this was discussion in the normal sense of the term. The pattern followed was that one should read and another explain the passage by extempore paraphrase. This would be followed by each member of the cell in turn voicing his "opinion", which, if he were at all in the way of "striving", would most certainly always coincide completely with what the book said. Whereupon the cell leader or another prisoner would commence his little speech with: "What the last 'tung hsioh' has expressed I feel is most 'accurate' and find myself in complete agreement with him, except that I would like to add ..." whereupon he would give some aspect that had been omitted. The peculiar part of this discussion, then, was that the conclusion was at the beginning instead of the end. It was no more than going through the motions of rationalising the authority of the text-book, which was always "right". The demand of the authorities was that there should be a unanimous conclusion at the end of a session of discussions but this, only and inevitably, was a ratification of the "infallible" teachings of Marx concerning the particular point in question. Faced with divergent opinions, which were few, once any new "tung hsioh" realised what he was facing, the cell leader would piously say: "If we cannot solve your problem, there are plenty of books in the prison, and if the books cannot solve your problems, then we can ask the Government officials. The People's Government under the leadership of the Communist Party has solved the problems of a nation as big as China; it would be strange indeed if it could not solve yours." For about twenty hours of "learning time" the five cell members raged at me on the question of evolution. The Marxist develop-

the teaching of Darwin is the very core of their atheistic
concepts. Apparently to disbelieve the idea that Labour
as solely responsible for man's position above the beasts was
considered a most reactionary "heresy". My "tung hsiohs" did
just about all in their power, apart from rending their garments,
to convince me of "their" viewpoint. By their harsh words and
fierce attitudes, they displayed how "progressive" were their
concepts, and how totally enraged they were at the words of this
imperialist in their midst, who dared to resist indoctrination and
reform by preaching Christian beliefs. The controversy stretched
over days and at night I lay down with my mind in a whirl.
This was the beginning of the notorious "brain-washing".
Warders began to take note of me. They were always hard on
people who were holding out against the "learning". All the
prisoners now viewed me with a growing hatred. " 'A backward
element' in our cell holds us all up," someone said.

Every Saturday a meeting for criticism and self-criticism was
held in the cell. Chang Li and I were the main targets. Each evening had been devoted to pounding Chang Li with verbal abuse in
order to make him confess something he was supposed to be hiding.
Diao was positively vitriolic. The vilest criminal on the face of the
earth could hardly have been more reviled. I found out, as time
went by, that this was quite a common occurrence. The authorities never interfered in such cases, on the principle that you must
not quell the indignation of the masses, the masses in the prison, of
course, being the prisoners. In fact, this ragging and nagging was
an integral part and vital weapon of the thought reformation
process and was heavily relied on by the Government as a means of
wearing down resistance. Chang Li had come through this week
of torture, biting his lip with almost uncontrollable rage. Now he
and I, as chief rebels, were the objects of attack. Every prisoner
must say something. If he does not take part in "learning" and all
the meetings, that is taken as a symptom of some grave malady of
mind which must be routed out. It thus seemed better to say a
few words and be harangued for a while, than to say nothing.
First there is "self-criticism". There being obvious targets in the
cell, the other prisoners make short work of their own criticisms.
This is a typical example: "As to the daily life, I must confess that

this week in mopping the floor, I did not do so well as I might. This is because my thoughts are not sufficiently concentrated on the daily routine. I am thinking all the while of my case. I must correct this in future, as negligence to duty affects everyone. We are living communally and I must have due regard to the common hygiene. Not to do so would be a breach of regulation No. 8. I must be for ever struggling against self-centredness, which is the besetting sin of the bourgeoisie, and seek to establish proletariat thinking which emphasises the "masses'" life. It is obvious in many things I have not changed my class standpoint. In future I promise to observe the prison rules more thoroughly, to "learn" harder, relating principle to practice, and to seek to be of "help" to other "tung hsiohs" so that we can all progress together towards our "new life". I can think of nothing else this week, but will be glad for any opinions which "tung hsiohs" could express in regard to my many faults."

After a few such colourless self-criticisms, the big questions were taken up. Chang Li in these meetings was called upon to review his attitude of "learning" and "reflection on his crime" in the past week. Chang Li would mumble a few words about his resisting spirit being very wrong, that he would do his best but could not think of anything new to say. Then Diao would begin: "What have the 'tung hsiohs' to say about that? He obviously needs our help." A ruthless flow of both muddled and ordered criticism by several would be the result. This was comprised of a medley of bandied Communist phrases, harping on class standpoint, the timidity of the petty bourgeoisie, the evils of the KMT and blessings of the new regime, the honesty and justice of the People's Government, etc., and the policy towards counter-revolutionaries. The underlying emphasis of the criticism, was always rooted in the Marxist concept that in the progress of history there was a determining law of development. This was independent of the human mind and inherent in the existence of things. The Communists claimed by reason of their dialectical approach to the universe to be able to discern and co-operate with this law. In every society in history, there were contradictions existing, that must result in a new society being born. Our indoctrination text-book outlined this to us in no uncertain terms. At each stage of history there was the progressive class. These were the oppressed and those out for increased production for a higher standard of living. By siding with the progressive class at any given stage of history, you caught on to that factor that sooner or later must be triumphant, overthrow the old, and establish the new. In New China this had been achieved. It was fruitless, a prisoner would be told, to try and reverse history; you must march on, embrace the new regime and its ideology, or be for ever "backward". There would come a time, when if you persisted in reactionary thinking and living, you would just be crushed by the onward march of the masses. In Britain and America the capitalist system was said to have reached its highest form, namely imperialism, and thus was on the verge of collapse. The only thing for a Britisher, apparently, was to desert the sinking ship of the bourgeoisie and establish strong links with the proletariat world front for the establishing of a "people's Britain".

This bombardment of abstraction was turned on at nearly every meeting like some half worn-out gramophone record. It would be followed by a common plea that such a backward "tung hsioh" be compelled to review his attitude again, making use of the valuable opinions just offered him. Chang Li would stagger in for the second round. After another hashed self-criticism he would be told it was quite inadequate. He must think things over again and be prepared to make a proper review the following evening. With me at first they were more restrained, but as weeks went by these occasions became more exacting. The most virulent attacks were made on my faith, which was always identified with imperialism. Diao also expressed himself strongly. He criticised first my attitude regarding my crime. My main fault was "Cho Hsing Bing", which means "the impatience sickness". Only by patient and thorough reflection could my crime be fully confessed. He also gave a homily on the hindrance that my faith was to my progress towards the people's standpoint. Afterwards he said to me in English, "you can take the first part but the second I had to say, because of the others." I became baffled and confused under the constant circus of this tragic tomfoolery. Diao naturally was not to be trusted. Under Regulation eighteen he was obliged to report my propagation of Christian teaching. About three times I was warned about it. "This is a prison," Mr. Fan postulated, "not a Gospel Hall."

Another aspect that was now brought home to me very forcibly was that the Government viewed reform and one's progress in it as inseparable from one's crime. Thus a big criminal who reformed himself quickly and thoroughly in the prison would have his sentence reduced from, say, fifteen years to perhaps three. I saw an actual instance of this later on. On the other hand, a man who originally had a very small crime, should he resist indoctrination continually, would have no certainty that he would ever leave the prison. In fact there were times when this was definitely asserted. It was quite clear that the situation for me was even more hopeless than I had imagined. Not only did they want my confession but they wanted my soul. In my mind great conflicts arose. I found myself speaking straight out, but sometimes beginning to fence off my persecutors. The environment was so inescapable, Compromise haunted me but I fought on. The iron grip of Satan was determined to crush my faith and my spirit. Mr. Hu now sought a special book written by Mr. Ai Tze Chi to refute my faith in the Bible. Diao searched out special articles in the communist magazine called "Learning", to give scientific backing to what he propounded. Meanwhile my food was maintained at reasonable levels. "We are not like the imperialists, who so ill-treat their prisoners. If you are cold we give you clothes to wear. Because you are a foreigner we give you better food than the others. We know that you have been used to a better diet than us. Yet how do you reward us, just you reflect upon it?"

My mind recalls a picture of a Chinese torture, in a book of my childhood days. There the victim was placed in a small wooden box which must have crushed and crippled him. The lid was shut fast and, through a tiny hole, food was put in his mouth. In this way he would live but become hopelessly deformed. It seemed to me that this was what was happening now. In the Satanic framework of Marxism, I was being closed up but yet kept alive. What would it mean? Deformity, apostasy, or insanity? If one said one wanted to live, then there was only the threat of death. Yet if one was prepared to die, and I had told them, "Settle my case as you please," then, in perversity, they would insist that

I live and that I learn to live as they demanded I should. To a man without convictions, this process was not necessarily painful, but to one in whom by God's grace Christ and His Word had found their place, it was excruciating. If I were to come out to His glory it would be an instance of the acorn breaking the tombstone in its thrust to the light. Nothing of human fortitude could do it. God's life in me was the only factor of victory. His mighty arm moving in answer to prayer could take me out of the lion's mouth. By this time, unbeknown to me, across the world, the cries of thousands were beseiging the Throne of Grace. Sometimes Diao would look at me and say," You are strong," and I testified of Christ my strength.

Day by day Chang Li went downhill. I was seeing how not to conduct oneself under pressure. The officials constantly interviewed him on his attitude towards the Government and Diao kept every evening's proceedings carefully in mind and wrote a daily report. A patient with such a "high temperature" needed drastic measures to cool him down. The day came. Chang Li had been out for an interview. From the corridor came the dread sound of iron chains being dragged along the floorboards. We looked at the doorway. There stood Chang Li, literally drooping with horror. On his feet were heavy manacles and a thick iron chain. His hands were handcuffed behind his back, with small rough Chinese handcuffs. No one spoke. He hobbled across to his bedding pile and with great difficulty sat down. The last few inches he just dropped. Diao was the first to break the very awkward silence. "You must strive to get them off now!" Chang Li shook his head weakly. "They will never come off." "Oh, yes, they will. There is not one prisoner, who has not eventually through 'striving' managed to shed his shackles."

Chang Li now entered a period of interrogation which was terrible to witness. It continued every day with constant raging meetings in the cell. These were really "struggle" meetings, except that they were a persistent feature, rather than a special pressure for a few days only. The "squeezing toothpaste" process began. This was a favourite phrase in the prison. Each prisoner explained the policy of the Government to him and begged him to say what he was hiding, Diao pointed out that the People's

Government never arrested a person unless there was a definite proof of guilt. With the masses organised nothing could remain unnoticed. Chang Li became even more aggravated and cried out in defiant mockery: "Yes! I am a secret agent, so is my wife and so are all my children!" This came to the ears of the officials under the unfailing system of Regulation 18 and his case became more severe. I was astonished. In a way I felt sorry for him, and yet I felt he was acting unwisely. At night it was dreadful. Having to relieve himself, with his hands handcuffed, he would afterwards be criticized for disregarding the common hygiene. Then at night, when it was cold, hardly anybody dared cover him with his bedding, lest they should be found sympathising with such a "stubborn" reactionary. I did so on one occasion and a prisoner said: "You did that as standing on religious ground." Once Mr. Hu had me out and asked me point blank: "Do you sympathise with Chang Li? Do you think he deserves this treatment?" I murmured something about if he were guilty of hiding a crime against the people, then of course he deserved it. The Government came to detest my evasive answers, as indeed I did myself. There was hardly a day without new mental conflicts. Now followed the most awful act of all, eight days and seven nights of continuous interrogation. I believe there was one break of a day in between, but otherwise no break longer than two hours. It was maintained by different interrogators right round the clock. Each time he had to walk a considerable distance to the court until the iron manacles made great sores in his flesh. These were given no adequate attention and took months to heal. I also remember how he caught a cold and being unable to wipe his nose, he would bend forward and draw his face across the knee of his trousers until the mucus came out onto the cloth. Under the strain Chang Li began to fabricate the most incredible stories, which annoyed and distressed us, because it was so stupid. The material had to be taken down in the cell by the university lecturer and it only increased his own suffering. In the end the Government abandoned his case for the time being, having failed to extort the confession they desired but he was left in chains.

Through all this crisis I was living and sleeping next to him. There was no doubt a reason for this, because I was the next on

the list. The grouping of prisoners in the cells was always deliberate
and was a means of introducing subtle pressures. Our cell leader
changed and the reformed KMT General tung hsioh, took over.
We were also joined by another tung hsioh, the captain of a
Yangtse steamer. He was an old fellow and somewhat cantankerous.
As a result of this and the spreading of outside news in the prison,
he had been handcuffed behind his back. By his stubborn ways
he greatly incensed the prisoners and I remember once, on
account of some superstitious talking, the cell leader took hold
of the captain's head and banged it against the wall where he sat.
He was of course quite defenceless. At evening the cell-leader
made a brief self-criticism and thus dismissed his unauthorised
violence. The old captain had months before the handcuffs came
off and he found then that one of his arms was deformed. He was
unable to lift it above his head. At this time also, a big struggle
meeting was held in prison against a French Catholic Father and
a young Japanese woman, both accused of being spies. Practically
the entire prison, numbering several hundred men at that time,
were massed to "criticize", shout and rave at these two. The
Catholic answered bravely: "You can execute me but I will never
accept your thought reform." "What shall we do to him?" the
official asked the assembled prisoners. "Put him in handcuffs and
manacles", was the unanimous decision of the assembled convicts.
This was immediately carried out. The Japanese girl was then
made to speak before all those men, as to her attitude towards the
confession of her crimes. When many criticisms had been voiced,
she said she would think over the "tung hsiohs" opinions. The
vote of the prisoners was that she should be given a chance, but
within a fortnight she was handcuffed.

In "learning", I had tried to emphasise that I did condemn
imperialism, and when I said that much modern Christianity in the
west had departed to a great extent from the original teachings of
Christ and had even at times condoned British expansion abroad,
they felt I had made a big step forward. I said that wherever I
had been influenced by that spirit, then I wanted to get back to
the original Spirit of Jesus Himself. When I enlarged on this from
history, quoting a few examples, the official said that I had
made some progress, but that my reform was much too slow. This

was a signal for their new offensive. All the pressure of the recent events plus a certain slight yielding on one point of indoctrination meant that the time was ripe. The KMT General was really a much better man as cell leader than Diao. God was gracious to me in this. I was cross-examined much of the time in the cell and then frequently interrogated in the court and sometimes interviewed afterwards as well. My whole history from before I left England right to the time of capture was scrutinised, in a way never done before. Every detail was covered in both the cell and the court. I had to write out a complete statement of my activities and contacts. It covered 33 closely written pages of succinct English. Much of this was the product of "ch'i fa". "Ch'i fa" is what some have called seduction. In the realm of thought, it is merely the process of provoking another by apposite suggestion to think of things, which on his own he would have found difficult or perhaps impossible to recall. In the prison setting, "ch'i fa" of course became a sinister force. There was a definite seductive significance to it and it was a big instrument used, both by officials and prisoners, to obtain a confession or, a bigger confession from a person under questioning. Allurement by perhaps, auto-suggestion might be a better definition of the communists' ch'i fa. English seems to be devoid of a suitable word. Each paragraph had to be read to the prisoners and then criticised, analysed and often scrapped, then rewritten until finally passed by the whole cell. Each thing had to be stated from the people's standpoint until, instead of being a missionary, who in certain points may have slipped up or been compromised politically, I became an international spy carrying on espionage under the cloak of religion. We had some terrible scenes. Black became white, white became black and moral and spiritual values a blurr of words.

The first statement was eventually passed and I was told by the official that it showed some progress but not enough. New pressure began. A fortnight's struggle meetings were convened by my interrogators. After the year alone and all that it meant, followed by these last strenuous months of thought-warfare, this latest effort was a severe blow. In the cell I had to review my attitude and go over all sorts of obscure points in my case, while the other prisoners goaded and provoked me. When I simply sat and said nothing, which I found a good weapon for parts of the time, the "tung hsiohs" would become almost like raving lunatics, and one even spat at my face. Some days it went on morning, afternoon and evening. It was a nightmare from start to finish. My chief interrogator, a new official this time, came and sat in the cell towards the end of the fortnight. His words were terrible. I had been told during these meetings that, by my refusal to disclose my alleged British Government relations, I was definitely "testing the law with my body", and now my interrogator spoke solemnly to the whole cell. "Some criminals," he said, "wait until they get to the firing squad and then squeal. Bull is a man like that. The meetings can stop now. Just leave him." Mr. Fan also interviewed me. He said very seriously and quietly: "In Peking we have definitely executed foreigners who plotted against the life of Mao Tse Tung. We do execute foreigners when necessary. You simply *must* realise this."

I came to the conclusion, with the stoppage of the meetings and the statement of my interrogator, that, after I had now been nearly eighteen months in the hands of the Communists, they had almost certainly decided to sentence me to death. It seemed as if a great burden had fallen from my shoulders. I had come, by reason of the hell on earth which the "learning" and various meetings had meant to me, to that most abnormal state of mind in which to die would be a glorious escape. The "tung hsiohs" caught me whistling. They asked me why I did so. It was the habit to ask for the thoughts of anyone who exhibited the slightest unusual behaviour. All thought must be open. "What do you think of the interrogator's remarks?" they enquired. "I take it that I have been sentenced to death." As I said this they began to laugh, although it was not cruelly.

Up to now I had continued in prayer, but the meditation of Scripture had become almost impossible. On Sundays I had tried to go over portions in my mind, as that day was mostly left free for reading and needlework, but the pressure of my circumstances so wearied and hurt the mind that I gradually found myself unable to concentrate. Now the devil launched another attack. One day I gave thanks for food, as was my custom. I was mercilessly attacked. "It is not God, Who gives you that. It is the toil of the hard-working Chinese people." It was reported and the official informed me very forcibly that in this prison no expression whatsoever of religious faith in one's daily life was allowed. On another occasion when I mentioned the Name of Jesus, the university lecturer cried out in blasphemy. They would give no place even to His Name. When they found out I still prayed, they called the warder and I had to stand up. This was a common form of humiliation. The prisoner might have to stand for an hour or two amongst his sitting cell-mates like a naughty boy in school until told to sit down. "You are not to pray," the warder ordered. "There is no religious freedom for you here, that is reserved for the people. Do you understand?" "I understand," I replied impassively without expressing my promise that I would stop. The patience God gave me to go on day by day in quietness before my accusers and tormentors is a marvel to me now, as I reflect upon it. It was His work and His alone. Although I was so weak and faltering, yet prayer was winning. Satan was being held at bay. My armour was still on me and the shield of faith in my hand. His love, which predestined and foreknew, had called me and justified me and according to His promise would glorify me,* until found in the image of His Son. This unbreakable chain of five great links stretching from eternity to eternity must outlive all the chains of men and Satan. No indoctrination could thwart His redeeming love. I remembered in the cell once, that simple verse coming to me until its thoughts filled my eyes with tears:

> "He can break every fetter,
> He can break every fetter,
> He can break every fetter,
> He can set you free."

* Rom. 8. 29-30.

CHAPTER XVIII

STRAIT-JACKET THE SANE!

"His soul came into iron." Psalm 105.

> How to endure, when all around us die
> Nations and gracious cities, homes and men,
> And the sweet earth is made a filthy den
> Beneath whose roof, black, belching vultures fly.
> How to endure the darkness, when the sky
> Is totally eclipsed by evil, when
> Foul grinning Chaos spreads its reign again
> And all good things in senseless ruin lie.
> Must we be hard as stone? It wears to dust.
> As stiff as oaks? But they untimely break.
> As pitiless as steel? It turns to rust,
> And time from pyramids will ruins make.
> In violence, decay, starvation, need,
> What can endure? Only the living Seed.
>
> Kenneth Boulding, *The Naylor Sonnets.*

FROM time to time the prison was rent from end to end with a campaign. These sometimes coincided with the big national campaigns and purges or, on the other hand, were mere internal special efforts in the course of the "thought reform". The first prison campaign, so far as I was concerned, had been in December 1951, when we had all studied "the law governing the Suppression of Counter-revolutionaries". Prior to this we had only known the policy of the Government in general terms, as "Suppression and leniency combined", and through the general slogan of "clemency to the repentant and judgment on the impenitent". Now the various classes of crime were clearly delineated in black and white and each prisoner was encouraged to estimate how long his sentence should be. Rumour-spreading received the lowest sentence, being only three years. Almost all other sentences ranged from five years to execution, according to the seriousness of the crime, although for nearly every crime execution was possible. Prisoners viewed this hope-shattering document with grave misgivings. One "tung hsioh" told us that, at another prison, he had heard sentences announced. Apart from two of just a year or eighteen months, all were fairly long. Ten to fifteen years was quite common. Officials encouraged us to learn "Article fourteen", which said that those who made a frank confession and showed true evidence of repentance would receive lenient judgment and in some cases even be exempt from judgment. If we "strived" for the fourteenth article we had nothing to fear. On this ground a new drive for prisoners' confessions was initiated throughout the prison. The official came to our cell and asked me before the others: "What do you think your punishment should be, according to the Law?" "At the lightest eleven years (I should have said fourteen I found out afterwards), and at the heaviest, execution," I said in all seriousness. From the standpoint of the People's Government this was in fact the position.

In April 1952, another nationwide campaign, this time against all manner of illicit practices, was in full swing. It had two aspects. These were the three anti's, Anti-corruption; Anti-Waste; Anti-Bureaucracy. The main target of this aspect of the campaign was to purge Government Departments of all undesirable staff and unreliable cadres. The other aspect was the five anti's, which were directed against tax evasion, misappropriation of Government funds, theft of Government property, bribing of Government staff and the unlawful obtaining and use of Government economic secrets. This aspect was directed against such bourgeois classes as had been allowed a place in the revolution, but who were only concerned with personal profits, rather than national construction. These purges, in many ways, did China a lot of good, as I think any who knew China under the KMT will agree, but the extreme scale on which they were conducted was staggering. For instance, in Tientsin alone, there were thirty thousand exposures received by the Government, and the books we studied told us that eighty per cent of the bourgeois classes had been found guilty on various charges. This campaign brought the workers into a position of unassailable power in industry on practical issues, as the Land Reform campaign had brought the peasants into unassailable control of the land.

H

In the prison it was one of the biggest conflagrations ever. The raucous cries of the struggle meetings in numerous cells went on all day and often far into the night. The prison sounded just like a lunatic asylum. Some meetings were carried on until four in the morning, the unfortunate victims being taken from the cell to another to allow the exhausted "chi chi fen tzu", that is, zealous prisoners, to rest, while a new group continued the pressure. One man endured six weeks' struggle meetings with a break of only one day in between. He stood before his tormentors until his feet were swollen. Sometimes in such cases a man might be made to stand with his toes turned inwards or his hands held out for a long time. Petty indignities but very trying. These were mostly the prisoners' ideas in which the authorities rarely intervened. Chains, handcuffs and manacles were a common sight. Many in fear confessed where their treasures were hidden. It was stated that a Japanese girl-spy, wife of a very rich Chinese, handed over 300,000 U.S. Dollars and that Wang Ling Chi, the ex-KMT Army Commander-in-Chief, living in the prison, handed over one and a half tons of gold. When one considers the gross disparity of privilege between rich and poor in old China, it is little wonder that China had a revolution. The wholesale corruption and oppression of the poor has always brought the righteous judgment of God on a land thus full of iniquity. Yet we have no cause for complacency. The deeds of the west in China, in many cases, are too shameful to record and the treatment of foreign nationals to-day is due, at least in part, to seeds of distrust, hatred, dishonesty and immorality sown by some of the baser elements of the white races. We should never forget that under good rule a Communist-led revolution is a virtual impossibility. Chang Li encountered further struggle meetings because he could not explain his radio business and the old hard-bitten river captain handed over all his possessions of any value. "You are sure you are willing for the People's Government to have these things?" the official asked him. "You must be personally willing." "Yes, I am perfectly willing," he said, without a murmur.

In the beginning of May, I was transferred to another cell. It was situated downstairs on the north side and adjoining the courtyard, so was rather dull. I had not been there long, when another campaign began. This was a drive for the tightening of prison discipline. Everyone had to think how he had transgressed the regulations during the past six months and also how other prisoners had transgressed them. The big drive against offenders was on the usual lines. Meetings were held for exposure. This evidence was collected by officials and analysed and then we all had meetings for confession. Each one of us had to rack our minds for all the details of our past movements in the prison and then make a confession to the others in the cell, receive their criticism and judge ourselves. As with political questions, some would conceal what they had done or fail to remember. These prisoners' inadequate confessions usually resulted in struggle meeting tactics being applied. After a hectic two or three weeks a big struggle meeting was held in the courtyard, at which some two hundred or more attended. Eight major offenders were hauled up and some handcuffed or put in chains. Our cell leader lost his position and one of the other "tung hsiohs", a very strong-willed and disliked fellow, came tumbling down from his "progressive" pedestal and had to make a long self criticism before us.

So the pressure on the mind was maintained. If it was not one thing it was another and, as to our cases, we were mostly still in suspense. In June, I was suddenly called from the cell at night. This had only happened once since I had been in the new prison. I knew it was serious. It was a glorious tropical night. The air was full of the sounds of insects. I was taken to a distant hut on the hillside. My interrogator was furious with me. I was made to stand for reflection whilst the officials vacated the court. Once before, I had been nearly seven hours in the interrogation room and I thought that, like Chang Li, I would now be questioned all through the night. As I stood there alone under the vigilant eye of the guard, who would not allow me to move an inch, I could see some big cockroaches crawling over the floor. My mind began to think of the end. "Is this the way to death?" Yet God is so full of love towards us. He holds back the enemy time and again. The lions were chained. Before very long my interrogator returned, still quite adamant, but he let me go back to my cell after a short lecture. He said that I sat before him as a piece of wood or stone. I stumbled back in the darkness. I always tried to be obedient with the guards. Chang Li on one occasion had become enraged with a guard, holding a fixed bayonet. Pulling open his vest to expose his chest he had shouted at the warder: "Go on, kill me now!" For a Christian this attitude was impossible. I dared not be proud, when crushed under His hand of discipline, but could only consider Him who endured such contradiction of sinners against Himself and Who, when He suffered, threatened not.

In August large numbers of prisoners were transported from the prison to elsewhere. Some went to "reform through labour" camps. A few were released and others went to other prisons to confess their crimes under even more rigorous conditions. The situation was very tense. No one of course knew whether there were to be executions or not. The prison now seemed half empty and the top floor was eventually cleared, all prisoners being housed on the ground floor. Whether because of this or for other reasons, I never found out, but Mr. Hu came into the cell and announced to me that I would be permitted to exercise with the other prisoners every morning in the courtyard. Since my arrival in Chungking in January, 1951 I had been given no exercise. It was now August, 1952. God was caring for me. If I had continued much longer I have little doubt my health would have been affected. Looking back one can see how, time and again, His restraining hand moved in answer to the great volume of prayer on my behalf. Before the summer finished, I was also allowed two baths outside. To sit in cold water in the hot tropical sun, looking out at the hills, was as good as a breath of freedom. How we learn to thank the Lord through tribulation.

A new phase of study had been in progress for some time now. Originally no newspapers had been allowed in the prison, but the official Chungking paper, *The New China Daily News*, was now a subject for communal reading and discussion. At first I was forced to sit in silence with another prisoner in our cell during the morning, no doubt because my question still remained unsettled. I needed time to continue reflecting. I used to do what needlework I could to pass the hours. Whilst in the prison I cut out and stitched up several pairs of shorts out of a tablecloth and a medical apron I had in my baggage. I also patched up my corduroy trousers, quilt and other clothing with much painstaking care, until my work was admired by the other prisoners. There were also many books which I read, although I used to think it was almost like self-poisoning. On the other hand, if I did not keep abreast of the other prisoners in the knowledge of the indoctrination material, the meetings became intolerable and my persecution more acute. At twelve the other prisoners returned from the newspaper reading, held in another big cell, and reported on the news to us. In Communist papers all news is for "education". It is primarily printed not to report events but for political instruction. I began to get an insight into the new society as described by its own masters. The achievements and statistics claimed in reconstruction were most arresting although the blustering self praise and pride in self effort, thoroughly nauseating. The impressive water conservancy projects, the laying of railways, erection of factories, the increased production in cotton and rice and the general stabilising of the country's economy, were great strides forward and one rejoiced for the Chinese people, for any measure of truth in these reports of improvement in their tragic lot. The whole nation was being energised. The masses in their millions stirred by exacting emulation drives, were beginning to raise at least something from the rubble of the years. All this was so necessary but what of the more important side of life? This was most disturbing.

It was evident, from what I learned and read, that this vast nation of some five hundred million souls, by means of a determined, well organised programme of propaganda, conducted on a scale unprecedented in history, was being re-orientated in its whole thinking to accept the Marxist way of life. In the rise of Mao and his Communist party, a philosophy and an administration had been welded into a single authority. In such a state "heresy" is but a step to "treason", disloyalty to the "ideal" the seed of disloyalty to the realm. Here is ground for the direst tyranny in the name of the greatest good. The rule and religion of Mahommed, the authority and creed of the inquisition and the god-king and lamaism of Tibet, in their different ways illustrate the same principle. All these human kingdoms follow the same pattern and are but Satanic counterfeits of the Kingdom of Heaven, in which Christ in perfect righteousness shall be both ruler of the people and yet object of their worship. Now, in China, by the government-backed agencies of the press, radio, education, entertainment and, most important of all, the discussion group, the indoctrination was proceeding. In university, factory, school and office, town and village, yes, even in the church and the home, by means of "learning" discussion groups, basic lessons in Marxism were being thrust upon the people. Under the fierce glare of the nationwide campaigns, failure to attend, disinterestedness or stubborn resistance to reception of the new teaching would arouse a dangerous suspicion. Such a coolness or antagonism, if related to some thoughtless word of criticism in the factory, an error at work, or a failure in duty, could all too easily bring forth the cry from the "enthusiasts" of "saboteur" or "counter-revolutionary". It is here that the freedom of thought and faith receives a death-blow. It is not so much through any law, for that asserts such freedom, but by the social pressure brought to bear upon each member of the community, where good citizenship is measured solely by loyalty to the Marxist ideal. This authority claims to stand for the peoples' highest good and views all thought foreign to its own system and ideals with hostility, and in fact, though veiled at present, has every intention of achieving or expediting its obliteration.

Mao Tse Tung stated that one of the prime duties of the state, following the military success of the revolution, was to carry out the thought reform of the intellectuals. In the papers, the clever, though often very stilted, "self criticisms" of some of the more prominent intellectuals were held up as examples for us. By a prolonged and most penetrating campaign in the colleges and universities, all thought independent of Marxism was so denounced and traduced as to intimidate all but the most courageous into silence. At the other end of the scale, that very large section of the Chinese population that was illiterate prior to the "liberation" was now being taught to read by greatly improved methods, which brought the complete solving of the problem of illiteracy within reach of this generation. For this great army of new readers, so far as I could see, the ONLY literature available was along Marxist, and where necessary, technical lines. One other factor was the Government-directed "reform" of the Church, whereby "imperialist" influences were purged out and, needless to say, principles of the Communist version of nationalism brought in. In the home all life and production was being brought to centre on Mao Tse Tung and the state, by means of his portrait and a "patriotic pact" signed by the family. I was deeply conscious, as I came in contact with all this material, of the great spiritual and intellectual perils that seemed to be overwhelming so great a nation. In the prison I regretted more and more how I was being tempted to speak in their language and view so much from the Communist standpoint. I am convinced, after more than three years in their hands, that not only must we never yield an inch on our basic faith in Christ but, in the assertion of our heavenly citizenship and all that that involves practically, we must be absolute. On our knees, we must search out, whether in China or England, that which belongs to God and that which belongs to Caesar. Today in China it is through the ever increasing claims of the state that the Christian who is determined to stand can yet find himself seduced. Let us also remember it is of course just as unthinkable for a Christian to serve imperialism as Communism. We serve the Lord Christ. For the believer His interests are supreme.

In our review of the articles in the papers, everything had to be discussed with reference to our particular political needs. This was hard for me, because in the eyes of the "tung hsiohs" I was an imperialist diehard. The alleged U.S.A. bacteriological warfare, American aggression in Korea and maltreatment of Chinese nationals by the Hong Kong Government, etc., all needed a self-criticism on my part, as being allied in political outlook to these affairs. I hated it all but became ruthlessly efficient in speech-making along orthodox lines in those things which did not fundamentally touch my faith. My Chinese became both fluent and colloquial. I mastered nearly all the pet phrases, and often the prisoners would say to some poor unfortunate un-educated Chinese "tung hsioh": "You see, even a foreigner can express himself better than you." This may be to my condemnation. Often I rebuked myself for bowing to expediency, for hypocrisy and even compromise in my own mind. It was fighting all the time, emphasising the political issues, agreeing to the condemnation of aggression and analysing British Capitalism and its abuses as portrayed in their literature.

My main purpose was to keep off the philosophical side of "thought reform". Every person was supposed to become a materialist. Once we started on this line life became impossible, and my crime was aggravated. All opposition was viewed not as a testimony, but as persistence of the imperialist standpoint and a refusal to come over to the people's side. My soul's arms and legs were gradually being forced into a mental strait-jacket. When my prayer life had been attacked so viciously, I had found it necessary to stop praying in the normal way, and just hold myself before the Lord, lifting my heart to Him without utterance, knowing He understood my dilemma. Yet how mighty is the witness of His Spirit within us, once we are His. We do not deserve His grace but He pours it upon us, as and when He will. I remember lying on my bed one night, when suddenly, like a mighty flood rising behind a dam of logs and refuse on the reach of some river, the power of God's Spirit rose up within me and, breaking all before Him, caused a torrent of passionate words to pour forth from my heart to God upon His Throne.

In October a new terror presented itself. The Governor assembled us on the first of the month. It was New China's National Foundation Day. In Peking nearly half a million people were parading before the "Gate of Heavenly Peace" to cry: "Long live Mao Tse Tung!" We in the prison also had a "celebration". As at New Year time, oranges, sweets and cigarettes were distributed to the prisoners, and we received a lecture on our thoughts. After the lecture we had a joint meeting and a campaign began. This time it was to be "Thought examination". It lasted six weeks. The group to which I was attached included about twenty "tung hsiohs". It began fairly mildly and worked up to a fantastic crescendo. Each man was required publicly, before the group, to relate the stages of his "thought reform" since arrest, the gradual influences brought to bear upon him, and the measure to which he had been brought to stand with the people. Past thoughts concerning the Communists must be exposed and criticised, outstanding problems aired and the future of one's means of "striving" clearly stated. A record was taken of the salient points of each speech and the criticisms voiced by those listening. This was a searching procedure for everyone. There was no way of escape, as far as I could see. This being the case, I jumped in quickly before the campaign rose to its height, and delivered a carefully planned and tabulated statement of my arrest and my changing impressions of the Communist policy and the P.L.A., contrasting them with what I had previously heard and read. I also stated something of my reactions, whilst under threat of death in connection with my question. I felt, in a way, that I was speaking independently of Christ, which hurt me. In another way I felt like a man running across a bridge before it collapsed. I skirted the whole basic issue of materialism. At the end I brought out one or two questions, which I said were still unsolved, such as the question of shedding of blood in the revolution and the question of class hatred. As to the future I said nothing. The result of this outwardly colourful but inwardly wretched statement was better than I had hoped. In a sense it was true, yet in a sense it was false, particularly in what was omitted. These terrible times in the prison I can now only commit to the Lord for His searching and cleansing. I do not know what one could do in such cases, but we know that our God is infinitely gracious and the blood of Jesus Christ, God's Son, cleanses us from all sin. The prisoners were quite reasonable as, whatever the value of the statement progressively, it was obvious that it was the product of meticulous thought. This perhaps more than anything calmed their attitude and, after various criticisms, running I suppose into three hours, I was left alone. The campaign now increased in intensity. One after another of the "tung hsiohs" found himself unable to pass the penetrating criticism and demands of the prisoners, under the eye of the officials, and as a result ran into "struggle meetings". One man had about five days' intensive barrage to make him state his thoughts clearly. Another endured a day or two, then aggravated everybody by talking nonsensically. He was a very highly educated person but answered like an ignoramus. This was very dangerous for him. The campaign was closed at this stage and I think the man received a heavy sentence shortly afterwards. The official, Mr. Liu, said: "Well, I expect you are all very tired." I guess we were. Mentally it was a great strain and only increased inward conflicts.

During this "thought examination" campaign and at other times, certain instances came to light of the corruption and distortion of prisoners' minds in their desperate efforts to gain merit and be thought "progressive". One man scribbled a reactionary slogan on the wall of the latrines and then promptly went to report it as a great find to the authorities. Then several men might gradually form into a clique and attack another prisoner constantly with vicious criticism, whilst among themselves they would criticise very lightly, thus gradually seeking to give the impression that the other prisoner or prisoners were backward, but they themselves making progress in reform. This practice, very common in different forms in the prison, was termed, "Hit others, elevate yourself". From magazines seen in the prison, it would seem that this is a frequent occurrence not only amongst reactionaries but also in the Communist Party itself. This malady, rooted deep in the corrupt nature of the human heart in departure from God, they have been unable to cure. "If any man be in Christ he is a new creation" is unthinkable to them. Another rather amusing incident was also divulged. One prisoner had an attack of asthma and, as is peculiar to that complaint, there came an evening when, to the ignorant eye, it would seem that he was about to expire, barely being able to draw his breath. The official was called. No sooner did he appear at the door than from the lips of the prisoner, as if it were his last words on earth, there broke out the piercing cry, "Down with Imperialism! Down with Imperialism!" It looked a most convincing case of real thought reformation but the next morning the attack had passed and he was much recovered! How the human mind twists and turns in such circumstances. My own battered mind would so easily look for a way out and devise means, but God would have His child even in these conditions, leave all completely in His hands.

Apart from the usual conflicts arising out of the demands of the thought reformation, there were often personal problems, which prisoners found it hard to face. The wives of counter-revolutionary convicts, because of the social slur attached to such a union, generally requested a divorce from the Government. The Government was always willing to grant it in such cases, this being an evidence of "Progressiveness" on the part of the wife. When a petition had been filed, then the prisoner was called for two or three interviews. He was expected to sign without a murmur, show no grief and generally "think through" to a full acceptance of the situation. On returning from signing such a document of divorce, he would be expected to make a review or criticism of his feelings in the cell, to the other prisoners. The content of this would be something along these lines. "In my past life, when my people were struggling against the oppression and tyranny of the Chiang Kai Shek clique and the imperialists, I actively engaged in serving the interests of the ruling classes. This is a great crime and I can only thank the People's Government for arresting me before I committed further crimes and thus giving me a chance to reform. It is obvious now that my wife is very progressive, has embraced the cause of the people and is in active production in the reconstruction of our country. I would not for one moment stand in her way. She has a glorious future and her association with me, a reactionary, can only retard her. My affection for her is purely feudal in character and must be resolutely put from my mind. Having 'learnt', in the prison and under the help received from the officials and my 'fellow students', I realise that true love between the sexes must be based on class love. I, with my reactionary standpoint not yet fully reformed, could find no real partnership with one like my wife, who has now so obviously adopted the proletariat standpoint. If I were released to-day I should probably be most embarrassed by my 'backward' condition if I were to meet her. I am glad that she can go forward unimpeded to her new life. The love we must foster now is the love of the proletariat and only on that basis seek a partner. Now my whole task is to seek to complete my reform and attain to new life myself."

November was given over to studying Sino-Russian relations, as teams of Soviet actors and scientists were touring China. Mass meetings were held everywhere to welcome the visitors and a nationwide campaign of education on the Soviet Union launched to coincide with the occasion. Politically, militarily, economically and culturally the Soviet Union is depicted as holding unquestioned superiority. To learn of her is the highest wisdom, to criticise her the most desperate reaction. For the Chinese to-day "Long live peace" is synonomous for "Long live the U.S.S.R." For them she is the head of the "peace camp" of the People's Democracies and champion of the peace-loving peoples of the world. To them Lenin's mandate "Power to the Soviets, Peace to the peoples" is the sum of it all. During this month and later all "wrong" thinking about Russia had to be corrected not only in the prison but throughout the whole country.

In December I made a bad mistake. I was caught glancing at the cell in which I believed Ford to be living and I also passed the door of the courtyard when he was exercising. This was disastrous. I had "peered round corners", thus breaking Regulation No. 3. As we were both British and had been captured in Tibet, this made it very serious and could be interpreted as an attempt at collusion. The result was almost catastrophic. An official enquiry was opened on my conduct. I had to be crossexamined on all matters pertaining to Ford since my arrest. It was futile in the extreme. Zealous prisoners were mobilised and the sessions soon reached struggle meeting proportions. I would be shouted at for a while, then sent out into another cell, while the prisoners decided on tactics, then brought back for more questioning. This would mean more shouting as I failed to comply with their wishes. The whole proceedings lasted three weeks, during which time I had to spend my little spare time mooning about, reflecting on my thoughts and everything I had heard or done or thought, concerning Ford, since arrest. At last the "hunt" was called off without a verdict. The case was never closed. So the wearying process went on.

Some might be tempted to ask what was the most exhausting factor? Was it the nagging, the noise, the scrutiny, or what was it? In a word, it was the combination of the whole circumstances of the prison, upon a man with no real possibility of relaxation. Firstly, there was the maintained suspense of the threat of execu tion or life imprisonment. This was made more excruciating by tantalising the prisoner with promises of pardon, if only he would reform himself more wholeheartedly and acknowledge his "crimes" more deeply. This state of tension was aggravated by almost incessant provocation and baiting, by attacks on his integrity and self respect in regard to his political default, and by investigation into his daily thought, conduct and observance of the regulations. From morning to night, day after day, month after month and year after year, it was "learning", mutual haranguing, criticism and struggle meetings, in one form or another. Every physical and mental movement was maintained under vigilant scrutiny by official, warder or fellow prisoner, all of whom, for fear of their own future would not dare to relent. By the system of reciprocal spying and reporting all ideas of friendship or exchange of confidence were excluded. Living constantly in this atmosphere of conflict, distrust and lack of love from any quarter, life for many became unbearable. In this unthinkable environment, interrogation often continued unabated, together with searching interviews as to the prisoner's reaction and attitude, and with exacting demands to remember the minutest details of actions and events that transpired years previously. These sufferings were in addition to the usual heartbreak of being shut within four walls, kept under strict discipline and feeding on a diet which was too deficient in vitamins to maintain full vitality. All of course is designed with one end in view, to bring the mind into absolute submission to the will and indoctrination of the Marxist way of life.

From January, 1953 to May, I fell into a series of minor slip-ups on various points, resulting in a more or less maintained tension. I would say something "reactionary" and then have a thought examination meeting for several nights running. For instance in the course of a discussion I suggested that the Korean war had stimulated China's industry. This meant that I was accused of vindicating American aggression on the ground that it helped forward Chinese reconstruction. The whole thing was utterly absurd but these constant naggings, on top of all I had already endured, further weakened me. The crowning point of these minor but exhausting episodes was when Stalin died. That day, when most prisoners put on progressive long faces in mourning for the people's leader and teacher, I was found humming whilst in the corridors. This was viewed as imperialist delight at the death of such an enemy. This, together with a somewhat aggressive and forthright statement that I held to my Christian faith and would never be able to "reform" my thinking in that realm caused the Government to arrange their most diabolical and veiled attack on my faith in God. It happened at the end of May, 1953.

I was now in such a state of mental fatigue that I had become frightened of my symptoms. It seemed, at times, as if a great knot was fixed in my forehead and could not be untied, or as if some big clot had become stuck there and could not be removed. When I spoke or was questioned my whole face flushed and I felt my cheeks burning like fire. I felt unable to meditate on the Scriptures or pray except with the greatest difficulty. In the prison were various prisoners in different stages of nervous disorder. Two were considered insane, another just eccentric and several just on the verge of breakdown. The insane ones I saw on occasions. It was heartbreaking to see them. One was rather violent and was kept most of the while in chains. He never washed but lived alone in a far corner of a big cell amongst filthy rags. His great cry was for execution. One day, when the guard would not let him get a drink from an urn of water used for washing, he bellowed out: "You won't let me get a drink, you won't let me be executed and you won't let me commit suicide!" Warders and officials came running in and hushed him up. I personally thought he was very sensible at times. The other insane prisoner, whose originally slight mental trouble was now very serious, would give the guards a difficult time. His classic remark was revolting, yet a most cynical commentary on the whole place and system. He stood by his cell door asking to be excused. He said in a slow deliberate voice: "Bao Gao! My excrement and urine have increased, I request reform!" There were other ugly stories of this poor demented creature. I said to a fellow-prisoner, who was not too progressive: "I think the main thing for us now is to try and keep ourselves from going mad," and he thoroughly agreed.

At such a time as this, the last great attack began. Apart from political questions my faith was directly attacked. It was deemed a necessary step, it would seem, on the assumption that I was an imperialist and my Christianity therefore, of necessity, imperialistic in nature. They were terrible days. Another three weeks followed of the foulest of meetings. Within the first two days they reached struggle meeting proportions on the question of my attitude alone. I had to review and review my attitude as being proud, because I had dared to say that no one in the cell could deal with the question of my faith. Racial superiority was hashed up again and a multitude of remarks I had made during past weeks. The Stalin question was discussed repeatedly. Then I had to make statements as to my belief in God. This I would normally have been glad to do, but not in circumstances where the pearls of divine truth would be trampled underfoot and my tormentors turn again to rend me. The basic issues of the standpoints of materialism and its differences with the Christian faith were searched out. Moses and then the Lord Himself were taken up from the revolutionary standpoint. Whilst they failed to destroy my faith, yet the outcome was that I had to agree to consider the claims of materialism objectively. For me this was a retreat as, up to that time, although I had read so much and heard so much, I had wholly refused to do this. I felt I could hardly go on under the strain any more. I was now brought to the verge of collapse and began to tread the very brink of apostasy. My mind seemed unable to cope with the thoughts and the circumstances that now surrounded me. I could only wish for death. Then it was that God on His Throne, in answer to the prayers of what must have been, by that time, the ten thousands of His people in all the five continents, intervened. It seemed as if throughout the heavenly places, where the great spiritual warfare was in progress, His great commandment went out: "Thus far and no further." In utter faithfulness to His own promises, He would not suffer me to be tempted above that which I was able. The three weeks came to an end and the pressure ceased.

In the summer I was given some work to do, binding books, making cardboard boxes and painting covers. About the middle of September Mr. Liu called me. "Pack up everything you have with you." I did so, but I knew not what to think. My case had

come to no settlement. Even this year there had been several
fresh interrogations but with no clear result. In the Spring my
interrogator had been most sarcastic. "You think we will release
you, but I tell you, you are dreaming. We shall never surrender
to you. You must surrender to us." This was his last word to me.
What would become of me now? Where were they taking me?
Outside the prison all my belongings, including my bedding and
the boxes brought from Gartok and Batang, now all moth-eaten
and mouldy after the years, were placed in a pile. I boarded a
waiting truck and was driven into Chungking. What thoughts
surged through my mind! As the prison in the hills fell behind, it
seemed impossible that it was two years and two months since I
entered those doors. Where I had seen the handcuffed prisoner
that first day, was now standing the big prison cookhouse. The
chimneys had not been for corpses. All around in the spacious
grounds were crops and vegetables growing. A number of
prisoners were working. They had "striven" well to be able to
labour. Away in the distance, where the hills dropped away I
could see the wide waters of the Jarlin river. It looked very
beautiful to my hungering eyes. The lorry lurched downhill past
the palm I used to spy from my window. I did not yet know
whether it was the victor's palm or not. The limestone quarries
had been greatly developed in the two years. We came to the road
and passed on to Chungking. Most of the people seemed better
dressed. There were no beggars, the road was made up and good
modern buses swept along the tree-lined streets. Much building
was in progress and I caught a sight of the People's Palace of
Culture and some new workers' dwellings. China was making
strides in national reconstruction. How right the revolution
seemed in some ways, yet I was too weak to think. I could only
drink in the sight of people and moving things and hope against
hope for the miracle of freedom.

In Chungking we stopped under a very dark awning. I instinctively looked at the windows of the building. My heart sank.
They were barred. "Come this way," a voice gruffly ordered me
and I struggled up a long flight of steps with a piece of luggage.
On the second floor of a three-storey building I was thrust into
a very poorly-lit cell. As I passed another cell door the voice of

a prisoner, whom I recognised as having lived with me in the other prison, muttered to his cell mates: "Here comes British Imperialism."

I sat down but dare not move. I was very soon aware that this prison was different. I was horrified to find that no movement was permitted except by permission of the warder. The guards seemed exceptionally harsh. Almost immediately I had to acquaint myself with the new regulations. I was relieved to find them somewhat similar to the previous place. For the next few months I was virtually in solitary confinement again. Another Chinese prisoner was placed with me to watch me and attend to our prison duties. Apart from brief periods of relaxation, I sat crosslegged on my bedding on the floor, from six in the morning till ten at night. My fellow-prisoner and I were not permitted to converse freely. We had to confine our conversation to bare necessities and often the guard would interrupt us and shout us into silence again. My food was no longer a special diet but was lowered for the second time. It was now the same as all other Chinese prisoners, meat once a month instead of twice a week and other days just rice and vegetables. At first I found the complete denial of movement a trying thing but then gradually I forgot about it and began to enjoy the stillness and the absence of pressure by other prisoners. Furthermore, the second day after I arrived, a summary of my interrogations was produced for me to sign. This gave me hope that my case was moving towards completion.

In the healing quietness I examined myself as to my faith. All the waves and billows of the past three years had gone over me. Satan had brought to bear every device upon me. My mind had been so battered and was now so fatigued that I hardly knew how to think. Yet, as in that dark cell my vision cleared, I could not explain it nor did I need to do so. I knew that I believed my Saviour risen from the dead. I knew He was the Son of God. I knew He had shed His blood for me. I had been shaken, torn and wounded but I was conscious still, that round about me were His everlasting arms. I knew within my heart the witness of His Spirit, triumphant still, standing yet inviolable to all the foe's assault. I knew that underneath my feet, impregnable, unshaken and strong as ever, was the Rock of Ages, Jesus Christ my Lord. And there as I sat, from the very well springs of my soul surged up the words that God is pleased to honour above all human utterance, "I believe."

CHAPTER XIX

WHEN IRON GATES YIELD

... kept in prison: but prayer was made without ceasing of the Church unto God for him ... the iron gate opened ... of his own accord. He said, Now I know of a surety that the Lord hath ... delivered me ... from all the expectation of the people ..." Acts 12.

THE life of the prisoners in the Chunking prison was even more intense than in the one in the hills. Indoctrination was incessant. The "learning" periods were very long and lasted all day except Sunday. The guards' scrutiny was constant and every movement checked. Our cell was gloomy but peaceful. In all the other cells in the same block as ourselves, the war against "reactionary" thought waged unceasingly. In the next cell to us was a typical "cell-leader" dictator. One poor fellow under him was half-crazed and subject to relentless nagging. In the day there was little respite for anyone and at night often a warder would wake up prisoners because the bedding was over their face or they were turning over with too much movement. I was shouted at several times when asleep. My fellow-prisoner whispered to me: "Up to some months back we were not allowed to turn over at night unless we 'bao gao'ed'.—Now the Government is merciful to us," he added. Although the light was so poor and the eyestrain severe, yet we kept our noses to the books provided for our "self education", otherwise it only meant falling foul of the warders. After the second meal, there was a short period of recreation permitted as at the other prison, and we were allowed to play chess. This was a relaxation for which we were profoundly grateful. Days went by and then an official came to see me. "What is the state of your 'learning'?" he enquired. "Still in the investigation stage" I replied. "I have not yet accepted your 'Dialectical Materialism'." I wondered what this would bring forth, yet I believed the Lord would have me say it, lest they should imagine they had broken me at the last session of struggle meetings. He looked at me perplexedly. "You should 'learn' more," he said. I could not help but feel that what I had just uttered would adversely affect my period of confinement, but I would not retract it, even if I had the opportunity. In the first few weeks at the new place, I also had an interview with another official. We talked together of my possible sentence. I said that I thought my verdict would soon be announced, but was puzzled by my interrogator's attitude, which seemed to give me no hope whatever unless I could elucidate the question of my political background. "Of course these matters need to be made clear," he said, "but when your sentence is announced, you will be satisfied." He went on to say, "Your faith is different from ours but we do hope that one day, when eventually you get back to England, you will speak well of the Communist Party and New China." Hope began to rise in my heart. Perhaps, after a sentence at a Labour Camp, I might even get back to England.

On November 11th, I remember it clearly because it was Europe's Armistice Day, my chief interrogator called me into a court-room and announced to me, after a severe lecture on my unchanged imperialist standpoint, that some move was afoot. "We are going to send you out of S.W. China," he said. I tried to judge what this statement might mean. "You will need some money for a railway fare and you had better think what is to be done about your baggage." I could not believe my ears but, as was my long cultivated habit, sat without a flicker on my face lest I betray my thinking. It was always a grim psychological duel in the court-room. The man speaking to me was the official who had said the Government would never surrender to me. I half sensed that he was fencing himself now, trying to put a good face on what, for him, was a personal defeat. It may be Peking, I thought, in which case the prospect of reopening my case at the Capital was very terrible. Yet the mention of a railway ticket meant that my relations with the Government were to undergo a change. I dared not speculate or build my hopes. The emotional upheaval of disappointment might reduce me to collapse in my overstrained condition. All I could do was struggle to hold an even keel whatever the future might hold.

On November 13th I was called in. The chief interpreter and

another official faced me across the black table of the court. The interpreter thundered: "We have your data. We are in possession of 'material' that reveals you have hidden something from the Government in your trial. Unless you acknowledge it there is no hope of a settlement of your case." These tactics did not catch me unawares. It was typical, and I replied immediately, clearing my ground: "If it is a question of British Government relations there is no hope of my making any further statement. If the point in question relates to something of my activities in China, I am willing to reflect again on all my activity." I spoke quietly and unruffled. This manner had gained for me the nickname of "India Rubber". Sustained patience was often termed "negative resistance", but it put the authorities in a difficult position as it did not "close the door", another phrase often used to condemn prisoners who refused to admit any possibility of further confession. I now gave them both a closed and an open door. If they wanted something to do with my activities in China, the interpreter might in his reply unwittingly disclose it. He made a poor reply for an interrogator, saying I must still think about the first point but that it was to do with a contact in Chungking. The next day I was interrogated and they probed my reactions to this new development. Another duel followed. My attitude was partly nonchalance, to show that I was hiding no crime and to show that I considered this question must be only some small point I had overlooked, and partly concern, inasmuch as this had to be settled before my question could be closed. O, how I hated it all. They concentrated on my relationship with John Ting, which the Lord helped to show was in no way political. I was given great clarity of mind and felt the sheer logic of what I was saying was definitely winning through. At last I was sent back to my cell.

As time moved on to December 1953, I recalled the passage on the rooftop at Batang. Something will have to happen soon, I mused, if the interpretation of that passage is to be fulfilled in the way I believed God was speaking to me at the time. I waited with expectation. On December 2nd an official called me out. Three years to the day the hand of God, which spans the eternities, moved in grace for one of his disciplined children. "God is not a man that He should lie." The official discussed with me questions relating to my baggage and then said to me: "The Government has come to a decision about your case. I want you to think of nothing else now. Just go on 'learning'." I had placed one foot on the farther side of Jordan. Death's waters could not claim me when Christ was leading. He must keep His Word. In view of everything there could be little doubt they were preparing me for release.

Whilst I waited for the hoped for day to dawn, I was interviewed by one of the Communist intelligentsia, a man holding a high post as an interpreter and employed on the writing of the legal summaries of westerners' cases in English. He spoke to me kindly and explained to me that, Yang, the official who had threatened me so severely with execution could not now be viewed as representing the Communist Party. The Party, he said, would have to educate him. I listened blankly. I might have been amused but it was too late.

On December 11th, in the early afternoon, the Governor of the prison came personally to my cell. He beckoned to me. I went forward and was hustled roughly by a warder with a tommy-gun on to the outer veranda. I walked along by the thick wooden bars. Suddenly a photographer snapped me and I was hurried on upstairs. More guards and more photographs. With an armed warder right on top of me, I was led into the court. At the black table sat two officials I had never seen before and also my chief interrogator. The scene was most dramatic. I was obviously going to be sentenced. I felt sure that the result would be victorious, yet in the back of my mind still came the thought. "You would be thoroughly shaken if they announced that you were to be executed." The indictment was read out. Conspiracy with traitors of China. Rumour mongering and the photographing of military objects. I was not asked to sign it, but to sign another paper that ratified the indictment as fact. Under indoctrination I had come to my rationalised conclusions of their phraseology. "Facts" were things viewed from the proletariat standpoint. "Crime" was transgression of their law. According to their own phraseology and as judged in their court under their law, the indictment was in complete keeping with the circumstances. I signed it for what it was worth. Cameras clicked again. The chief official acting as judge solemnly announced the verdict. "The People's Supreme Court of Justice of the Province of Sikang in the People's Republic of China, on account of your crimes committed against the people of the Republic, sentences you to be expelled immediately and for ever from the boundaries of this realm." On the order was the great red seal of the Sikang People's Government.

A gruff command and I marched through the poker faces down to my cell. I was followed by an official, who ordered me to bind up my bedding and oddments at once and proceed outside. I "bao gao'ed" for the last time and was admitted to the lower courtyard. My bedding roll and small zip fastener grip were searched. Every article of clothing was pulled out and placed in a jumbled heap for final examination. My whole person and the clothes I was wearing were gone over with great care. What, after three years, they expected to find on me, I do not know. Two other prisoners, both Chinese, were also undergoing the same process. Then ropes were brought out and the two Chinese were bound high up on their arms and around their backs. Their arms were allowed some play, and a long lead left at the back to be held by the guards. When all was ready, we staggered with our baggage down to a truck, waiting at the prison entrance. We were escorted by warders all the way. The other two were now hand-cuffed, but I was spared that ordeal. I walked in a dream. I must have looked a strange figure. I wore an old blue sports jacket of George's, out at the elbow, a grey pullover with zip fastener to the neck, a big well-patched pair of land army pantaloons and rough Tibetan woollen socks up to my knees, which were both coarse and dirty. On my feet I had a pair of shoes, that were just falling to pieces. I was unshaven.

At last we were packed into the truck and driven off. I wondered where we would be sleeping that evening. Knowing Chunking a little from previous trips, I judged we were making for the river. I was quite right in my reckoning. Unerringly, the truck found its way to the ferry crossing. As we descended from the truck and boarded the old junk at the riverside we were quite a spectacle. One old fellow of the people nearly walked into us, not looking where he was going. When he saw us, and especially when he had a sight of the handcuffs, he jumped for his life, making ridiculously hasty movements to get away from us, as if he had touched something contaminated. At first I thought the junk was to be our transport down river but it was only a kind of landing stage for the ferry launch, which soon bore us to the south bank of the Yangtse. We waited on the sandy shore until twilight. The lamps of the city, sprawling over the cliffs and hills of the peninsula on which it was built, lit up one by one, and twinkled into long broken pencils of light in the swiftly flowing waters. Little children crowded round us, only to be chased away by our now solitary guard. The one escorting official at last returned, having made all arrangements, and we moved on board the river steamer lying moored just off the shore. What a night! It seemed again as if I were a character in a play.

On the ship, one of the through corridors on the top deck was reserved for us and we laid out our bedding rolls. We each had a space about five feet by two. The official was very good to me. He said: "You know the result of your case, don't you?" I said: "Yes." "Well," he said. "Just you behave yourself and you'll be all right. We have not handcuffed you, so it's up to you." I needed no telling. It was arranged for us to have meals on deck just where we were. It was quite cold, being winter, but I had adequate covering and was so deliriously happy at the prospect of freedom, that nothing mattered. The following morning I woke early. We were slipping away downstream. The wind was very strong and the crew pulled down the canvassing, thus obscuring the view. How my eyes longed for the country! The next few days, with improved weather, the canvas was partially rolled up and I had the feast of years, a trip through the Yangste gorges. As I saw the handiwork of God, my Creator and Redeemer, so surpassingly beautiful, and lay there on the deck of the steamer, every moment a moment nearer freedom, something in me began to unwind. Only slightly at first, but more and more as days went by. It was an inexplicable sense of ease. Yet sometimes the thought would return, "You are not free yet," and the mind would begin to tense again.

On December 15th, we disembarked at Hankow. It was a bleak drizzly morning. We were taken immediately to a big Government establishment. In my mind was the great question:

"Will I be put in prison again?" After a meal in a kind of office waiting-room, we boarded the truck and were driven away to some place outside Hankow. High red walls loomed before us. I knew that once again we had arrived at a place of punishment. I looked at the great prison with growing dread. The official jumped out, came round the back, and motioning to the two handcuffed and bound Chinese said: "You two get down. You!" he said, pointing at me, "stay where you are!" My heart jumped for joy. I sat in the truck and watched my two fellow prisoners march in through the guarded gates. I wondered when they would ever come out of there again. God's mercy to me was unfathomable. The truck was driven off again, into the city, until we stopped at a shabby old railway hostel, where we put up for the night, although it was barely midday when we arrived there. How lovely it was to get into bed in the afternoon. The official now changed his attitude towards me and treated me more or less as a free man. He handed over to me all my bits and pieces, like my wrist watch, my cameras and my fountain pen. I repacked my luggage and changed into slightly more presentable trousers, although still very patched ones. In the zip-fastener bag was my Bible. "Shall I look at it?" I thought. In a very real sense I was still not free and the guard and official still talked to me on indoctrination material. I felt it better to provoke no trouble and leave it until that precious moment when, in freedom and quietness, I could turn its pages again after nearly three years.

We all slept late the next morning, had a lunch of stew, potatoes and "manto", and then proceeded to the station on the farther bank of the river. The train left at about six. The official walked with me up and down the platform. I had asked him regarding my passport on the boat. He had said: "You leave that to me." I hoped it would be all right. Suddenly two Police Inspectors accosted us. They wanted to know who I was. My official produced a letter and documents, which they took off with them. About half an hour later, they returned. All was in order. The locomotive roared in. It was the first train I had seen for six years. Our seats were in a fine modern coach, where by an ingenious system, two seats and two racks in the daytime became six bunks at night. It was good, after all the years within four walls, to hear

the rattle of the bogies underneath and to see the paddy fields
fleeting by outside. We turned in about ten and I knew little
more until the dawn. I lay on my bunk looking out of the window
to the fresh and awakening countryside. We had travelled south
all through the night. It was already much warmer. We were
passing through tea country. For a time we stopped at Henyang
junction and then journeyed on all day towards Canton. We
passed through Kwantung as the sun went down. It seemed that
dear old China arrayed herself in all her glory especially for me,
that last evening. It was a golden landscape of hills and valleys,
woodland streams and little plots sown by the peasants. My mind
was overwhelmed by its beauty. God made every clod of Chinese
soil and loves every one of her five hundred million sons. I could
say to His glory that I loved them still. I had lived and suffered as
one of them. I had wept with them through their revolution and
by His grace I was leaving them, longing only that they might
come to know Him too. That last golden sunset in the land of
China surely spoke of "the end of the Lord". "As for God," I
could say from the very depths of my soul, "His way is perfect."

At ten o'clock at night we alighted from the train. We stepped
into rickshaws and bowled silently along in the already deserted
streets of Canton. Through district after district of big modern
buildings we sped, until we came to a big compound. I was told
by the official to stand with my guard outside while he went in.
After some time we went into the garden of the place and sat in
a small pavilion. It was the police station. The soldier and I
waited a long while in the darkness. The Official reappeared.
Thank God, all formalities were successfully concluded and we
made our way to a small inn. December the nineteenth, 1953, we
were early at the Canton railway terminus, although the train
did not leave until about nine. It was crammed to capacity and
stopped at every station. The sun was very hot and the countryside was more tropical, with papua, pineapple plants and banana
palms quite frequently to be seen. Station by station, I was
moving towards the great moment. Year after year, I had lived
for this day. God knows all it had meant. With blow after blow,
I had been spiritually and psychologically bludgeoned, until I
was dazed and broken in mind and spirit, but none had been able

to pluck me from my Shepherd and His Father's hand. In the crisis, I had found my faith and love at times too weak to hold Him fast, but the final triumph was not to be in my hold of Him, but in His hold of me. His love would never let me go. He would keep that which I had committed unto Him. In His own time and way, He was determined and able, to make me all the man, that He had planned that I should be. I was broken, but I had proved His Word unbreakable.

Just before two, the engine ground to a halt before the frontier. A somewhat officious uniformed person led us to the Customs barrier. My paltry belongings were searched yet again. I asked for my passport. "I have no passport for you," the official said. It was their final deception. There was much over which I might have fretted. I had but a "mildewy" fifteen and fivepence in money, which had remained with me my whole stay in China, unexchanged. It was totally inadequate for my immediate needs. For all that I had been told, Hong Kong would be bankrupt. I could count on no friends or missionaries being there, but I knew all things were in His hand. I somehow felt He would prove Himself again, as I stepped into liberty. I repacked my darned garments back into the grip. My name was scrawled on a piece of paper and sent through to the British authorities. I waited for the word to move forward. A distracted Chinese woman went past as I stood. It would seem that there was some irregularity in her papers, for she was weeping very bitterly. I turned and the official beckoned me on. I stood now within six feet of the barbed wire barrier. I could see the spotlessly white office buildings of the British frontier post. Above them fluttered the Union Jack in brilliant sunshine. On the farther side I could see one or two people walking about, then suddenly a man came striding towards the narrow gap in the barbed wire. I was signalled through; People's China had yielded up her prey; but a few steps and all was over.

A loveable fellow with a French accent put out a great big friendly hand and with beaming face spoke to me those unforgetable words: "Welcome to Freedom." In his other hand he had a visiting card. "Do you know this man?" he asked. I glanced at the name. "Raymond J. Guyatt." O, how great is our God! None other than a Christian from my own Church near London, a young fellow with whom I had been brought up since childhood and a very dear and close friend for many years. "He is in Hong Kong," the man said, "and is waiting to receive you." I tried to speak but found that, after almost four years without speaking English to a fellow countryman, my first sentences were all jumbled up with Chinese. I could have wept, but God made me strong and I did not break down. It took me about a quarter of an hour to gain full control of my emotions. I was in a daze and overwhelmed by kindness. I had known no human love for years. I sat in the immigration office. "Have you a passport?" "No, it has been confiscated," I told them. The man with a French accent, who proved to be a Catholic Father, authorised to meet any foreigner expelled from China at the border, kindly filled in a form for me. He was so sympathetic and kept telling everybody on duty: "That man has been in prison three years." The immigration officer smiled as I signed the form and said: "Just go to the Immigration Office in Hong Kong on Monday." The question of my passport was at least temporarily settled. "Now come and have something to eat," my Catholic friend suggested. We went into a cool airy café and he ordered the loveliest egg sandwiches I had ever seen and glasses of orangeade. It was my first bread since 1949.

Within half an hour I was on the train, with another Catholic Father who undertook to see me right into Hong Kong. It took about forty-five minutes to Kowloon. Crowds of forces folk piled on the train. I was silent and shrank back into my corner. Suddenly to see a crowd of English boys made me feel as if I were no longer one of them. Their faces looked so fresh and their clothes so clean and smart. I looked through the window as we came to the coast. The sea was wonderful. At Kowloon the Catholic Father quickly bought me a ticket and we crossed the straits to Hong Kong. The thousands of people, the harbour, the magnificent peak and the great city fascinated me. Once on the wharfside, before I knew what was happening, I was in a taxi racing through the busy streets. Ten minutes brought us to a block of flats. We climbed to the third floor and rang the bell. A young English woman cautiously opened the door, astonished to find a tramp in the custody of a Catholic Father waiting to come in. There was a brief moment of awkwardness for we were complete strangers to one another, then she said: "Yes, I am Mrs. Guyatt." "I am Geoff. Bull" was the simple reply and I stepped across the threshold of that little home, where prayer had been made for me so often. I was in the bathroom when Raymond came in from the city a little later. At the doorway our eyes met. Just two words broke out from our lips, "Geoff!" "Ray!" We could say no more. We knew that prayer had conquered. God had brought me through.

*   *   *   *   *

The 24,000 ton steamer "R.M.S. Chusan" slipped her moorings and began to move slowly and gracefully out from the great harbour. On the quayside, were groups of Christians waving and waving, as the width of water between us increased. At last only a few white handkerchiefs could be seen and the mountains of China began to recede. I stood high up on one of the decks gazing into the distance. I had known six weeks of freedom. There had been nights when I could only lie on my pillow and cry out I knew not what. There had been that first hallowed reading of the Scripture in Corinthians: "I will destroy the wisdom of the wise and will bring to nothing the understanding of the prudent." There had been my first walk in the hills and that day when I had looked at the flowers and did not know I could pick them, had clutched a leaf and begun to cry. Then, on one of the island shores I had paddled and with friends cooked sausages over a camp fire on the beach. I had too sat at the Lord's table on the Lord's Day and remembered Him in the breaking of bread, who was broken for me. I had stood with my Chinese brothers and sisters in Christ and sung "All hail the power of Jesus' Name". These experiences, more precious to me than words can tell, were healing and strengthening, yet my soul was still restless. An hour passed and the land fell away on the sky-line. Now there was only the great unfettered dome of the heavens, and all around the mighty sea unusually still and calm. The voices of the struggle meetings could be heard no more and the hum of the city was left far behind. Alone with the Lord I suddenly became conscious of a great silence, a silence I had not known since those days when so often, from some high Tibetan pass, I had scanned the farthest hills. The peace of God possessed and garrisoned my heart anew and, as night came on, I looked out once more towards a boundless horizon. It seemed like the end of a book and yet may be for me, it was only His beginning.

> Rise my soul Thy God directs Thee,
> Stranger hands no more impede;
> Pass thou on; His hand protects thee,
> Strength that has the captive freed.